HAPPY FATHERS DAY
2013

LOVE
KRISTEN

Gary Belsky
& Neil Fine

This edition published in 2009 exclusively for Hallmark Cards, Inc., under license from ESPN Books, a division of ESPN Publishing.

Visit us on the Web at www.Hallmark.com.

Book design: Rogers Eckersley Design (RED), José Antonio Contreras

ISBN: 978-1-59530-026-3

BOK2128

Printed in China

For Ari, Elly, Emily, Mo, Shara, Sara, Adir, Sam, Zevvy, Ani, and Noa—11 ways to get through editing a book.

— G.B.

For Zeke and Edie, because they still think I have all the answers.

—N.F.

Almost

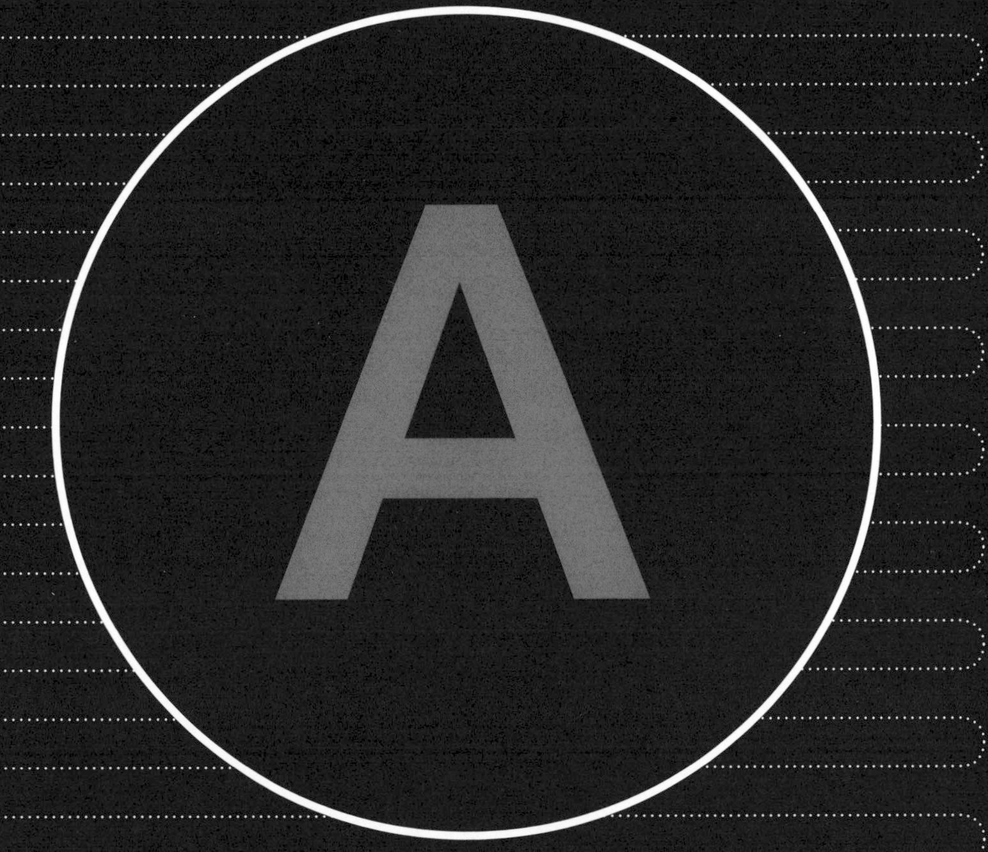

Autocratic

A B C D E F G H I J K L M N O P Q R S T U V W X Y Z

Almost There

Pitchers Who Lost A Perfect Game With One Out To Go

Hooks Wiltse
July 4, 1908
New York Giants (vs. Philadelphia Phillies)
George McQuillan was hit by a pitch, but Wiltse threw a 10-inning no-hitter and the Giants won 1-0.

Tommy Bridges
August 5, 1932
Detroit Tigers (vs. Washington Senators)
Dave Harris singled, but the Tigers won 13-0.

Billy Pierce
June 27, 1958
Chicago White Sox (vs. Washington Senators)
Ed Fitz Gerald doubled, but the White Sox won 3-0.

Milt Pappas
September 2, 1972
Chicago Cubs (vs. San Diego Padres)
Larry Stahl walked, but Pappas threw a no-hitter and the Cubs won 8-0.

Milt Wilcox
April 15, 1983
Detroit Tigers (vs. Chicago White Sox)
Jerry Hairston singled, but the Tigers won 6-0.

Ron Robinson
May 2, 1988
Cincinnati Reds (vs. Montreal Expos)
Wallace Johnson singled, but the Reds won 3-2.

Dave Stieb
August 4, 1989
Toronto Blue Jays (vs. New York Yankees)
Roberto Kelly doubled, but the Blue Jays won 2-1.

Brian Holman
April 20, 1990
Seattle Mariners (vs. Oakland A's)
Ken Phelps homered, but the Mariners won 6-1.

Mike Mussina
September 2, 2001
New York Yankees (vs. Boston Red Sox)
Carl Everett singled, but the Yankees won 1-0.

American Expressed

Baseball Scoring Symbols

Bill Shannon has been an MLB scorer since 1980 and is the lead official scorer in New York. Here is the shorthand he uses for his scorekeeping:

1 Pitcher
2 Catcher
3 1st baseman
4 2nd baseman
5 3rd baseman
6 Shortstop
7 Left fielder
8 Center fielder
9 Right fielder
10 Designated hitter
- Single
= Double
≡ Triple
≣ Home run

SH Sacrifice bunt *(sacrifice hit)*
SF Sacrifice fly
HBP Hit by pitch
E Error
E_T Throwing error
PB Passed ball
F Foul ball
U Unassisted putout *(usually first base only)*
L Line drive, as in L-9
***** Extraordinary play
K Swinging strikeout
ꓘ Called third strike

PH Pinch hitter
PR Pinch runner
P Popout to infielder
BB Walk *(base on balls)*
IW Intentional walk
▲ Bunt
SB Stolen base
OS Caught stealing
FC Fielder's choice
PO Pickoff
WP Wild pitch
BK Balk
INT Interference
OBS Obstruction

American Pine Language

Split, Spare and Strike Names in Bowling

SPLITS AND SPARES

Baby Split: 2-7 or 3-10, 4-5 or 5-6.
Bed Posts, Mule Ears, Snake Eyes: 7-10.
Big Four: 4-6-7-10.
Big Five, Greek Church: Three pins on one side, two on the other.
Bucket: 2-4-5-8 for righthanders, 3-5-6-9 for lefties.
Clothesline: 1-2-4-7 or 1-3-6-10.
Double Wood, Sleeper: 1-5, 2-8, 3-9.
Fast Eight: 4-7 or 6-10.
Lily, Sour Apple: 5-7-10
Picket Fence, Picket Rail: 1-2-4-7 or 1-3-6-10 spares.
Pocket Split: 8-10 for righties, 7-9 for lefties.

STRIKES

Double: Two strikes in a row.
String: Three or more consecutive strikes.
Turkey: Three strikes in a row.
Six-pack: Six strikes in a row.
Blow the Rack: All 10 pins go in the pit.
Brooklyn: A strike that comes after the ball hits the side opposite the one the bowler intended to hit. (It's called a "Jersey" in Brooklyn.)
Pack: A flush, solid strike.

A

B

C

D

E

F

G

H

I

J

K

L

M

N

O

P

Q

R

S

T

U

V

W

X

Y

Z

Ancient Links Lingo

Golf Club Names You Won't Hear Anymore

MODERN CLUB NAME	OBSOLETE EQUIVALENT
Putter	Blank
2-Wood	Brassie
3-Wood	Spoon
4-Wood	Baffing Spoon/Baffy
1-Iron	Cleek
2-Iron	Mid-Iron
3-Iron	Mid-Mashie
4-Iron	Mashie Iron
5-Iron	Mashie
6-Iron	Spade Mashie
7-Iron	Mashie Niblick
8-Iron	Pitching Niblick
9-Iron	Niblick
Pitching Wedge	Jigger

Annie's Pitch

Susan Sarandon's Speech From *Bull Durham*

"I believe in the Church of Baseball. I've tried all the major religions, and most of the minor ones. I've worshipped Buddha, Allah, Brahma, Vishnu, Shiva, trees, mushrooms, and Isadora Duncan. I know things. For instance, there are 108 beads in a Catholic rosary and there are 108 stitches in a baseball. When I learned that, I gave Jesus a chance. But it just didn't work out between us. The Lord laid too much guilt on me. I prefer metaphysics to theology. You see, there's no guilt in baseball, and it's never boring … which makes it like sex. There's never been a ballplayer slept with me who didn't have the best year of his career. Making love is

"You see, there's no guilt in baseball, and it's never boring … which makes it like sex."

like hitting a baseball: You just got to relax and concentrate. Besides, I'd never sleep with a player hitting under .250 unless he had a lot of RBIs or was a great glove man up the middle … Y'see, there's a certain amount of 'life wisdom' I give these boys. I can expand their minds. Sometimes when I've got a ballplayer alone, I'll just read Emily Dickinson or Walt Whitman to him. The guys are so sweet, they always stay and listen. Of course, a guy will listen to anything if he thinks it's foreplay. I make them feel confident. They make me feel safe, and pretty. What I give them lasts a lifetime; what they give me lasts 142 games. Sometimes it seems like a bad trade. But bad trades are part of baseball—who can forget Frank Robinson for Milt Pappas, for God's sake? It's a long season and you got to trust it. I've tried them all, I really have, and the only church that truly feeds the soul, day in, day out, is the Church of Baseball."

Annual Achievements

Sports Illustrated's SPORTSMAN OF THE YEAR

1954 Roger Bannister
1955 Johnny Podres
1956 Bobby Morrow
1957 Stan Musial
1958 Rafer Johnson
1959 Ingemar Johansson
1960 Arnold Palmer
1961 Jerry Lucas
1962 Terry Baker
1963 Pete Rozelle
1964 Ken Venturi
1965 Sandy Koufax
1966 Jim Ryun
1967 Carl Yastrzemski
1968 Bill Russell
1969 Tom Seaver
1970 Bobby Orr
1971 Lee Trevino
1972 John Wooden/ Billie Jean King
1973 Jackie Stewart
1974 Muhammad Ali
1975 Pete Rose
1976 Chris Evert
1977 Steve Cauthen
1978 Jack Nicklaus
1979 Willie Stargell/ Terry Bradshaw
1980 U.S. Olympic Hockey Team
1981 Sugar Ray Leonard
1982 Wayne Gretzky
1983 Mary Decker
1984 Edwin Moses/ Mary Lou Retton
1985 Kareem Abdul-Jabbar
1986 Joe Paterno
1987 Eight Athletes Who Care (Bob Bourne/ Judi Brown King/Kip Keino/Dale Murphy/ Chip Rives/Patty Sheehan/Rory Sparrow/Reggie Williams)
1988 Orel Hershiser
1989 Greg LeMond
1990 Joe Montana
1991 Michael Jordan
1992 Arthur Ashe
1993 Don Shula
1994 Bonnie Blair/Johann Olav Koss
1995 Cal Ripken Jr.
1996 Tiger Woods
1997 Dean Smith
1998 Mark McGwire/ Sammy Sosa
1999 World Cup Champion U.S. Women's Soccer Team
2000 Tiger Woods
2001 Randy Johnson/ Curt Schilling
2002 Lance Armstrong
2003 Tim Duncan/David Robinson
2004 Boston Red Sox
2005 Tom Brady
2006 Dwyane Wade
2007 Brett Favre

Anthem Roll Call

"Star-spangled Banner" Performers At The Super Bowl

I Universities of Arizona and Michigan Bands
II Grambling State University Band
III Anita Bryant (Pledge of Allegiance by NASA astronauts)
IV Al Hirt (Pledge by NASA astronauts)
V Tommy Loy
VI U.S. Air Force Academy Chorale
VII Andy Williams and the Little Angels of Holy Angels Church of Chicago (Pledge by NASA astronauts)
VIII Charley Pride
IX Grambling State University Band with Mardi Gras Chorus
X Tom Sullivan
XI Vicki Carr (sang "America the Beautiful")
XII Phyllis Kelly
XIII The Colgate Thirteen
XIV Cheryl Ladd
XV Helen O'Connell
XVI Diana Ross
XVII Leslie Easterbrook
XVIII Barry Manilow
XIX Children's Choir of San Francisco
XX Wynton Marsalis
XXI Neil Diamond
XXII Herb Alpert
XXIII Billy Joel
XXIV Aaron Neville
XXV Whitney Houston
XXVI Harry Connick Jr. (American Sign Language performance by Lori Hilary)
XXVII Garth Brooks (ASL performance by Marlee Matlin)
XXVIII Natalie Cole with Atlanta University Center Chorus (ASL performance by Atlanta Falcons cheerleader Courtney Keel Foley)
XXIX Kathie Lee Gifford (ASL performance by Heather Whitestone)
XXX Vanessa Williams (ASL performance by Mary Kim Titla)
XXXI Luther Vandross (ASL performance by Erika Schwarz)
XXXII Jewel (ASL performance by Phyllis Frelich)
XXXIII Cher (ASL performance by Speaking Hands)
XXXIV Faith Hill (ASL performance by Briarlake Elementary School Signing Choir)
XXXV Backstreet Boys (ASL performance by Tom Cooney)
XXXVI Mariah Carey with the Boston Pops Orchestra (ASL performance by Joe Narcisse)
XXXVII Dixie Chicks (ASL performance by Janet Maxwell)
XXXVIII Beyoncé (ASL performance by Súzanna Christy)
XXXIX Navy, Air Force, Army, and Coast Guard Choirs, with the U.S. Army Herald Trumpets (ASL performance by Wesley Tallent)
XL Aaron Neville and Aretha Franklin accompanied by Dr. John (ASL performance by Angela LaGuardia)
XLI Billy Joel

Apples Close To The Tree

Baseball's Father-Son All-Stars

There have been more than 100 father-son combinations in Major League Baseball history, but only 14 of these pairs have made the cut as All-Stars since the game's inception in 1933.

FATHER	SON
Sandy Alomar: California Angels (1970)	**Sandy Alomar Jr.:** Cleveland Indians (1990-92, 1996-98)
Sandy Alomar: California Angels (1970)	**Roberto Alomar:** San Diego Padres (1990), Toronto Blue Jays (1991-95), Baltimore Orioles (1996-98), Cleveland Indians (1999-01)
Felipe Alou: San Francisco Giants (1962), Atlanta Braves (1966, 1968)	**Moisés Alou:** Montreal Expos (1994), Florida Marlins (1997), Houston Astros (1998, 2001), Chicago Cubs (2004), San Francisco Giants (2005-06)
Gus Bell: Cincinnati Reds (1953-57)	**Buddy Bell:** Cleveland Indians (1973), Texas Rangers (1980-82, 1984)
Bobby Bonds: San Francisco Giants (1971, 1973), New York Yankees (1975)	**Barry Bonds:** Pittsburgh Pirates, (1990, 1992), San Francisco Giants (1993-98, 2000-04)
Ray Boone: Detroit Tigers (1954, 1956)	**Bob Boone:** Philadelphia Phillies (1976, 78-79), California Angels (1983)
Bob Boone: Philadelphia Phillies (1976, 1978-79), California Angels (1983)	**Bret Boone:** Cincinnati Reds (1998), Seattle Mariners (2001, 2003)
Bob Boone: Philadelphia Phillies (1976, 1978-79), California Angels (1983)	**Aaron Boone:** Cincinnati Reds (2003)
Joe Coleman: Philadelphia A's (1948)	**Joe Coleman Jr.:** Detroit Tigers (1972)
Ken Griffey: Cincinnati Reds (1976-77, 1980)	**Ken Griffey Jr.:** Seattle Mariners (1990-99), Cincinnati Reds (2000, 2004)
Jim Hegan: Cleveland Indians (1947, 1949-52)	**Mike Hegan:** Seattle Pilots (1969)
Randy Hundley: Chicago Cubs (1969)	**Todd Hundley:** New York Mets (1996-97)
Vern Law: Pittsburgh Pirates (1960)	**Vance Law:** Chicago Cubs (1988)
Gary Matthews: Atlanta Braves (1979)	**Gary Matthews Jr.:** Texas Rangers (2006)

Approved Attire

Official NBA Player Dress Code

General Policy: Business Casual

Players are required to wear Business Casual attire whenever they are engaged in team or league business.

Business Casual Attire Means:

- A long or short-sleeved dress shirt (collared or turtleneck), and/or a sweater
- Dress slacks, khaki pants, or dress jeans
- Appropriate shoes and socks, including dress shoes, dress boots, or other presentable shoes, but not including sneakers, sandals, flip-flops, or work boots

Exceptions To Business Casual

There are the following exceptions to the general policy of Business Casual attire:

A. Players In Attendance At Games But Not In Uniform
Players who are in attendance at games but not in uniform are required to wear the following additional items when seated on the bench or in the stands during the game:

- Sport coat
- Dress shoes or boots, and socks

B. Players Leaving The Arena
Players leaving the arena may wear either Business Casual attire or neat warm-up suits issued by their teams.

C. Special Events Or Appearances
Teams can make exceptions to the Business Casual policy for special events or player appearances where other attire is appropriate—e.g., participation in a basketball clinic.

Excluded Items

The following is a list of items that players are not allowed to wear at any time while on team or league business:

- Sleeveless shirts
- Shorts
- T-shirts, jerseys, or sports apparel (unless appropriate for the event [e.g., a basketball clinic], team-identified, and approved by the team)
- Headgear of any kind while a player is sitting on the bench or in the stands at a game, during media interviews, or during a team or league event or appearance (unless appropriate for the event or appearance, team-identified, and approved by the team)
- Chains, pendants, or medallions worn over the player's clothes
- Sunglasses while indoors
- Headphones (other than on the team bus or plane, or in the team locker room)

A B C D E F G H I J K L M N O P Q R S T U V W X Y Z

A B C D E F G H I J K L M N O P Q R S T U V W X Y Z

Athletic Promise

Olympic Oaths

Since the Antwerp Games of 1920, an athlete from the Olympic host country has taken a pledge on behalf of all participating athletes. The original oath was just 43 words, but in 2000 it was expanded to reflect changes in the sports world. Here is the new version, along with the oath that, since 1972, has been taken by one official on behalf of all:

ATHLETES

"In the name of all the competitors, I promise that we shall take part in these Olympic Games, respecting and abiding by the rules which govern them, committing ourselves to a sport without doping and without drugs, in the true spirit of sportsmanship, for the glory of sport and the honor of our teams."

OFFICIALS

"In the name of all the judges and officials, I promise that we shall officiate in these Olympic Games with complete impartiality, respecting and abiding by the rules which govern them, in the true spirit of sportsmanship."

Autocratic Rules 

NASCAR's Original Bylaws

When William "Big Bill" France moved to Daytona Beach, Florida, in 1936, it wasn't to revolutionize auto racing in America. But having worked on a pit crew at the Indianapolis 500, France did think he could bring some organization to the rough world of stock cars, with its band of underfinanced promoters and drivers. After many stops and restarts, France turned this motley collection into the National Association for Stock Car Auto Racing. Here are the 35 original rules from NASCAR's inaugural 1948 season:

1. Cars eligible—1937 models and up through 1948. '37 and '38 models must have four-wheel hydraulic brakes.
2. Later models must be run in the same model chassis.
3. Foreign manufactured cars will not be permitted.
4. If a car is a convertible type, it must be run with top up and in proper place and must be equipped with safety hoops mounted to frame.
5. All cars must have full stock fenders, running boards, and body if so equipped when new, and not abbreviated in any way other than reinforcement.
6. Stock bumpers and mufflers must be removed.
7. Crash bars may be used no wider than frame, protruding no farther than 12 inches from body.
8. All doors must be welded, bolted, or

strapped shut. Doors blocked will not be permitted.

9. Fuel and oil capacities may be increased in any safe manner. Any extra or bigger tanks must be concealed inside car or under hood.

10. Wheelbase, length, and width must be stock.

11. All cars must have safety glass. All headlight and taillight glass must be removed.

12. All cars must have full windshield in place and used as windshield. No glass or material other than safety glass may be used.

13. Cars must be equipped with rear view mirror.

14. All cars must be subject to safety inspection by Technical Committee at any time.

15. All cars must have four-wheel hydraulic brakes or any brake manufactured after 1947.

16. Piston displacement in any car is limited to 300 cu. in., except where motor is used in same body and chassis it was designed and catalogued for. Under 300 cu. in. motors may be interchanged in same manufacturer's line.

17. Any block can be oversize. The only truck blocks permitted to be used in any Stock Car will be 100 H. P. Ford Blocks, which are fundamentally same as passenger car. These may only be used in models up to 1947 Fords. (Stock interchangeable passenger car blocks must be used in all cars through 1947.)

18. Cars may be run with or without fan or generator.

19. Any flywheel may be used.

20. Any part may be reinforced.

21. Any interchangeable wheel or tire size may be used.

22. Any rear end arrangement may be used.

23. Any radiator may be used, providing stock hood will close and latch properly. Hoods must have safety straps. All cars must have hoods on and must be stock hood for same model car.

24. Any type battery ignition may be used, excluding magnetos.

25. Any type of manufactured spark plug may be used.

26. Any model manufactured flat type cylinder heads may be used. Cylinder heads may be machined to increase compression.

27. Heads allowed with overhead valves only when coming as standard or optional equipment from factory.

28. Any valve springs may be used.

29. Multiple carburetion will be permitted. Any type carburetion may be used.

30. Superchargers allowed only when optional on stock equipment by manufacturer.

31. Water pump impellers may be cut down.

32. Altered camshafts will be permitted.

33. Altered crankshafts may be used.

34. All drivers must be strapped in and must wear safety helmets. Belt must be bolted to frame at two points and must be aviation latch type quick-re lease belt.

35. Regulation crash helmets must be used.

Ballpark

Building

A B C D E F G H I J K L M N O P Q R S T U V W X Y Z

Ballpark Beginnings

The Original Rules Of The Knickerbocker Base Ball Club

People argue all the time about the birthplace of baseball, a version of which was played in England long before the American Revolution and even longer before Abner Doubleday. But the game as most play it today almost certainly has its origins in the following rules, codified in 1845 by Alexander Cartwright of New York's Knickerbocker Base Ball Club, which had been playing its version of "base ball" since the beginning of the decade.

1ST Members must strictly observe the time agreed upon for exercise, and be punctual in their attendance.

2ND When assembled for exercise, the President, or in his absence, the Vice-President, shall appoint an Umpire, who shall keep the game in a book provided for that purpose, and note all violations of the By-Laws and Rules during the time of exercise.

3RD The presiding officer shall designate two members as Captains, who shall retire and make the match to be played, observing at the same time that the players put opposite to each other should be as nearly equal as possible, the choice of sides to be then tossed for, and the first in hand to be decided in like manner.

4TH The bases shall be from "home" to second base, forty-two paces; from first to third base, forty-two paces, equidistant.

5TH No stump match shall be played on a regular day of exercise.

6TH If there should not be a sufficient number of members of the Club present at the time agreed upon to commence exercise, gentlemen not members may be chosen in to make up the match, which shall not be broken up to take in members that may afterwards appear; but in all cases, members shall have the preference, when present, at the making of the match.

7TH If members appear after the game is commenced, they may be chosen in if mutually agreed upon.

8TH The game to consist of twenty-one counts, or aces; but at the conclusion an equal number of hands must be played.

9TH The ball must be pitched, not thrown, for the bat.

10TH A ball knocked out of the field, or outside the range of the first and third base, is foul.

11TH Three balls being struck at and missed and the last one caught, is a hand out; if not caught is considered fair, and the striker bound to run.

12TH If a ball be struck, or tipped, and caught, either flying or on the first bound, it is a hand out.

13TH A player running the bases shall be out, if the ball is in the hands of an adversary on the base, or the runner is touched with it before he makes his base; it being understood, however, that in no instance is a ball to be thrown at him.

14TH A player running who shall prevent an adversary from catching or getting the ball before making his base, is a hand out.

15TH Three hands out, all out.

16TH Players must take their strike in regular turn.

17TH All disputes and differences relative to the game, to be decided by the Umpire, from which there is no appeal.

18TH No ace or base can be made on a foul strike.

19TH A runner cannot be put out in making one base, when a balk is made on the pitcher.

20TH But one base allowed when a ball bounds out of the field when struck.

Bandwagon Jumpers

Music Groups Named After Athletes Or Teams

Gnarls Barkley may deny being named after Charles Barkley, but other artists proudly hail their athlete namesakes.

- **Abdoujaparov**[1] (Most recent release: Ultra Cool, 2005)
- **Bettie Serveert**[2] (Bare Stripped Naked, 2006)
- **Busta Rhymes**[3] (The Big Bang, 2006)
- **The Delgados**[4] (The Complete BBC Peel Sessions, 2006)
- **Falco**[5] (Nachtflug 2005)
- **Kaiser Chiefs**[6] (Maximum Kaiser Chiefs: The Unauthorised Biography of the Kaiser Chiefs, 2006)
- **Koufax**[7] (Hard Times Are in Fashion, 2005)
- **Sugar Ray**[8] (The Best of Sugar Ray, 2005)
- **Cream Abdul Babar**[9] (Covering Track Marks, 2004)
- **Pele**[10] (Elephant, 2003)
- **Vida Blue**[11] (The Illustrated Band, 2003)
- **Babe Ruth**[12] (Grand Slam: The Best of Babe Ruth, 2004)
- **Luscious Jackson**[13] (Electric Honey, 1999)
- **Johan**[14] (Johan, 1998)
- **Throneberry**[15] (Squinting Before the Dazzle, 1998)

[1]Named for Djamolodine Abdoujaparov, Uzbek pro cyclist (1991 Tour de France points competition winner); [2] Betty Stove, Dutch pro tennis player (1977 Wimbledon finalist); [3]George "Buster" Rhymes, University of Oklahoma and Minnesota Vikings wide receiver (1981-87); [4]Pedro Delgado, Spanish pro cyclist (1988 Tour de France winner); [5] Falko Weissflog, East German ski jumper (1978 Worlds bronze medalist); [6]Kaizer Chiefs soccer club, South Africa; [7]Sandy Koufax, Brooklyn/Los Angeles Dodgers pitcher (1955-66); [8]Sugar Ray Leonard, pro boxer (1976-91); [9]Kareem Abdul-Jabbar, Milwaukee Bucks/Los Angeles Lakers center (1969-89); [10]Pelé, Brazilian soccer star (1956-74); [11]Vida Blue, Oakland A's/San Francisco Giants/Kansas City Royals/San Francisco Giants pitcher (1969-83);[12]George Herman "Babe" Ruth, Boston Red Sox/New York Yankees/Boston Braves pitcher/ outfielder (1914-35); [13]Lucious "Luke" Jackson, Philadelphia 76ers forward (1964-72); [14]Johan Cruyff, Dutch soccer star (1964-84); [15]Marv Throneberry, New York Yankees/Kansas City A's/Baltimore Orioles/New York Mets first baseman (1955, 1958-63)

A B C D E F G H I J K L M N O P Q R S T U V W X Y Z

Banner Carriers

The Most Common College Nicknames ...

1. Eagles (64; examples include: Biola University, Boston College)
2. Tigers (46; Louisiana State University, Occidental College)
3. Bulldogs (40; Yale University, The Citadel)
4. Lions (37; Columbia University, Mars Hill College)
5. Wildcats (33; University of Arizona, Cazenovia College)
6. Warriors (32; Winona State University, Hendrix College)
7. Cougars (31; University of Houston, Columbia College)
7. Panthers (31; University of Pittsburgh, York College)
9. Crusaders (30; Susquehanna University, Clarke College)
10. Pioneers (27; Transylvania University, Point Park University)
11. Knights (24; Fairleigh Dickinson University, Martin Luther College)
12. Bears (21; Brown University, Shaw University)
12. Falcons (21; U.S. Air Force Academy, St. Augustine's College)
14. Saints (20; Marymount University, Emmanuel College)
15. Cardinals (19; Ball State University, Otterbein College)
16. Hawks (18; Monmouth University, Shorter College)
16. Rams (18; Colorado State University, Shepherd University)
18. Vikings (17; Cleveland State University, Augustana College)
19. Golden Eagles (16; Marquette University, College of Southern Idaho)
19. Spartans (16; Michigan State University, D'Youville College)

... And Some Of The Most Uncommon

Auggies (1; Augsburg College)
Banana Slugs (1; University of California, Santa Cruz)
Battlin' Beavers (1; Blackburn College)
Bloodhounds (1; John Jay College of Criminal Justice)
Blueboys (1; Illinois College)
Chanticleers (1; Coastal Carolina University)
Eutectics (1; St. Louis College of Pharmacy)
Fords (1; Haverford College)
Gorloks (1; Webster University)
Ichabods (1; Washburn University)
Judges (1; Brandeis University)
Jumbos (1; Tufts University)
Nanooks (1; University of Alaska-Fairbanks)
Otters (1; Cal State Monterey Bay)
Paladins (1; Furman University)
Pelicans (1; Spalding University)
Phantoms (1; East-West University)
Pilgrims (1; New England College)
Profs (1; Rowan University)
Silverswords (1; Chaminade University)
Stormy Petrels (1; Oglethorpe University)
Violets (1; New York University)
White Mules (1; Colby College)

Source: Pete Fournier, *The Handbook of Mascots and Nicknames*, 2nd edition

Baseball Originals

THE FOUNDING TEAMS OF MAJOR LEAGUE BASEBALL

Baseball in its present two-league structure essentially dates to 1901, when the upstart American League (descendent of the Western League) undertook a bidding war with the older National League (founded in 1876) for the best players. The two circuits eventually reached a peace settlement, paving the way for the first World Series in 1903.

NATIONAL LEAGUE

Boston Beaneaters (founded 1876; now Atlanta Braves)
Chicago Orphans (1876; now Chicago Cubs)
New York Giants (1883; now San Francisco Giants)
Philadelphia Phillies (1883)
Pittsburgh Pirates (1887)
Brooklyn Superbas (1890; now Los Angeles Dodgers)
Cincinnati Reds (1890)
St. Louis Cardinals (1892)

AMERICAN LEAGUE

Baltimore Orioles (1901; now New York Yankees)
Boston Americans (1901; now Boston Red Sox)
Chicago White Sox (1901)
Cleveland Blues (1901; now Cleveland Indians)
Detroit Tigers (1901)
Milwaukee Brewers (1901; now Baltimore Orioles)
Philadelphia Athletics (1901; now Oakland A's)
Washington Senators (1901; now Minnesota Twins)

Basketball Nightmare

THE ORIGINAL OLYMPIC DREAM TEAM ROSTER

When international basketball rules—which had barred NBA players from Olympic participation—were changed in 1989, the United States assembled a juggernaut team composed of its most gifted NBA players (and one token college star). This so-called Dream Team won the 1992 gold medal, beating its eight opponents by an average of 44 points. Here is the roster (and their teams):

Magic Johnson (Los Angeles Lakers)
Michael Jordan (Chicago Bulls)
Charles Barkley (Philadelphia 76ers)
Larry Bird (Boston Celtics)
Clyde Drexler (Portland Trail Blazers)
Patrick Ewing (New York Knicks)
Christian Laettner (Duke University)
Karl Malone (Utah Jazz)
Chris Mullin (Golden State Warriors)
Scottie Pippen (Chicago Bulls)
David Robinson (San Antonio Spurs)
John Stockton (Utah Jazz)

Belt Bucklers

WWE Champions And Their Signature Moves

On January 25, 1963, promoter Vince J. McMahon broke away from the National Wrestling Alliance to form the World Wide Wrestling Federation. With "Nature Boy" Buddy Rogers as its first champion, the Federation dominated the Northeast. In the 1980's, McMahon's son, Vince K. McMahon, took it nationwide with events such as WrestleMania. Today, World Wrestling Entertainment (the name was changed in 1999) dominates the business. Here's a list of champs and the moves that put them on top:

April 29, 1963 **BUDDY ROGERS** (Figure-Four Leg Lock)
May 17, 1963 **BRUNO SAMMARTINO** (Backbreaker)
January 18, 1971 **IVAN KOLOFF** (Flying Knee Drop)
February 2, 1971 **PEDRO MORALES** (Boston Crab)
December 1, 1973 **STAN STASIAK** (Heart Punch)
December 10, 1973 **BRUNO SAMMARTINO** (Backbreaker)
April 30, 1977 **SUPERSTAR BILLY GRAHAM** (Bear Hug)
February 20, 1978 **BOB BACKLUND** (Atomic Knee Drop)
December 26, 1983 **THE IRON SHEIK** (Camel Clutch)
January 23, 1984 **HULK HOGAN** (Leg Drop)
February 5, 1988 **ANDRÉ THE GIANT** (Big Boot)
March 27, 1988 **RANDY SAVAGE** (Flying Elbow Drop)
April 2, 1989 **HULK HOGAN** (Leg Drop)
April 1, 1990 **ULTIMATE WARRIOR** (Warrior Slam)
January 19, 1991 **SGT. SLAUGHTER** (Cobra Clutch)
March 24, 1991 **HULK HOGAN** (Leg Drop)
November 27, 1991 **UNDERTAKER** (Tombstone)
December 3, 1991 **HULK HOGAN** (Leg Drop)
January 19, 1992 **RIC FLAIR** (Figure-Four Leglock)
April 5, 1992 **RANDY SAVAGE** (Flying Elbow Drop)
September 1, 1992 **RIC FLAIR** (Figure-Four Leglock)
October 11, 1992 **BRET HART** (Sharpshooter)
April 4, 1993 **YOKOZUNA** (Bonzai Drop)
April 4, 1993 **HULK HOGAN** (Leg Drop)
June 13, 1993 **YOKOZUNA** (Bonzai Drop)
March 20, 1994 **BRET HART** (The Sharpshooter)
November 23, 1994 **BOB BACKLUND** (Cross Face Chicken Wing)
November 26, 1994 **DIESEL** (Jackknife Powerbomb)

November 19, 1995 **BRET HART** (Sharpshooter)
March 31, 1996 **SHAWN MICHAELS** (Sweet Chin Music)
November 17, 1996 **SID** (Powerbomb)
January 19, 1997 **SHAWN MICHAELS** (Sweet Chin Music)
February 16, 1997 **BRET HART** (The Sharpshooter)
February 17, 1997 **SID** (Powerbomb)
March 23, 1997 **UNDERTAKER** (Tombstone)
August 3, 1997 **BRET HART** (Sharpshooter)
November 9, 1997 **SHAWN MICHAELS** (Sweet Chin Music)
March 29, 1998 **STONE COLD** (Stone Cold Stunner)
June 28, 1998 **KANE** (Chokeslam)
June 29, 1998 **STONE COLD** (Stone Cold Stunner)
November 15, 1998 **THE ROCK** (The People's Elbow)
January 4, 1999 **MANKIND** (Mandible Claw)
January 24, 1999 **THE ROCK** (The People's Elbow)
January 31, 1999 **MANKIND** (Mandible Claw)
February 15, 1999 **THE ROCK** (The People's Elbow)
March 28, 1999 **STONE COLD** (Stone Cold Stunner)
May 23, 1999 **UNDERTAKER** (Tombstone)
June 28, 1999 **STONE COLD** (Stone Cold Stunner)
August 22, 1999 **MANKIND** (Mandible Claw)
August 23, 1999 **TRIPLE H** (Pedigree)
September 16, 1999 **MR. McMAHON** (none used)
September 26, 1999 **TRIPLE H** (Pedigree)
November 14, 1999 **BIG SHOW** (Chokeslam)
January 3, 2000 **TRIPLE H** (Pedigree)
April 30, 2000 **THE ROCK** (The People's Elbow)
May 21, 2000 **TRIPLE H** (Pedigree)
June 25, 2000 **THE ROCK** (The People's Elbow)
October 22, 2000 **KURT ANGLE** (Angle Slam)
February 25, 2001 **THE ROCK** (The People's Elbow)
April 1, 2001 **STONE COLD** (Stone Cold Stunner)
September 23, 2001 **KURT ANGLE** (Angle Slam)
October 8, 2001 **STONE COLD** (Stone Cold Stunner)
December 9, 2001 **CHRIS JERICHO** (Walls of Jericho)
March 17, 2002 **TRIPLE H** (Pedigree)
April 21, 2002 **HULK HOGAN** (Leg Drop)
May 19, 2002 **UNDERTAKER** (Tombstone)
July 21, 2002 **THE ROCK** (The People's Elbow)
August 25, 2002 **BROCK LESNAR** (F-5)
November 17, 2002 **BIG SHOW** (Chokeslam)
December 15, 2002 **KURT ANGLE** (Angle Slam)
March 30, 2003 **BROCK LESNAR** (F-5)
July 27, 2003 **KURT ANGLE** (Angle Slam)
September 18, 2003 **BROCK LESNAR** (F-5)
February 15, 2004 **EDDIE GUERRERO** (Frog Splash)
June 27, 2004 **JBL** (Clothesline From Hell)
April 3, 2005 **JOHN CENA** (STFU)
January 8, 2006 **EDGE** (Spear)
January 29, 2006 **JOHN CENA** (STFU)
June 11, 2006 **ROB VAN DAM** (Five-Star Frog Splash)
July 3, 2006 **EDGE** (Spear)
September 17, 2006 **JOHN CENA** (STFU)

Bespoked Style

Tour de France Dress Code

Jerseys of various designs are presented to leaders after each stage of bicycling's premier event.

YELLOW JERSEY

A new yellow jersey is awarded to the leader in the overall standings, who wears it during the next stage and until he no longer leads the classification. (Introduced in 1919)

GREEN JERSEY

A new green jersey is awarded to the leader in the points standings, who wears it during the next stage and until he no longer leads the classification. (Introduced in 1953, in honor of Tour's 50th anniversary)

RED POLKA-DOT JERSEY

A new red polka-dot jersey is awarded to the King of the Mountains, who wears it during the next stage and until he no longer leads the classification. The best climber is determined by adding the points plus bonuses won in all mountain and hill climbs. (The designation began in 1933 and the polka-dot jersey was introduced in 1975)

WHITE JERSEY

A new white jersey is awarded to the highest-ranking rider under the age of 25. The rider wears the jersey during the next stage and until he no longer leads the classification. There is also an overall winner in the Young Riders classification. (Introduced in 1975, it was dropped in 1989 and reinstated in 2000)

YELLOW HELMET

The riders of the team that is leading in the standings each wear a yellow helmet during the following stage and until the team no longer leads the classification. The general team classification is determined by adding each team's best three individual times for the prologue and every stage, excluding bonus points.

RED NUMBER

The most aggressive rider in each stage wears a red number during the following stage (other riders wear a black number on a white background). The honor is given to the rider who shows the most aggressive attacks during breakaways or leads the chase to catch a breakaway. The recipient for each stage and the overall race is decided by a panel chaired by the race manager or Tour organizer.

Note: If a rider leads in more than one classification, he wears only the highest-ranking jersey. Jerseys rank in the following order: yellow, green, red polka-dot, and white. Riders occupying the next position in rankings wear the corresponding classification jerseys.

Best In Show

MAJOR LEAGUE BASEBALL'S ALL-CENTURY TEAM

In 1999, MLB asked fans to vote for the best players of the 20th century: two for each infield position, two catchers, six pitchers, and nine outfielders. A panel of experts added five more that the fans overlooked (*).

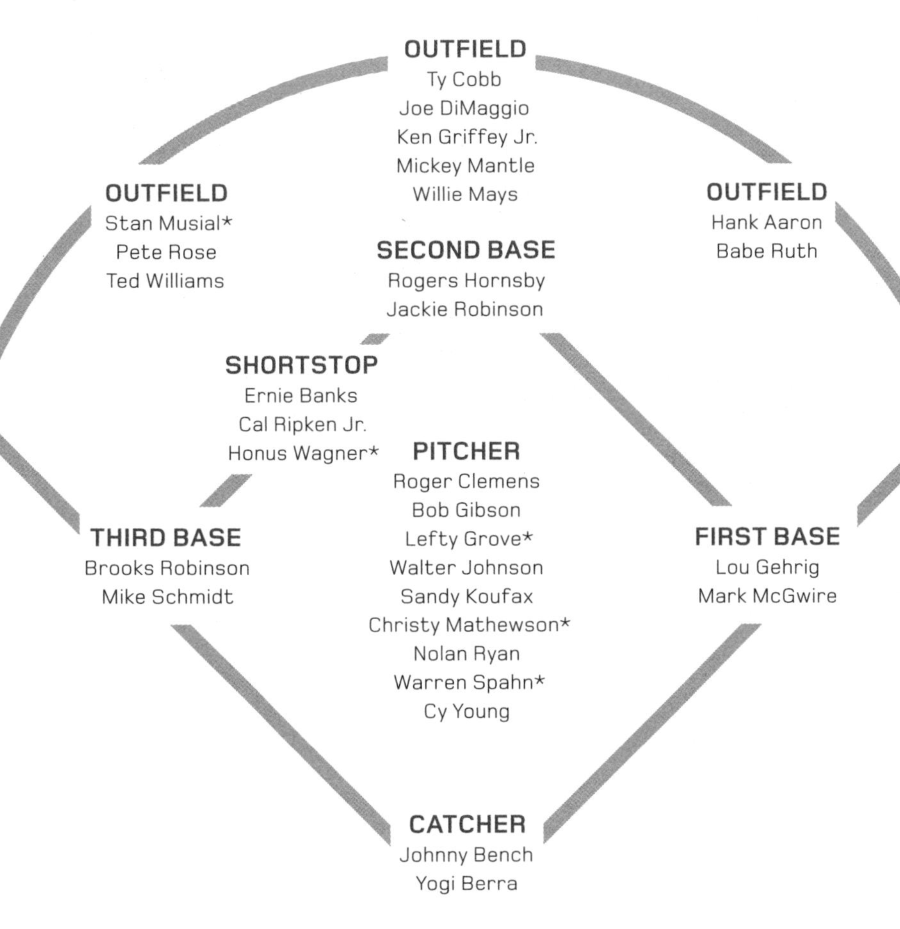

Building Codes

Name Origins Of Stadiums

These days, most sports facilities are named for the highest bidder, but there are still a few that are known (officially or otherwise) by something other than a corporate moniker, the name of the team it houses, or the city in which it is based. Here are some:

BRADLEY CENTER
(Milwaukee Bucks)
For Harry Lynde Bradley, a local businessman whose daughter funded construction costs

FENWAY PARK
(Boston Red Sox)
Located in the Fenway section of Boston

HUBERT H. HUMPHREY METRODOME
(Minnesota Twins, Minnesota Vikings)
For famed senator, vice president, and presidential candidate Hubert Humphrey

JACOBS FIELD
(Cleveland Indians)
For former team owner Richard Jacobs

JOE LOUIS ARENA
(Detroit Red Wings)
For the boxing champ, who grew up in Detroit

LAMBEAU FIELD
(Green Bay Packers)
For founder E.L. "Curly" Lambeau

KAUFFMAN STADIUM
(Kansas City Royals)
For former owner Ewing Kauffman

MADISON SQUARE GARDEN
(New York Knicks, New York Rangers)
An earlier iteration of the building was next to Madison Square Park

PAUL BROWN STADIUM
(Cincinnati Bengals)
For team founder Paul Brown

RFK STADIUM
(D.C. United)
For the late Senator Robert F. Kennedy

ROSE GARDEN ARENA
(Portland Trail Blazers)
Portland is known as the City of Roses

RALPH WILSON STADIUM
(Buffalo Bills)
For the team's first owner

SOLDIER FIELD
(Chicago Bears)
Built to honor veterans of World War I

WRIGLEY FIELD
(Chicago Cubs)
For one-time club owner William Wrigley Jr.

Campus

Cut

A
B
C
D
E
F
G
H
I
J
K
L
M
N
O
P
Q
R
S
T
U
V
W
X
Y
Z

Campus Credit

MAJOR COLLEGE FOOTBALL AWARDS

Chuck Bednarik Award (defensive player)
Fred Biletnikoff Award (receiver)
Bobby Bowden Award (student-athlete)
Buck Buchanan Award (Division I-AA defensive player)
Dick Butkus Award (linebacker)
John Gagliardi Trophy (Division III player)
Lou Groza Award (placekicker)
Ray Guy Award (punter)
Heisman Memorial Trophy (best player)
Ted Hendricks Award (defensive end)
Harlon Hill Trophy (Division II player)
Vince Lombardi/Rotary Award (lineman)
Ronnie Lott Trophy (defensive player, for performance and personal attributes)
John Mackey Award (tight end)
Manning Award (quarterback, includes bowl game performance)
Maxwell Award (best player)
Bronko Nagurski Trophy (defensive player)
Davey O'Brien Award (quarterback)
John Outland Trophy (interior lineman)
Walter Payton Award (Division I-AA offensive player of the year)
Dave Rimington Trophy (center)
Mosi Tatupu Award (special teams player)
Jim Thorpe Award (defensive back)
Johnny Unitas Golden Arm Award (senior quarterback)
Doak Walker Award (running back)

Canton Classics

INAUGURAL INDUCTEES INTO THE PRO FOOTBALL HALL OF FAME

The Pro Football Hall of Fame in Canton, Ohio, was founded in 1963. Here is the original 17-member class, and the first inductee by position:

ORIGINAL CLASS

Sammy Baugh: QB; Washington Redskins (1937-52)
Bert Bell: league administrator and owner; Philadelphia Eagles, Pittsburgh Steelers (1933-59)
Joe Carr: league administrator (1921-39)
Earl "Dutch" Clark: QB; Portsmouth Spartans, Detroit Lions (1931-38)
Harold "Red" Grange: HB; Chicago Bears, AFL New York Yankees, NFL New York Yankees (1925-34)
George Halas: founder, owner, coach; Decatur Staleys, Chicago Staleys, Chicago Bears (1920-83)

Mel Hein: C; New York Giants (1931-45)
Wilbur "Pete" Henry*: T; Canton Bulldogs, New York Giants, Pottsville Maroons (1920-28)
Robert "Cal" Hubbard*: T; New York Giants, Green Bay Packers, Pittsburgh Pirates (1927-36)
Don Hutson: End; Green Bay Packers (1935-45)
Earl "Curly" Lambeau: founder, player, coach; Green Bay Packers, Chicago Cardinals, Washington Redskins (1919-53)
Tim Mara: founder, administrator; New York Giants (1925-59)
George Preston Marshall: founder, administrator; Boston Braves, Boston Redskins, Washington Redskins (1932-69)
John "Blood" McNally: HB; Milwaukee Badgers, Duluth Eskimos, Pottsville Maroons, Green Bay Packers, Pittsburgh Pirates (1925-38)
Bronko Nagurski: FB; Chicago Bears (1930-37, 1943)
Ernie Nevers: FB; Duluth Eskimos, Chicago Cardinals (1926-31)
Jim Thorpe: HB; Canton Bulldogs, Cleveland Indians, Oorang Indians, Rock Island Independents, New York Giants, Chicago Cardinals (1915-28)

BY POSITION

HALFBACK: Harold "Red" Grange; Earl "Curly" Lambeau, John "Blood" McNally, Jim Thorpe (1963)
FULLBACK: Bronko Nagurski, Ernie Nevers (1963)
QUARTERBACK: Sammy Baugh, Earl "Dutch" Clark (1963)
CENTER: Mel Hein* (1963)
GUARD: Mike Michalske*, New York Yankees, Green Bay Packers; 1926-35, 1937 (1964)
OFFENSIVE TACKLE: Wilbur "Pete" Henry*; Robert "Cal" Hubbard* (1963)
WIDE RECEIVER: Don Hutson (1963)
TIGHT END: Mike Ditka, Chicago Bears, Philadelphia Eagles, Dallas Cowboys; 1961-72 (1988)
DEFENSIVE TACKLE: Art Donovan, Baltimore Colts, New York Yankees, Dallas Texans, Baltimore Colts; 1950-61 (1968)
DEFENSIVE END: Andy Robustelli, Los Angeles Rams, New York Giants; 1951-64 (1971)
LINEBACKER: Chuck Bednarik*, Philadelphia Eagles; 1949-62 (1967)
SAFETY: Emlen Tunnell, New York Giants, Green Bay Packers; 1948-61 (1967)
CORNERBACK: Dick "Night Train" Lane, Los Angeles Rams, Chicago Cardinals, Detroit Lions; 1952-65 (1974)
PLACEKICKER: Lou Groza*, Cleveland Browns; 1946-67 (1974); Jan Stenerud, Kansas City Chiefs, Green Bay Packers, Minnesota Vikings; 1967-85 (1991)
COACH: George Halas (1963), Curly Lambeau (1963)
COMMISSIONER: Bert Bell (1963)
OWNER: Tim Mara, George Preston Marshall (1963)
SUPERVISOR OF OFFICIALS: Hugh "Shorty" Ray (1966)

*Two-way player

A B C D E F G H I J K L M N O P Q R S T U V W X Y Z

Canvas Regulations

Original Marquess Of Queensberry Rules For Boxing

In 1867, British sportsman and journalist John Graham Chambers wrote the Marquess of Queensberry Rules, the basis of boxing as we know it today. The rules were so named because they were sanctioned by John Sholto Douglas, the ninth Marquess of Queensberry. On August 29, 1885, the first United States title fight under these rules took place in Cincinnati, when John L. Sullivan defeated Dominick McCaffery in six rounds.

1. To be a fair stand-up boxing match in a 24 foot ring or as near that size as practicable.

2. No wrestling or hugging allowed.

3. The rounds to be of three minutes' duration and one-minute time between rounds.

4. If either man fall through weakness or otherwise, he must get up unassisted, ten seconds be allowed him to do so, the other man meanwhile to return to his corner, and when the fallen man is on his legs the round is to be resumed and continued until the three minutes have expired. If one man fails to come to the scratch in the ten seconds allowed, it shall be in the power of the referee to give his award in favour of the other man.

5. A man hanging on the ropes in a help less state, with his toes off the ground, shall be considered down.

6. No seconds or any other person to be allowed in the ring during the rounds.

7. Should the contest be stopped by any unavoidable interference, the referee [is] to name the time and place as soon as possible for finishing the contest, so that the match must be won and lost, unless the backers of both men agree to draw the stakes.

8. The gloves to be fair-sized boxing gloves of the best quality and new.

9. Should a glove burst, or come off, it must be replaced to the referee's satisfaction.

10. A man on one knee is considered down, and if struck is entitled to the stakes.

11. No shoes or boots with springs allowed.

12. The contest in all other respects to be governed by the revised rules of the London Prize Ring.

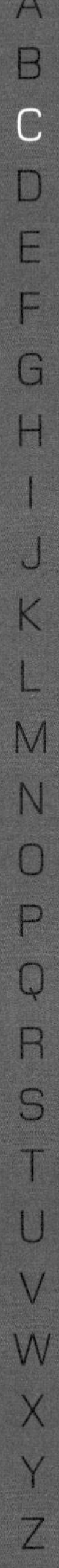

Captain Cover

Magazine Covers That Have Featured Michael Jordan

Baseball Card Price Guide
Basketball Digest
Beckett Baseball Monthly
Beckett Basketball Monthly
Beckett Sports Collectibles
Cigar Aficionado
Details
Digital Diner
Disney Adventures
Ebony
Ebony Man
Entertainment Memorabilia Magazine
ESPN The Magazine
Esquire
Fortune
GamePro
Gold Collectors Series Magazine
GQ
Hoop Magazine
Hoops NBA Yearbook
Inside Sports
Inside Stuff
Jet
Legends
Men's Fitness
Newsweek
Petersen's Basketball Preview
SLAM
Sport
Sports Card Trader
Sports Illustrated
Sports Illustrated for Kids
Sports Market Report
Street & Smith's Pro Basketball
Super Sports Basketball Scene
The Green Magazine
The Investor's Journal
The Sporting News
Time
Trading Cards
Travel + Leisure Golf
Tuff Stuff
TV Guide
TV Sports Calendar
Vibe
WWF Magazine

★ Center Cities

State Capitals With Big Four Sports Teams

Atlanta: Braves (1966)
Falcons (1966)
Hawks (1969)
Thrashers (1999)

Boston: Red Sox (1901)
Bruins (1924)
Celtics (1946)

Columbus:
Blue Jackets (2000)

Denver: Broncos (1960)
Nuggets (1967)
Rockies (1993)
Avalanche (1995)

Indianapolis:
Pacers (1967)
Colts (1984)

Nashville: Titans (1998)
Predators (1998)

Phoenix: Suns (1968)
Cardinals (1988)
Coyotes (1996)
Diamondbacks (1998)

Raleigh:
Hurricanes (1999)

Salt Lake City:
Jazz (1979)

Sacramento:
Kings (1985)

St. Paul: Wild (2000)

Center Of Attention

Nicknames For Wilt Chamberlain

According to Robert Cherry, author of Wilt: Larger Than Life, *the great NBA center had many nicknames bestowed upon him by friends and foes alike, not to mention the ones he gave himself. Here are eight, with their origins:*

Wilt the Stilt: Dubbed by Philly sportswriter Jack Ryan, in obvious reference to Chamberlain's height.

Dippy; Dipper: Family and friends called him this because he had to dip his head through the low doorways of his native West Philadelphia home.

Big Dipper: Derived from Dippy. Chamberlain liked it much more than Wilt the Stilt, which he felt made him seem a freakish, awkward animal.

Uncle Wiltie; Wiltie: What Chamberlain sometimes called himself.

Whip: Harlem Globetrotters teammates called Chamberlain this in a bow to his prodigious manhood.

Wilton Norman Chamberlain: His given name, and the one that Bill Russell called him. The Boston Celtics center and Chamberlain's archrival would often dial him up on the phone and say, "Wilton Norman Chamberlain, this is William Felton Russell calling."

Cereal Stars

Everyone Who Has Appeared On A Wheaties Box

More than 1,400 athletes, teams, and other notables (circus family, fighter pilot, lion tamer, movie stuntman, and even a fictional character or two) have appeared on national or local Wheaties cereal boxes—on the front, side, or back—since Lou Gehrig became the first in 1934. Here, according to General Mills, are all of them:

Hank Aaron, Kareem Abdul-Jabbar, Felix Adler,[1] Andre Agassi, Troy Aikman, Michelle Akers, Muhammad Ali, Ethan Allen,[2] Johnny Allen, Marcus Allen, Sandy Alomar, Mike Alstott, Leonel Alvarez, Luis Alves, Ignacio Ambriz, Ottis Anderson, Sparky Anderson, Carolyn Anthony,[1] Luke Appling, B.J. Armstrong, Jack Armstrong,[3] Lance Armstrong, Morrie Arnovich, Arthur Ashe, Steve Atwater, Red Auerbach, Gene Autry,[4] Earl Averill, Max Baer, Jeff Bagwell, Chris Bailey, Laurie Baker, Capt. R. L. Baker, George Barclay, Tom Barrasso, Marty Barry, Sam Barry, Bob Bartlett,[5] Mengke Bateer, Alice Bauer, Marlene Bauer, Sammy Baugh, Mark Bavaro, Myriam Bedard, Jody Beerman, Sheldon Beise, Beau Bell, James "Cool Papa" Bell, Madison "Matty" Bell, Edward A. Bellande,[6] Johnny Bench, Andy Benes, Brooke Bennett, Cornelius Bennett, Edgar Bennett, Patty Berg, Wally Berger, Bonnie Berning, Yogi Berra, Raymond Berry, Bernie Bierman, Craig Biggio, Chauncey Billups, Larry Bird, Alana Blahoski, Drew Bledsoe, Barry Bonds, Zeke Bonura, Amanda Borden, Bill Bordley, Lou Boudreau, Phil Bourque, Bruce Bowen, William Boyd,[4] Terry Bradshaw, Tom Brady, Branco, Denny Brauer, Tommy Bridges, Heine Brock, Derrick Brooks, Johnny Mack Brown,[4] Mack Brown, Tim Brown, Troy Brown, Isaac Bruce, Jane Buch, Don Budge, Mark Buehrle, Jay Buhner, Marc Buoniconti, Nick Buoniconti, Ellis Burks, Heidi Bush, Dick Butkus, Butterfly Unit,[1] Wally Butts, Karyn Bye, Earnest Byner, Red Cagle, Dolph Camilli, Ken Caminiti, Roy Campanella, Elden Campbell, Ezra Canty, Harry Carey,[4] James H. Carmichael,[6] Chris Carpenter, Cris Carter, Kevin Carter, Bill Cartwright, Ron Cey, Sammy Chagolla, Wilt Chamberlain, Evelyn Chandler, Joey Cheek, Mark Chmura, Amy Chow, Earl "Dutch" Clark, Gary Clark, Speedy Claxton, Roberto Clemente, Harlond Clift, Ben Coates, Mickey Cochrane, Paul Coffey, Con Colleano,[1] Rip Collins, Antoinette Concello,[1] David Cone, Michael Cooper, Joey Cora, Ray "Crash" Corrigan,[4] Bob Cousy, Colleen Coyne, Roger Craig, Joe Cronin, Jim Crowley, (Speed) Cummings, Kiki Cuyler, John Daniels, Harry Danning, Ed Danowski, Gordon S. Darnell,[6] Bob Davies, Curt Davis, Eric Davis, Glenn Davis, Terrell Davis, Dominque Dawes, Darryl Dawkins, Lowell "Red" Dawson, Ned Day, Dizzy Dean, Paul Dean, Bill DeLancey, Jack Del Rio, Frank Demaree, (Speed) Dempsey, Jack Dempsey, Leslie Deniz, Paul Derringer, Detroit Pistons (2004), Detroit Shock (2006), Katlin Detsch, Joanna de Tuscan, Donna deVarona, Bill Dickey, Babe Didrikson, Charlie Diehl,[2] Joe DiMaggio, Tom Dolan, Chris Doleman, Tony Dorsett, Abner Doubleday, Stacy Dragila, Clyde Drexler, Joe Dumars, Tim Duncan, Tricia

........➤

Cereal Stars, continued from page 33

Dunn, Leo Durocher, Dale Earnhardt , Bill Elliott, John Elway, Bob Errey, Julius Erving, Boomer Esiason, Chris Evert, Betty Fairfield,[3] Jeremy Farnan, Marshall Faulk, Jane Fauntz, Brett Favre, Tom Fears, Bob Feller, Tammie Ferguson, Danny Ferry, Lou Fette, Nancy Filimonczuk, Jennifer Finzel, Leonard Flowers, Tyron Floyd, Lew Fonseca, Barry Foster, Tremaine Fowlkes, Jimmie Foxx, A.J. Foyt, Irvin Frailey, Gretchen Fraser, Walt Frazier, Mal B. Freeburg,[6] Benny Friedman, Frank Frisch, Denise Fuller, Peter Gagarin, Andres Galarraga, Sherry Galloway, Kevin Garnett, Justin Gatlin, Lou Gehrig, Charles Gehringer, Althea Gibson, Josh Gibson, Kirk Gibson, Randy Gilhen, Mlle. Gillette, Manu Ginobili, Ty Gleason,[2] Terry Glenn, Lefty Gomez, Juan Gonzalez, Joe "Flash" Gordon, Goose Goslin, Otto Graham, Cammi Granato, Red Grange, Horace Grant, A.C. Green, Hank Greenberg, "Mean Joe" Greene , Kevin Greene, Wayne Gretzky, Ken Griffey Jr., Lefty Grove, Ralph Guldahl, Tony Gwynn, Stan Hack, Odell Hale, Darvin Ham, Richard Hamilton, Hanson & Garrigan, Capt. R. G. Hanson,[6] Franco Harris, Marvin Harrison, Gabby Hartnett, Charles Hartwig, Joe Hauser, John Havlicek, Eric Heiden, Doug Heir, Rollie Hemsley, George Hendry, Arnie Herber, Dorothy Herbert,[1] Billy Herman, Jim Hershberger, Ben Hogan, Merril Hoge, Nat Holman, Mike Holmgren, Joe Horlen, Desmond Howard, Dixie Howell, Kent Hrbek, Carl Hubbell, Sarah Hughes, Lindsey Hunter, The Flying Hutchinsons,[1] Don Hutson, Adele Inge, Michael Irvin, Cecil Isbell, Qadry Ismail, Francis Jackson, Stephen Jackson, Capt. Terrell Jacobs,[1] Peter Jacobsen, Joe Jacoby, Irving Jaffee, Jaromir Jagr, Mike James, Ned Jarrett, Ab Jenkins, Bruce Jenner, Lynn Jennings, Derek Jeter, Brad Johnson, Keyshawn Johnson, Lee Johnson,[2] Magic Johnson, Mr. and Mrs. Martin Johnson,[7] Michael Johnson, Pepper Johnson, Randy Johnson, Robert Johnson, Vinnie Johnson, Brent Jones, Howard Jones, K.C. Jones, Tom Jones,[2] Buck Jordan, Michael Jordan, Jackie Joyner-Kersee, George Kell, Jim Kelly, Ralph Kercheval, Andy Kerr, Steve Kerr, Bob Kessler, Ralph Kiner, Katie King, Harry Kipke, Chuck Klein, Kit Klein, Jack Knight[6], Bernie Kosar, Stan Kostka, Jack Kramer, Jim Lachey, Bill Laimbeer, Carnell Lake, Sean Landeta, Steve Largent, Barry Larkin, Frank Larson, Ty Law, Bobby Layne, Bill Lee, Mario Lemieux, Bob Lemon, Darrell Lester, Carl Lewis, John "Buddy" Lewis, Gene Lillard, Lawson Little, Greg Lloyd, Kenny Lofton, Ernie Lombardi, Vince Lombardi, Troy Loney, Luc Longley, Shelley Looney, Ronnie Lott, Ed Lubanski, John Lugbill, Johnny Lujack, H. Lund,[8] Todd Lyght, John Lynch, George Maddox, Greg Maddux, Rick Mahorn, Phil Mahre, Steve Mahre, Gus Mancuso, Jack Manders, Tony Manero, Lloyd Mangrum, Charles Mann, Matt Mann,[2] Peyton Manning, Ed Manske, Mickey Mantle, Heinie Manush, Alice Marble, Dan Marino, Marty Marion, Johnny "Pepper" Martin, Edgar Martinez, Lizbeth Martinez, Pedro Martinez, Tino Martinez, Tom Matte, Willie Mays, Cynthia Mazur, Tim McCarver, Frank "Buck" McCormick, Barney McCosky, Tim McCoy,[1] Michael McCrary, Bucko McDonald, Wellington P. McFail,[6] Henry McGee, Mark McGwire, Jessie McLeod, Hugh McManus, Dave McMillan, Marie

McMillan,[1] Bo McMillin, Mary T. Meagher, Joe Medwick, Sue Merz, Jose Mesa, Eddie Michaels, George Mikan, Darko Milicic, Lisa Brown Miller, Shannon Miller, Wayne Miller, Lawyer Milloy, Billy Mills, Minnesota Twins (1987), Johnny Mize, Dominique Moceanu, Regis Monahan, Art Monk, Joe Montana, Warren Moon, Joe Moore, John Moore, Byron Morris, Hal Morris, J. H. Morrisey,[8] Monk Moscrip, Wally Moses, Vicki Movsessian, Fred Muller, Van Lingle Mungo, George Murray, Stan Musial, Mike Mussina, George I. Myers,[6] Randy Myers, Bronko Nagurski, Joe Namath, Steve Nash, Bert Nelson,[1] Byron Nelson, Cindy Nelson, Ernie Nevers, Hal Newhouser, Bobo Newsom, New York Giants (1990), (Speed) Nichols, Jack Nicklaus, Nicola, Hideo Nomo, Carl Nordly,[2] Ken Norton, Jay Novacek, Bart Oates, Dan O'Brien, Davey O'Brien, Jack O'Brien, Neil O'Donnell, Jonathan Ogden, Megan O'Hara, Apolo Anton Ohno, Mehmet Okur, Shaquille O'Neal, David Ortiz, Tom Osborne, Mel Ott, Eiji Oue, Jesse Owens, Orlando Pace, Brian Paek, Leroy "Satchel" Paige, Rafael Palmeiro, Arnold Palmer, Jim Palmer, Brad Park, Tony Parker, Benny Parsons, Joe Paterno, Lynn Patrick, Carly Patterson, Jimmy Patterson, John Paxson, Isabelle Payne, Walter Payton, Drew Pearson, Lee Petty, Richard Petty, Jaycie Phelps, Michael Phelps, Roman Phifer, Mike Piazza, Frank Pietrangelo, Andy Pilney, Scottie Pippen, Jim Pollard, Tayshaun Prince, Kirby Puckett, Rene Pugnet,[9] Albert Pujols, Raymond Radcliff, Maria Rasputin,[1] Ronald Reagan, Andre Reed, Harold "Pee Wee" Reese, Repenski Troupe,[1] Dorothy Lee Resseguie, Mary Lou Retton, Kim Rhodenbaugh, Jerry Rice, Bob Richards, Bobby Richardson, Mark Richt, Jose Rijo, Freddy Rincon, Cal Ripken Jr., Phil Rizzuto, William W. Robbins, Brooks Robinson, David Robinson, Jackie Robinson, John J. Robinson, Ricardo Rocha, Bill Rodgers, Dennis Rodman, Alex Rodriguez, Elwin "Preacher" Roe, Jennie Rooney,[1] Malik Rose, Pete Rose, Al Rosen, Norman Ross, Tom Ross, L. T. Rowe, Charles "Red" Ruffing, Babe Ruth, Nolan Ryan, Mark Rypien, Chris Sabo, Sacramento Monarchs (2005), Joan Benoit Samuelson, San Antonio Spurs (2003), San Antonio Spurs (2005), Ryne Sandberg, Barry Sanders, Deion Sanders, Ricky Sanders, Cael Sanderson, Gene Sarazen, Wes Schulmerich, Barbara Ann Scott, Byron Scott, Todd Scott, Briana Scurry, Shannon Sharpe, Wilbur Shaw, William Sheperd, Karen Sheridan, Don Shula, Al Simmons, Phil Simms, Arnie Simso,[2] Singer and Harris and Hall, Antowain Smith, Bruce Smith, Dick Smith, Elinore Smith, Emmitt Smith, Lee Smith, Neil Smith, Ozzie Smith, Riley Smith, Steve Smith, John Smoltz, Sam Snead, Duke Snider, Larry Snyder, Paul Sorrento, Warren Spahn, Truman Spain, Chris Spielman, Eddie Stanky, Bart Starr, Arnold Statz, Roger Staubach, Kevin Stevens, (Speed) Stevenson, Victor Stewart, Sam Stillings, Dave Stockton, Elvis Stojko, M.W. Stoker,[10] Kerri Strug, Harry Stuhldreher, (Speed) Sullivan, Peter Taglianetti, Shirley Temple,[4] Texas Western Basketball Team (1966), Joe Theismann, Yancey Thigpen, Frank Thomas, Isiah Thomas, Thurman Thomas, Reyna Thompson, Melanie Toftum, Cecil Travis, Tom Tresh, Lee Trevino, Harold "Hal" Trosky, Sarah Tueting, Lewis S. Turner,[6]

........➤

Cereal Stars continued from page 35
Twin Zephyrs, Grover Tyler,[6] Gretchen Ulion, Johnny Unitas, USA Men's Olympic Hockey Team (1980), USA Women's Olympic Gymnastics Team (1996), USA Women's Olympic Hockey Team (1998), Carlos Valderrama, Amy Van Dyken, Jimmy Vasser, Arky Vaughan, Zoilo Versalles, Michael Vick, Ellsworth Vines, Maribel Vinson, Joe Vosmik, Dwyane Wade, Wallace Wade, Lynn Waldorf, David Walker, Doak Walker, Gerald "Gee" Walker, Ben Wallace, Rasheed Wallace, Wallenda Troupe,[1] Bucky Walters, Darrell Waltrip, Paul Waner, Cotton Warburton, Lon Warneke, Glenn S. Warner, Roy H. Warner,[6] Charles Wasicek, Bob Waterfield, Ricky Watters, Tom Weiskopf, Johnny Weismuller,[4] David Wells, Billy Welu, Jerry West, Mark Wheaton, Ed White, Jo Jo White, Reggie White, Pinky Whitney, Sandra Whyte, Laura Wilkinson, Bernie Williams, Esther Williams, Ted Williams, Corliss Williamson, Kevin Willis, Dan Wilson, Hack Wilson, Robert Wilson, Dave Winfield, Tiger Woods, Rod Woodson, James Worthy, Kristi Yamaguchi, Cale Yarborough, Rudy York, Steve Young, Hugo and Mario Zacchini,[1] Alex Zanardi

[1]circus star; [2]amateur coach; [3]fictional character; [4]movie star; [5]polar explorer; [6]aviator; [7]big-game hunters; [8]railroad engineer; [9]boat captain; [10]trick rodeo rider

Cooperstown Pioneers

Inaugural Inductees Into The Baseball Hall Of Fame

Like football, the first baseball Hall of Fame class did not include a player from each position. Here are the original members (inducted in 1936), listed in order of votes received, as well as the first inductees, by position:

ORIGINAL CLASS

Ty Cobb: CF; Detroit Tigers, Philadelphia Athletics (1905-28)

Babe Ruth: OF, P; Boston Red Sox, New York Yankees, Boston Braves (1914-35)

Honus Wagner: SS; Louisville Colonels, Pittsburgh Pirates (1897-1917)

Christy Mathewson: P; New York Giants, Cincinnati Reds (1900-16)

Walter Johnson: P; Washington Senators (1907-27)

BY POSITION

FIRST BASE (1939): Cap Anson (Rockford Forest Citys, Philadelphia Athletics, Chicago White Stockings/Colts; 1871-97); Lou Gehrig (New York Yankees; 1923-39); George Sisler (St. Louis Browns, Washington Senators, Boston Braves; 1915-30)

SECOND BASE (1937): Napoleon Lajoie (Philadelphia Phillies, Philadelphia Athletics, Cleveland Indians; 1896-1916)

SHORTSTOP (1936): Honus Wagner

THIRD BASE (1945): Jimmy Collins (Louisville Colonels, Boston Beaneaters, Boston Red Sox, Philadelphia Athletics; 1895-1908)

LEFT FIELD (1945): Fred Clarke (Louisville Colonels, Pittsburgh Pirates; 1894-1915), Ed Delahanty (Philadelphia Quakers, Cleveland Infants, Philadelphia Phillies, Washington Senators; 1888-1903); Jim O'Rourke (Middletown Mansfields, Boston Red Stockings, Boston Red Caps, Providence Grays, Buffalo Bisons, New York Giants, New York Giants Players League, Washington Senators; 1872-1904)

CENTER FIELD (1936): Ty Cobb

RIGHT FIELD (1936): Babe Ruth

CATCHER (1939): Buck Ewing (Troy Trojans, New York Gothams/Giants, New York Giants Players League, Cleveland Spiders, Cincinnati Reds; 1880-97)

PITCHER (1936): Walter Johnson; Christy Mathewson

RELIEF PITCHER (1985): Hoyt Wilhelm (New York Giants, Cleveland Indians, St. Louis Cardinals, Baltimore Orioles, Chicago White Sox, California Angels, Atlanta Braves, Chicago Cubs, Los Angeles Dodgers; 1952-72)

MANAGER (1937): John McGraw (Baltimore Orioles NL & AL, New York Giants; 1899-1932); Connie Mack (Pittsburgh Pirates, Milwaukee/Western League, Philadelphia Athletics; 1894-1950)

Cut Men

Songs With Titles Or Lyrics That Mention Athletes

SONG	ATHLETE
Slide, Kelly, Slide (Maggie Cline; 1889)	Mike "King" Kelly
Let's Go Joe (Cab Calloway and His Orchestra; 1942)	Joe Louis
Did You See Jackie Robinson Hit That Ball? (Buddy Johnson; 1949)	Jackie Robinson Satchel Paige Roy Campanella Don Newcombe Larry Doby
Say Hey [The Willie Mays Song] (The Treniers; 1954)	Willie Mays
Mrs. Robinson (Simon & Garfunkel; 1967)	Joe DiMaggio
Hurricane (Bob Dylan; 1975)	Rubin Carter
Rapper's Delight (The Sugarhill Gang; 1979)	Muhammad Ali
Let It Flow [for Dr. J] (Grover Washington Jr.; 1980)	Julius Erving
Centerfield (John Fogerty; 1985)	Joe DiMaggio, Ty Cobb, Willie Mays
I Think I Can Beat Mike Tyson (DJ Jazzy Jeff and the Fresh Prince; 1989)	Mike Tyson
Magic Johnson (Red Hot Chili Peppers; 1989)	Magic Johnson A.C. Green Kareem Abdul-Jabbar James Worthy Byron Scott
We Didn't Start the Fire (Billy Joel; 1989)	Joe DiMaggio Sugar Ray Robinson Roy Campanella Mickey Mantle Sonny Liston Floyd Patterson Rocky Marciano
Vogue (Madonna; 1990)	Joe DiMaggio
Scenario (A Tribe Called Quest; 1991)	Bo Jackson Joe Namath
Jump Around (House of Pain; 1992)	John McEnroe
Tie Goes to the Runner (Public Enemy; 1992)	Jim Brown
The Chase, Part II (A Tribe Called Quest; 1993)	Vinny Testaverde
Protect Ya Neck (The Jump Off) (Wu-Tang Clan; 1993)	Pete Sampras Jesse Owens Jackie Joyner-Kersee
What's Up Doc? (Can We Rock) (Fu-Schnickens with Shaquille O'Neal; 1993)	Dick Butkus Christian Laettner Alonzo Mourning Randy Savage Bruce Lee

SONG	ATHLETE
Alright Hear This (Beastie Boys; 1994)	Bobby Knight
Ty Cobb (Soundgarden; 1996)	Ty Cobb
4, 3, 2, 1 (LL Cool J; 1997)	Roy Jones Jr. Michael Jordan Ken Griffey Jr.
Lie to Kick It (2Pac; 1997)	Michael Jordan Mike Tyson
Sweet Beatrice (Adam Sandler; 1997)	Guy Lafleur Robert Parish
Gettin' Jiggy Wit It (Will Smith; 1997)	Shaquille O'Neal Muhammad Ali
Just Don't Give A... (Eminem; 1997)	Marty Schottenheimer Mike Tyson
I-76 (G. Love & Special Sauce; 1997)	Charles Barkley Larry Bird Maurice Cheeks Julius Erving Moses Malone Andrew Toney Darryl Dawkins Bobby Jones Allen Iverson Jerry Stackhouse
Let It Rain (Xzibit; 1998)	Jack Nicklaus Cassius Clay
What Would Brian Boitano Do? (*South Park: Bigger, Longer & Uncut* Soundtrack; 1999)	Brian Boitano

SONG	ATHLETE
Michael Jordan (Five For Fighting; 2000)	Michael Jordan
Heroes (Jill Sobule; 2000)	Babe Ruth
Loaded (Ricky Martin; 2000)	Sammy Sosa
Mighty Healthy (Ghostface Killah; 2000)	Derek Jeter
Live From the Streets (Angie Martinez; 2001)	Latrell Sprewell
Heart of the City (Ain't No Love) (Jay-Z; 2001)	Randall Cunningham
The Whole World (OutKast; 2001)	Randy Moss
Wayne Gretzky (Goldfinger; 2002)	Wayne Gretzky
This Is Who I Am (Lil' Kim; 2003)	Wilt Chamberlain
Piazza, New York Catcher (Belle & Sebastian; 2003)	Mike Piazza
Act a Fool (Master P featuring Lil Jon; 2004)	Sam Cassell
My Hood (Elliott Ness featuring P. Diddy; 2004)	Walter Payton

Double

D

Dubious

A B C D E F G H I J K L M N O P Q R S T U V W X Y Z

Double Headers

Players Who Won Championships In College And The Pros In Consecutive Years

BASKETBALL

Bill Russell (University of San Francisco, 1956; Boston Celtics, 1957)
Henry Bibby (UCLA, 1972; New York Knicks, 1973)
Magic Johnson (Michigan State University, 1979; Los Angeles Lakers, 1980)
Billy Thompson (University of Louisville, 1986; Los Angeles Lakers, 1987)

FOOTBALL

Tony Dorsett (University of Pittsburgh, 1976; Dallas Cowboys, 1977)
Danny Stubbs (University of Miami, 1987; San Francisco 49ers, 1988)
Derrick Lassic (University of Alabama, 1992; Dallas Cowboys, 1993)
William Floyd (Florida State University, 1993; San Francisco 49ers, 1994)
Tyrone Williams (University of Nebraska, 1995; Green Bay Packers, 1996)
Brian Griese (University of Michigan, 1997; Denver Broncos, 1998)
Marquise Hill (Louisiana State University, 2003; New England Patriots, 2004)

Note: 1965-97, AP poll used to determine national champion; 1998-2004, BCS ranking

Drama Kings, Part One

Athletes Who Act

It's one thing to take a dive to draw a penalty. It's quite another to pretend to be someone else entirely. Here are some athletes who have had decent success on the big—or little—screen (along with their "signature" movies or shows):

Kareem Abdul-Jabbar *(Game of Death, Airplane!)*
Muhammad Ali *(Freedom Road)*
Ray Allen *(He Got Game)*
Lyle Alzado *(Ernest Goes to Camp)*
André The Giant *(The Princess Bride)*
Barry Bonds *(Beverly Hills, 90210)*
Brian Bosworth *(Stone Cold)*
Terry Bradshaw *(Failure to Launch)*
Jim Brown *(The Dirty Dozen)*
John Cena *(The Marine)*
Wilt Chamberlain *(Conan the Destroyer)*
Roger Clemens *(Kingpin)*
Vlade Divac *(Juwanna Mann)*
Julius Erving *(The Fish That Saved Pittsburgh)*
Rick Fox *(Oz)*
Rosey Grier *(The Thing with Two Heads)*
Tony Hawk *(CSI: Miami)*
Hulk Hogan *(Rocky III)*
Allan Houston *(Black and White)*
Michael Irvin *(The Longest Yard)*
Howie Long *(3000 Miles to Graceland)*
Cam Neely *(Dumb and Dumber)*
Merlin Olsen *(Father Murphy)*
Shaquille O'Neal *(Kazaam)*
Roddy Piper *(They Live)*
The Rock *(The Scorpion King)*

Drama Kings, Part Deux

Actors Who Were Athletes

Known now mostly for their film and television roles, these thespians were serious athletes in a previous life. Here they are, with their signature role(s) and jock chops:

Randall "Tex" Cobb *(Fletch Lives, Raising Arizona)*: Heavyweight boxer, 1977-93

Chuck Connors *(The Rifleman)*: Boston Celtics forward, 1946-1948; Chicago Cubs first baseman, 1951

Mark Harmon *(St. Elsewhere, NCIS)*: UCLA quarterback, 1972-73

Alex Karras *(Webster, Blazing Saddles)*: Detroit Lions defensive tackle, 1958-62, 1964-70

Ed Marinaro *(Hill Street Blues)*: Minnesota Vikings, New York Jets, Seattle Seahawks running back, 1972-77

Burt Reynolds *(The Longest Yard, Deliverance)*: Florida State running back, 1954

Woody Strode *(Spartacus, The Man Who Shot Liberty Valance)*: Los Angeles Rams defensive end, 1946

Bob Uecker *(Major League, Mr. Belvedere)*: Milwaukee Braves, St. Louis Cardinals, Philadelphia Phillies, Atlanta Braves catcher, 1962-67

Michael Warren *(Hill Street Blues)*: UCLA point guard, 1966-68

Carl Weathers *(Rocky, Rocky II)*: Oakland Raiders linebacker, 1970-71

Fred Williamson *(M*A*S*H)*: Pittsburgh Steelers, Oakland Raiders, Kansas City Chiefs defensive back, 1960-67

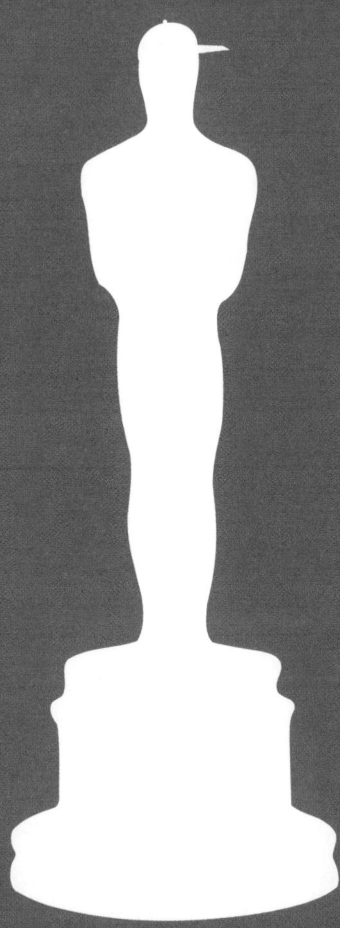

Dennis Rodman *(Double Team)*
John Salley *(Eddie)*
O.J. Simpson *(The Naked Gun)*
Kelly Slater *(Baywatch)*
Fran Tarkenton *(Hill Street Blues)*
Antonio Tarver *(Rocky Balboa)*
Lawrence Taylor *(1st & Ten, Any Given Sunday)*

A
B
C
D
E
F
G
H
I
J
K
L
M
N
O
P
Q
R
S
T
U
V
W
X
Y
Z

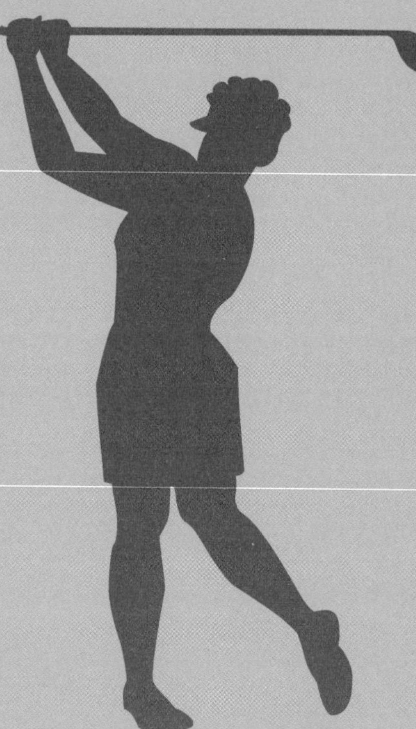

Driving Tests

Signature Golf Holes

Unlike football fields or basketball courts, golf courses have unique designs that offer a different challenge at every hole. Here are 18 of the most renowned holes in the world, with the features for which they are chiefly known:

The 2nd Hole at Valderrama Golf Club (Cadiz, Spain)
Par-4, 385 yards
Claim to fame: Large cork oak tree guards middle of fairway.

The 3rd Hole at Oakmont Country Club (Oakmont, Pennsylvania)
Par-4, 425 yards
"Church pews" bunker contains 12 rows of grass-covered ridges.

The 4th Hole at Banff Springs Golf Course (Banff, Alberta)
Par-3, 199 yards
Elevated tee shot over glacial lake to small, bowl-shaped "devil's cauldron" green.

The 4th Hole at Royal County Down Golf Club (Newcastle, Northern Ireland)
Par-3, 213 yards
Sea of gorse and greenside bunkers make hole daunting, but water and mountain views from elevated tee provide one of sport's best views.

The 5th Hole at Royal Melbourne Golf Club, Composite Course (Melbourne, Australia)
Par-3, 176 yards
Modeled after Eden Hole at St. Andrews (the 11th on the Old Course), a set of deep bunkers hug steeply sloped green, framed by native brush.

The 8th Hole at the Old Course at Royal Troon Golf Club (Troon, Scotland)
Par-3, 123 yards
"Postage stamp" green just 30 feet across at widest point and surrounded by five bunkers.

The 10th Hole at Pine Valley Golf Club (Pine Valley, New Jersey)
Par-3, 161 yards
"Devil's asshole," pot bunker from which best escape is a backward shot.

The 10th Hole at Winged Foot Golf Club, West Course (Mamaroneck, New York)
Par-3, 190 yards
Elevated "pulpit" green slopes downward, flanked by two bunkers.

The 13th Hole at Augusta National Golf Club (Augusta, Georgia)
Par-5, 510 yards
Rae's Creek runs along left side of fairway and cuts across front of green.

The 13th Hole at Medinah Country Club, Course No. 3 (Medinah, Illinois)
Par-3, 219 yards
Visually stunning from start to finish, featuring water, sand, oaks, and maples. But the aesthetics belie the hazards: a steeply sloping putting surface, three well-defined bunkers and Lake Kadijah, resting in front of the green.

The 16th Hole at Cypress Point Club (Pebble Beach, California)
Par-3, 218 yards
Tee shot atop cliff carries across the Pacific Ocean.

The 16th Hole at Merion Golf Club, East Course (Ardmore, Pennsylvania)
Par-4, 460 yards
End of fairway meets old limestone quarry filled with sand, rocks, and shrubs.

The 16th Hole at Shinnecock Hills Golf Club (Southampton, New York)
Par-5, 542 yards
Twenty bunkers line both sides of fairway that bends four times from tee to green.

The 16th Hole at TPC Scottsdale, Stadium Course (Phoenix, Arizona)
Par-3, 162 yards
Typically plebian turns into pandemonium every year for the FBR Open, when fans gather by the thousands—serenading approaching players, cheering good shots, and lustily booing bad ones—to create the rowdiest atmosphere in golf.

The 17th Hole at Carnoustie Golf Links, Championship Course (Carnoustie, Scotland)
Par-4, 433 yards
Barry Burn stream forms S-shaped coil through right half of fairway.

The 17th Hole at the Old Course at St. Andrews (St. Andrews, Scotland)
Par-4, 455 yards
Deep, cone-shaped "road bunker" cuts into left side of green.

The 17th Hole at TPC Sawgrass, Stadium Course (Ponte Vedra Beach, Florida)
Par-3, 132 yards
Wide island green in middle of lake.

The 18th Hole at Pebble Beach Golf Links (Pebble Beach, California)
Par-5, 543 yards
Left side of hole runs along shore of Stillwater Cove, 12 to 15 feet above water.

Dubious Distinction

NFL Rules Named After Players

Basketball has its Larry Bird Rule, but no sport is better known for insinuating players into its official regulations than the NFL. Here, courtesy of the Professional Football Researchers Association, are some famous rules unofficially named for the guys who inspired them:

Bronko Nagurski Rule: A forward pass can be made from anywhere behind the line of scrimmage. Enacted in 1933. Prior to the rule change, a pass had to be thrown from at least five yards behind the line. Named after Nagurski, a back for the Chicago Bears, who threw a controversial TD pass during the 1932 championship game.

Baugh/Marshall Rule: When a pass from your end zone strikes the goalpost, a touchback results. Enacted in 1945 (when goalposts were on the end zone line). Prior to the change, the same play resulted in a safety. Named for Washington Redskins Hall of Fame quarterback Sammy Baugh and owner George Preston Marshall, after a Baugh pass hit the goalpost and proved to be the difference in a 15-14 championship game loss to the Cleveland Rams in 1945.

Lou Groza Rule: No artificial medium can be used to assist in the execution of a kick. Enacted in 1956. Groza, a Cleveland Browns kicker, had always used a length of tape as a directional tool to help aim his kicks.

Fran Tarkenton Rule: A line judge becomes the sixth official. Enacted in 1965. Named after Minnesota Vikings quarterback Tarkenton, who scrambled so widely that a crew of five officials had a difficult time determining if he was behind the line of scrimmage when he threw.

Don Chandler Rule: A back judge and a field judge, each stationed under one upright of the goalpost, take the place of a single official standing in the middle to decide if a kick is good. Enacted in 1966. Chandler was a field goal kicker for the Green Bay Packers who made a questionable field goal in a 1965 playoff game.

Bubba Smith Rule: Rubber caps replace metal points at the bottom of first-down stakes. Enacted in 1973. Smith was an All-Pro defensive end for the Baltimore Colts, who was injured when he became entangled in first-down chains that would not give way because they were stuck firmly in the ground.

Ben Davidson Rule: A defender is prohibited from running or diving into, or throwing his body against or on a ball carrier who falls or slips to the ground untouched and makes no attempt to advance, before or after the ball is dead. Enacted in 1976. Davidson was an Oakland Raiders defensive end known for aggressive play.

Tom Dempsey Rule: A shoe on an artificial limb must have a kicking surface that conforms to that of a normal kicking shoe. Enacted in 1977. Dempsey, who was born with no toes on his right foot, kicked for the New Orleans Saints and four other NFL teams, and set the NFL record with a 63-yard field goal in 1970. Prior to the rule, his shoe had a flat, hard plate in front.

Deacon Jones Rule: No head-slapping. Enacted in 1977. Jones was a Los Angeles Rams defensive lineman who liked to slap the heads of rival offensive linemen. Jones had already retired when the rule was put into effect.

Mel Renfro Rule: The offense can "double touch" the ball before catching it. Enacted in 1978. Renfro was a Dallas Cowboys defensive back ruled to have tipped a ball in Super Bowl V after it was touched by Baltimore Colts wide receiver Eddie Hinton before being grabbed by tight end John Mackey, who took it 75 yards for a TD.

Greg Pruitt Rule: Tear-away jerseys are illegal. Enacted in 1979. Pruitt was a running back and kick returner with the Cleveland Browns and Oakland Raiders who purposely wore flimsy jerseys that came apart in the hands of defenders who grabbed them.

Ken Stabler Rule: On fourth down, or any down in the final two minutes of play, only the player who fumbles a ball can recover or advance it. Enacted in 1979. Stabler was an Oakland Raiders QB who won a game by purposely fumbling the ball forward to his tight end.

Lester Hayes Rule: No "stickum." Enacted in 1981. Hayes was an Oakland Raiders defensive back who coated his fingers with substances that made it easier for him to hold on to balls.

Mark Gastineau Rule: A 15-yard penalty is given for any prolonged, excessive, or premeditated celebration. Enacted in 1984. Gastineau, a defensive end for the New York Jets, was known for his over-the-top celebratory dances after sacking the quarterback.

Emmitt Smith Rule: Taking off one's helmet is not permitted on the field of play. Enacted in 1997. Smith was a Dallas Cowboys running back who liked to remove his helmet before he left the field, as a gesture of dominance or taunting.

Roy Williams Rule: No "horse-collar" tackles. Enacted in 2005. Williams is a Dallas Cowboys defensive back who liked to grab players by the neck of their shoulder pads.

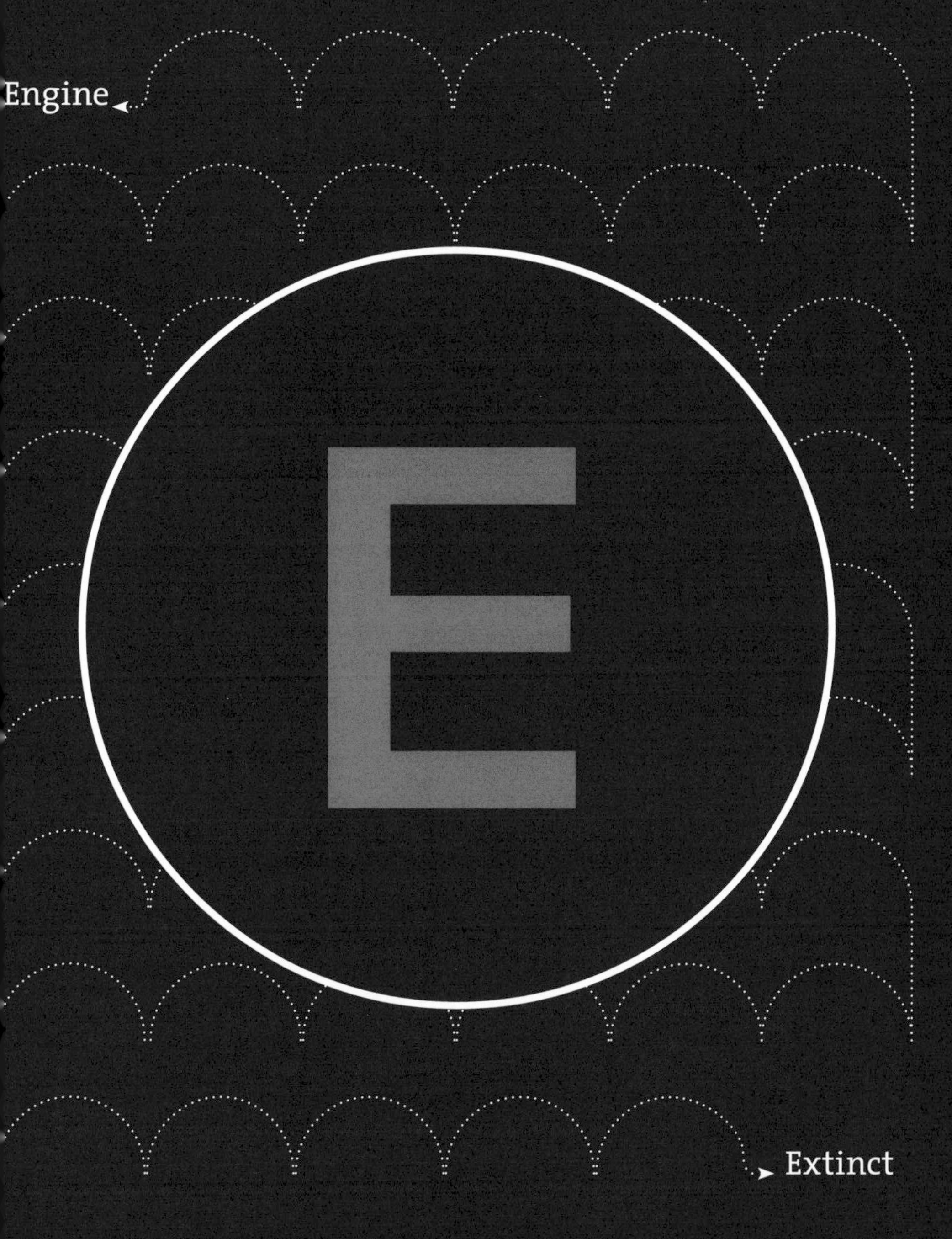
Engine
E
Extinct

Engine Starting

NASCAR's First "Strictly Stock" Season

Although the National Association for Stock Car Auto Racing sanctioned its first race in February 1948, the inaugural season of what we now call the Nextel Cup Series—originally known as the Strictly Stock Series—began 16 months later, in June 1949. Interestingly, for a sport with roots in races between Southern moonshine runners, its first season featured three races north of the Mason-Dixon Line.

STRICTLY STOCK RACE NO. 1

June 19, 1949
200 laps (150 miles)
at Charlotte Motor Speedway,
Charlotte, North Carolina
Jim Roper (1949 Lincoln/$2,000)

STRICTLY STOCK RACE NO. 2

July 10, 1949
40 laps (166 miles) at Beach and Road
Course, Daytona Beach, Florida
Red Byron (1949 Olds/$2,000)

STRICTLY STOCK RACE NO. 3

August 7, 1949
200 laps (200 miles) at Occoneechee
Speedway, Hillsborough, North Carolina
Bob Flock (1948 Olds/$2,000)

STRICTLY STOCK RACE NO. 4

September 11, 1949
200 laps (200 miles on a dirt track)
at Langhorne Speedway,
Langhorne, Pennsylvania
Curtis Turner (1949 Olds/$2,250)

STRICTLY STOCK RACE NO. 5

September 18, 1949
200 laps (100 miles)
at Hamburg Speedway,
Hamburg, New York
Jack White (1949 Lincoln/$1,500)

STRICTLY STOCK RACE NO. 6

September 25, 1949
200 laps (100 miles) at Martinsville
Speedway, Martinsville, Virginia
Red Byron (1949 Olds/$1,500)

STRICTLY STOCK RACE NO. 7

October 2, 1949
200 laps (100 miles) at Heidelberg
Raceway, Pittsburgh, Pennsylvania
Lee Petty (1949 Plymouth/$1,500)

STRICTLY STOCK RACE NO. 8

October 16, 1949
200 laps (100 miles) at North Wilkesboro
Speedway, North Wilkesboro,
North Carolina
Bob Flock (1949 Olds/$1,500)

Note: The first champion of NASCAR's premier series was Red Byron. He won two races and $5,800.

Engraved Errors

Spelling Mistakes On The Stanley Cup

After a team wins the NHL championship, club officials submit a list of names to the league to be engraved on the Stanley Cup. Once the NHL approves the list, it goes to a silversmith company in Montreal, where, since 1907, employees have engraved every single name. With more than 2,300 engravings made, there were bound to be a few mistakes.

- The name of Hall of Fame goaltender Jacques Plante is misspelled five different times, including "Jocko," "Jack," and "Plant."
- In 1951, Ted Kennedy of the Toronto Maple Leafs had his name misspelled "Kennedyy."
- In 1963, the Maple Leafs name itself was misspelled "Leaes."
- In 1972, the Bruins hometown was misspelled "Bqstqn."
- In 1975, the name of Montreal Canadien Bob Gainey was misspelled "Gainy."
- In 1981, New York Islanders was misspelled "Ilanders."
- In 1984, Edmonton Oilers owner Peter Pocklington had his dad's name, Basil, engraved on the Cup. After the fact, the NHL covered it with a series of X's.
- In 1996, Colorado Avalanche winger Adam Deadmarsh's name was fixed after it was originally engraved as "Deadmarch."
- In 2002, Detroit Red Wings goaltender Manny Legace's name was misspelled "Lagace" and later corrected.

Entry Points

No. 1 Picks In The Major League Baseball Draft

Credit the advent of the MLB draft to signing bonuses. Before the draft, teams bid against each other for young talent. But when the Los Angeles Angels gave University of Wisconsin outfielder Rick Reichardt a $250,000 bonus in 1964, owners decided to institute some sense of propriety. The Amateur Draft, renamed the First-Year Player Draft in 1998, paid immediate dividends for them. Rick Monday, the first player selected, signed for a reported $104,000, well below what he would have received under the old system.

1965 Rick Monday, OF; Kansas City A's from Arizona State University
1966 Steve Chilcott, C; New York Mets from Antelope Valley H.S. (Lancaster, California)
1967 Ron Blomberg, 1B; New York Yankees from Druid Hills H.S. (Atlanta)
1968 Tim Foli, INF; New York Mets from Notre Dame H.S. (Sherman Oaks, California)
1969 Jeff Burroughs, OF; Washington Senators from Woodrow Wilson H.S. (Long Beach, California)
1970 Mike Ivie, C; San Diego Padres from Walker H.S. (Decatur, Georgia)
1971 Danny Goodwin, C; Chicago White Sox from Peoria Central H.S. (Peoria, Illinois)
1972 Dave Roberts, INF; San Diego Padres from University of Oregon
1973 David Clyde, P; Texas Rangers from Westchester H.S. (Houston, Texas)
1974 Bill Almon, INF; San Diego Padres from Brown University
1975 Danny Goodwin, C; California Angels from Southern University

1976 Floyd Bannister, P; Houston Astros from Arizona State University
1977 Harold Baines, INF-OF; Chicago White Sox from St. Michaels H.S. (St. Michaels, Maryland)
1978 Bob Horner, 3B; Atlanta Braves from Arizona State University
1979 Al Chambers, OF; Seattle Mariners from John Harris H.S. (Harrisburg, Pennsylvania)
1980 Darryl Strawberry, OF; New York Mets from Crenshaw H.S. (Los Angeles)
1981 Mike Moore, P; Seattle Mariners from Oral Roberts University
1982 Shawon Dunston, SS; Chicago Cubs from Thomas Jefferson H.S. (New York)
1983 Tim Belcher, P; Minnesota Twins from Mount Vernon Nazarene College
1984 Shawn Abner, OF; New York Mets from Mechanicsburg H.S. (Mechanicsburg, Pennsylvania)
1985 B.J. Surhoff, C; Milwaukee Brewers from University of North Carolina at Chapel Hill
1986 Jeff King, INF; Pittsburgh Pirates from University of Arkansas
1987 Ken Griffey Jr., OF; Seattle Mariners from Moeller H.S. (Cincinnati)
1988 Andy Benes, P; San Diego Padres from University of Evansville
1989 Ben McDonald, P; Baltimore Orioles from Louisiana State University
1990 Chipper Jones, SS; Atlanta Braves from The Bolles School (Jacksonville, Florida)
1991 Brien Taylor, P; New York Yankees from East Carteret H.S. (Beaufort, North Carolina)
1992 Phil Nevin, 3B; Houston Astros from Cal State-Fullerton
1993 Alex Rodriguez, SS; Seattle Mariners from Westminster Christian H.S. (Miami)
1994 Paul Wilson, P; New York Mets from Florida State University
1995 Darin Erstad, OF-P; California Angels from University of Nebraska
1996 Kris Benson, P; Pittsburgh Pirates from Clemson University
1997 Matt Anderson, P; Detroit Tigers from Rice University
1998 Pat Burrell, INF; Philadelphia Phillies from University of Miami
1999 Josh Hamilton, OF; Tampa Bay Devil Rays from Athens Drive H.S. (Raleigh, North Carolina)
2000 Adrian Gonzalez, 1B; Florida Marlins from Eastlake H.S. (Chula Vista, California)
2001 Joe Mauer, C; Minnesota Twins from Cretin-Derham Hall H.S. (St. Paul, Minnesota)
2002 Bryan Bullington, P; Pittsburgh Pirates from Ball State University
2003 Delmon Young, RF; Tampa Bay Devil Rays from Adolfo Camarillo H.S. (Camarillo, California)
2004 Matthew Bush, SS; San Diego Padres from Mission Bay H.S. (San Diego)
2005 Justin Upton, SS; Arizona Diamondbacks from Great Bridge H.S. (Chesapeake, Virginia)
2006 Luke Hochevar, P; Kansas City Royals from independent league
2007 David Price, P; Tampa Bay Devil Rays from Vanderbilt University
2008 Tim Beckham, SS; Tampa Bay Rays from Griffin H.S. (Griffin, Georgia)

A B C D E F G H I J K L M N O P Q R S T U V W X Y Z

Equine English

A Glossary Of Horse Racing Slang

Acey deucy: Uneven stirrups.

Across the board: A bet on the same horse to win, place, and show.

Action: A horse's manner of moving.

Airing: Not running at best speed in a race.

Baby race: Race for two-year-olds.

Bad actor: Unruly horse.

Bad doer: Horse with poor appetite.

Blanket finish: Extremely close finish.

Blowout: Short, final workout, usually a day before a race, to sharpen a horse's speed.

Bobble: Bad step out of the starting gate, usually caused by the track breaking away from under a horse's hoof and causing him to duck his head or nearly go to his knees.

Breaking a maiden: First win.

Closer: Horse who runs best in the latter part of the race, coming from off the pace.

Cooling out: Restoring a horse, usually by walking, to normal temperature after becoming overheated in a race or a workout.

Gentleman jockey: Amateur rider, generally in steeplechases.

Hard boot: Kentucky horseman.

Hopped: Illegally stimulated.

Leaky roof circuit: Minor racetracks.

Monkey-on-a-stick: Riding with short stirrups.

Morning glory: Horse who performs well in morning workouts but not in races.

Mudder: Horse who runs well on muddy tracks.

On the Bill Daly: Horse who breaks in front and remains there through the finish. (From Father "Bill" Daly, old-time horseman who developed many great jockeys.)

Pocket: Horse running with other horses in front and alongside.

Straight as a string: Horse running at top speed.

Teaser: Horse used at breeding farms to find out if a mare is ready to receive a stallion.

Excess Volume

Capacity Of The World's Largest Stadiums

1. 250,000+ Indianapolis Motor Speedway (motor sports); Indianapolis, Indiana (built in 1909)

2. 223,000 Tokyo Racecourse (horse racing); Tokyo, Japan (1933)

3. 200,000 Shanghai International Circuit (motor sports); Shanghai, China (2004)

4. 168,000 Daytona International Speedway (motor sports); Daytona Beach, Florida (1959)

5. 167,000 Lowe's Motor Speedway (motor sports); Concord, North Carolina (1959)
6. 165,676 Nakayama Racecourse (horse racing); Chiba, Japan (1990)
7. 163,628 Churchill Downs (horse racing); Louisville, Kentucky (1895)
8. 160,000 Bristol Motor Speedway (motor sports); Bristol, Tennessee (1961)
9. 159,585 Texas Motor Speedway (motor sports); Forth Worth, Texas (1997)
10. 155,000 Istanbul Otodrom (motor sports); Istanbul, Turkey (2005)
11. 150,000 Rungnado May Day Stadium (multi-use); Pyongyang, North Korea (1989)
12. 144,000 Las Vegas Motor Speedway (motor sports); Las Vegas, Nevada (1996)
13. 143,231 Talladega Superspeedway (motor sports); Talladega, Alabama (1969)
14. 140,000 Dover International Speedway (motor sports); Dover, Delaware (1969)
14. 140,000 Nürburgring (motor sports); Nürburg, Germany (1927)
15. 139,877 Hanshin Racecourse (horse racing); Hyogo, Japan (1991)
16. 137,243 Michigan International Speedway (motor sports); Brooklyn, Michigan (1968)
17. 137,000 Autodromo di Monza (motor sports); Monza, Italy (1922)
18. 130,000 Flemington Racecourse (horse racing); Melbourne, Australia (1927)
18. 130,000 Rockingham Speedway (motor sports); Corby, England (2001)
19. 125,000 Silverstone Circuit (motor sports); Silverstone, England (1948)
20. 120,000 Circuit Ricardo Tormo (motor sports); Cheste, Spain (2000)
20. 120,000 EuroSpeedway Lausitz (motor sports); Klettwitz, Germany (2000)
20. 120,000 Hockenheimring (motor sports); Hockenheim, Germany (1932)
20. 120,000 Kyoto Racecourse (horse racing); Kyoto, Japan (1999)
20. 120,000 Saltlake Stadium (multi-use); Calcutta, India (1984)
21. 114,465 Estadio Azteca (multi-use); Mexico City, Mexico (1966)
22. 113,000 Atlanta Motor Speedway (motor sports); Hampton, Georgia (1997)
23. 112,029 Richmond International Raceway (motor sports); Richmond, Virginia (1946)
24. 107,501 Michigan Stadium (football); Ann Arbor, Michigan (1927)
25. 107,282: Beaver Stadium (football); University Park, Pennsylvania (1960)
26. 104,079 Neyland Stadium (football); Knoxville, Tennessee (1921)
27. 103,045 Jornalista Mario Filho (soccer); Rio de Janiero, Brazil (1950)
28. 102,329 Ohio Stadium (football); Columbus, Ohio (1922)
29. 100,200 National Stadium Bukit Jalil (multi-use); Kuala Lumpur, Malaysia (1998)

Note: Capacity figures are based on permanent and/or temporary seating and "walkabout" or standing-room-only admission, where applicable.

Executive Decisions

New York Yankee Managers Under The Boss

Since George Steinbrenner became principal owner of the New York Yankees in 1973, no baseball team has had a higher winning percentage (.562) or won more World Series (6). But all that success wasn't built on patience and a belief in continuity. In 33 seasons, The Boss has overseen 21 managerial changes, with five only guys enduring more than one tenure. Here's the list of Steinbrenner's 14 managers (and their career Yankee W-L records):

1973	Ralph Houk (80-82)
1974–75	Bill Virdon (142-124)
1975–78	Billy Martin (279-192)
1978	Dick Howser (0-1)
1978–79	Bob Lemon (82-51)
1979	Billy Martin (55-40)
1980	Dick Howser (103-59)
1981	Gene Michael (48-34)
1981–82	Bob Lemon (17-22)
1982	Gene Michael (44-42)
1982	Clyde King (29-33)
1983	Billy Martin (91-71)
1984–85	Yogi Berra (93-85)
1985	Billy Martin (91-54)
1986–87	Lou Piniella (179-145)
1988	Billy Martin (40-28)
1988	Lou Piniella (45-48)
1989	Dallas Green (56-65)
1989–90	Bucky Dent (36-53)
1990–91	Stump Merrill (120-155)
1992–95	Buck Showalter (313-268)
1996–2007	Joe Torre (1,173-767)
2008–present	Joe Girardi (89-73, through 2008)

Extinct Teams

Defunct Pro Football Franchises

As successful as the NFL is now, the history of pro football is littered with the carcasses of dead teams. Here are most of them (and their years of operation):

Chicago Tigers (1920)
Detroit Heralds (1920)
Cincinnati Celts (1921)
Washington Senators (1921)
Muncie Flyers (1920-21)
Detroit Tigers (1921)
Tonawanda Kardex (1921)
New York Giants (1921)
Cleveland Tigers/Cleveland Indians (1920-21)
Evansville Crimson Giants (1921-22)
Oorang Indians (1922-23)
St. Louis All-Stars (1923)
Toledo Maroons (1922-23)
Kenosha Maroons (1924)
Rock Island Independents (1920-25)
Rochester Jeffersons (1920-25)
Brooklyn Lions (1926)
Louisville Brecks/Louisville Colonels (1921-23, 1926)
Racine Legion/Racine Tornadoes (1922-24, 1926)
Los Angeles Buccaneers (1926)
Detroit Panthers (1925-26)
Columbus Panhandles/Columbus Tigers (1920-22, 1923-26)
Milwaukee Badgers (1922-26)
Hartford Blues (1926)
Kansas City Blues/Kansas City Cowboys (1924, 1925-26)

A B C D E F G H I J K L M N O P Q R S T U V W X Y Z

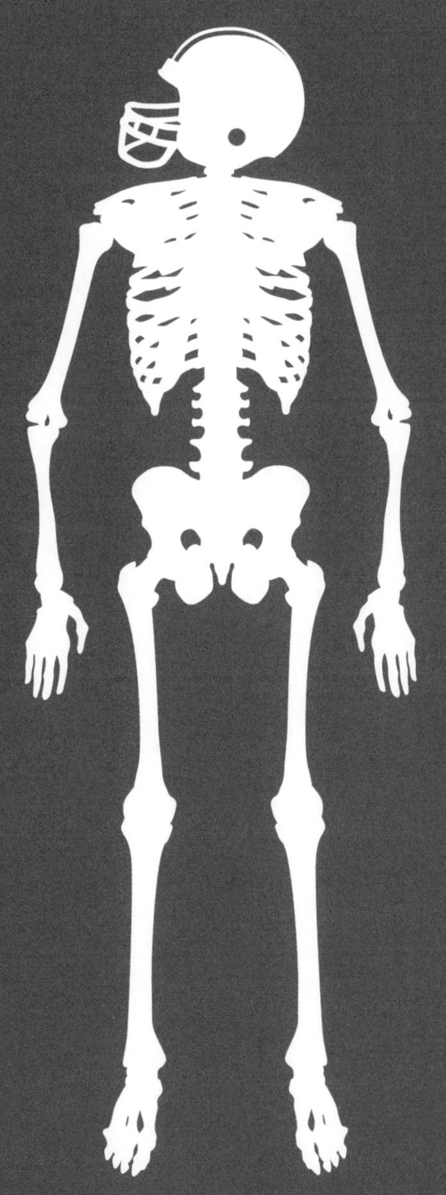

Hammond Pros (1920-26)
Akron Pros/Akron Indians (1920-25, 1926)
Canton Bulldogs (1920-23, 1925-26)
Duluth Kelleys/Duluth Eskimos (1923-25, 1926-27)
Cleveland Indians/Cleveland Bulldogs (1923, 1924-25, 1927)
New York Yankees (1927-28)
Detroit Wolverines (1928)
Pottsville Maroons/Boston Bulldogs (1925-28, 1929)
Dayton Triangles (1920-29)
Buffalo All-Americans/Buffalo Bisons/ Buffalo Rangers/Buffalo Bisons (1920-23, 1924-25, 1926-27, 1929)
Minneapolis Marines/Minneapolis Red Jackets (1921-24, 1929-30)
Orange Tornadoes/Newark Tornadoes (1929, 1930)
Providence Steam Roller (1925-31)
Frankford Yellow Jackets (1924-31)
Cleveland Indians (1931)
Staten Island Stapletons (1929-32)
St. Louis Gunners (1934)
Cincinnati Reds (1933-34)
Brooklyn Dodgers/Brooklyn Tigers (1930-43, 1944; merged with Boston 1945)
Boston Yanks (1944-48)
Baltimore Colts (1950)
New York Bulldogs/New York Yanks (1949, 1950-51)
Dallas Texans (1952)

Fairy

F

Fútbol

A B C D E F G H I J K L M N O P Q R S T U V W X Y Z

Fairy Tale Finish

Bill Murray's "Cinderella Story" Speech In *Caddyshack*

"What an incredible Cinderella story, this unknown comes outta nowhere to lead the pack, at Augusta. He's on his final hole, he's about 455 yards away, he's gonna hit about a two-iron, I think. Oh, he got all of that one! The crowd is standing on its feet here, the normally reserved Augusta crowd, going wild for this young Cinderella, he's come outta nowhere, he's got about 350 yards left, he's gonna hit about a five-iron, don't you think? He's got a beautiful backswing—that's—oh, he got all of that one! He's gotta be pleased with that, the crowd is just on its feet here, uh—he's the Cinderella boy, uh—tears in his eyes, I guess, as he lines up this last shot. He's got about 195 yards left, he's got about a—it looks like he's got about an eight-iron. This crowd has gone deathly silent, the Cinderella story, outta nowhere, a former greenskeeper now about to become the Masters champion. It looks like a mirac—it's in the hole!"

Fantasy Players

Official Names Of Major League Baseball Mascots

Arizona Diamondbacks: D. Baxter the Bobcat
Atlanta Braves: Homer and Rally
Baltimore Orioles: Orioles Bird
Boston Red Sox: Wally the Green Monster
Chicago White Sox: Southpaw
Cincinnati Reds: Mr. Red and Gapper
Cleveland Indians: Slider
Colorado Rockies: Dinger
Detroit Tigers: Paws
Florida Marlins: Billy the Marlin
Houston Astros: Junction Jack
Kansas City Royals: Sluggerrr
Milwaukee Brewers: Bernie Brewer
New York Mets: Mr. Met
Oakland Athletics: Stomper
Philadelphia Phillies: Phillie Phanatic
Pittsburgh Pirates: Pirate Parrot and Captain Jolly Roger
Minnesota Twins: T.C. Bear
St. Louis Cardinals: Fredbird
San Diego Padres: The Swinging Friar
San Francisco Giants: Lou Seal
Seattle Mariners: Mariner Moose
Tampa Bay Devil Rays: Raymond
Texas Rangers: Rangers Captain
Toronto Blue Jays: Ace and Diamond
Washington Nationals: Screech

Note: The Chicago Cubs, Los Angeles Angels of Anaheim, Los Angeles Dodgers, and New York Yankees do not have official mascots.

Fear Factors

Sports-Related Phobias

Agliophobia: fear of pain
Anginophobia: fear of choking
Arithmophobia: fear of numbers
Ataxiophobia: fear of muscle incoordination
Bromidrosiphobia: fear of personal odor
Chronomentrophobia: fear of clocks
Cyclophobia: fear of bicycles
Doxophobia: fear of receiving praise
Enissophobia: fear of criticism
Genuphobia: fear of knees
Gerascophobia: fear of growing old
Kakorrhaphiophobia: fear of defeat
Kopophobia: fear of fatigue
Ochlophobia: fear of crowds
Ophthalmophobia: fear of being stared at
Soteriophobia: fear of being dependent on others
Stasibasiphobia: fear of walking
Taurophobia: fear of bulls
Thermophobia: fear of heat
Topophobia: stage fright
Traumatophobia: fear of injury

Felt Tips

Differences Among Pool, Billiards, and Snooker

Players	Two or two teams of two	Two	Two
Balls	One cue ball, 15 numbered object balls that are colored or striped	One white cue ball, one spot white cue ball, one red object ball	One cue ball, 15 red object balls, six object balls of other colors (yellow, green, brown, blue, pink, black) with values of 2 to 7 points
Table	Six pockets (four in corners, two halfway down each long side)	No pockets	Six pockets (four in corners, two halfway down each long side)
Goal	Points are scored when balls are knocked into pockets; person or team that first reaches pre-determined point total for a game wins.	Points are scored when a player strikes three rails and the other cue ball in any order before hitting the red object ball.	Points are scored when various object balls (which have different values) are legally "potted" (in various orders based on the situation) or when opponent commits fouls, thus giving points away; person with the most points wins.

A B C D E F G H I J K L M N O P Q R S T U V W X Y Z

First On Ice

No. 1 Draft Picks Of The National Hockey League

Before 1963, any NHL team that sponsored a junior club had exclusive rights to players on those teams. To eliminate that monopoly on talent, the NHL began the amateur draft, in which all previously unsponsored amateur players 17 years of age and older were eligible to be drafted. In 1969, every junior of qualifying age (20) became available for selection. Today, the amateur draft is known as the entry draft, and any player from anywhere in the world, 18 or older, is eligible.

1963 Garry Monahan, C; Montreal Canadiens from the St. Michael's Juveniles of Toronto (age: 16 years, 7 months)
1964 Claude Gauthier, RW; Detroit Red Wings from Rosemount Midgets (N/A)
1965 Andre Veilleux, RW; New York Rangers from Montreal Junior B Canadiens (N/A)
1966 Barry Gibbs, D; Boston Bruins from Estevan Bruins (17 years, 7 months)
1967 Rick Pagnutti, D; Los Angeles Kings from Garson Native Sons (20 years, 6 months)
1968 Michel Plasse, G, Montreal Canadiens from Drummondville Rangers (20 years)
1969 Rejean Houle, RW; Montreal Canadiens from Montreal Junior Canadiens (19 years, 8 months)
1970 Gilbert Perreault, C; Buffalo Sabres from Montreal Junior Canadiens (19 years, 7 months)
1971 Guy Lafleur, RW; Montreal Canadiens from Quebec Remparts (19 years, 9 months)
1972 Billy Harris, RW; New York Islanders from Toronto Marlboros (20 years, 4 months)
1973 Denis Potvin, D; New York Islanders from Ottawa 67s (19 years, 7 months)
1974 Greg Joly, D; Washington Capitals from Regina Pats (20 years)
1975 Mel Bridgman, C; Philadelphia Flyers from Victoria Cougars (20 years, 1 month)
1976 Rick Green, D; Washington Capitals from London Knights (20 years, 3 months)
1977 Dale McCourt, C; Detroit Red Wings from St. Catharines Fincups (20 years, 4 months)
1978 Bobby Smith, C; Minnesota North Stars[1] from Ottawa 67s (20 years, 4 months)
1979 Rob Ramage, D; Colorado Rockies[2] from London Knights (20 years, 5 months)
1980 Doug Wickenheiser, C; Montreal Canadiens from Regina Pats (19 years, 2 months)
1981 Dale Hawerchuk, C; Winnipeg Jets[3] from Cornwall Royals (18 years, 2 months)

1982 Gord Kluzak, D; Boston Bruins from Nanaimo Islanders (18 years, 3 months)
1983 Brian Lawton, LW; Minnesota North Stars from Mount St. Charles (Rhode Island) H.S. (18 years, 11 months)
1984 Mario Lemieux, C; Pittsburgh Penguins from Laval Voisins (18 years, 8 months)
1985 Wendel Clark, LW/D; Toronto Maple Leafs from Saskatoon Blades (18 years, 7 months)
1986 Joe Murphy, RW; Detroit Red Wings from Michigan State University (18 years, 8 months)
1987 Pierre Turgeon, C; Buffalo Sabres from Granby Bisons (17 years, 10 months)
1988 Mike Modano, C; Minnesota North Stars from Prince Albert Raiders (18 years)
1989 Mats Sundin, C; Quebec Nordiques[4] from Nacka (Sweden) (18 years, 4 months)
1990 Owen Nolan, RW; Quebec Nordiques from Cornwall Royals (18 years, 4 months)
1991 Eric Lindros, C; Quebec Nordiques from Oshawa Generals (18 years, 3 months)
1992 Roman Hamrlik, D; Tampa Bay Lightning from Zlin ZPS (Czech Republic) (18 years, 4 months)
1993 Alexandre Daigle, C; Ottawa Senators from Victoriaville Tigres (18 years, 5 months)
1994 Ed Jovanovski, D; Florida Panthers from Windsor Spitfires (18 years)
1995 Bryan Berard, D; Ottawa Senators from Detroit Jr. Red Wings (18 years, 4 months)
1996 Chris Phillips, D; Ottawa Senators from Prince Albert Raiders (18 years, 3 months)
1997 Joe Thornton, C; Boston Bruins from Sault Ste. Marie Greyhounds (17 years, 11 months)
1998 Vincent Lecavalier, C; Tampa Bay Lightning from Rimouski Oceanic (18 years, 2 months)
1999 Patrik Stefan, C; Atlanta Thrashers from Long Beach Ice Dogs (18 years, 9 months)
2000 Rick DiPietro, G; New York Islanders from Boston University (18 years, 9 months)
2001 Ilya Kovalchuk, LW; Atlanta Thrashers from Moscow Spartak (Russia) (18 years, 2 months)
2002 Rick Nash, LW; Columbus Blue Jackets from London Knights (18 years)
2003 Marc-Andre Fleury, G; Pittsburgh Penguins from Cape Breton Screaming Eagles (18 years)
2004 Alexander Ovechkin, LW; Washington Capitals from Dynamo Moscow (Russia) (18 years, 9 months)
2005 Sidney Crosby, C; Pittsburgh Penguins from Rimouski Oceanic (17 years, 11 months)
2006 Erik Johnson, D; St. Louis Blues from U.S. National Team Development Program (18 years, 3 months)
2007 Patrick Kane, F; Chicago Blackhawks from London Knights (19 years, 8 months)

Note: [1]Now Dallas Stars; [2]Now New Jersey Devils; [3]Now Phoenix Coyotes; [4]Now Colorado Avalanche. Source: *NHL Official Guide and Record Book*

A B C D E F G H I J K L M N O P Q R S T U V W X Y Z

Five Unrelated Activities

THE EVENTS OF THE MODERN PENTATHLON

SHOOTING 20 shots with an air pistol from 10 meters away

FENCING One-hit bouts with an épée in a round-robin tournament

SWIMMING 200-meter freestyle race

RIDING Show-jumping obstacles over a 350- to 450-meter course

RUNNING 3,000-meter cross-country or road course run

Flying Objects

SPORTS WITH PROJECTILES

In most sports that involve hurling something through the air or on the ground, the projectile in question is some sort of ball. Here are some that aren't:

- Archery (arrows)
- Badminton (shuttlecock)
- Boomerangs (boomerang)
- Caber toss (caber)
- Curling (stone)
- Darts (darts)
- Disc golf (discs)
- Discus (discus)
- Footbag (footbag)
- Hockey (puck)
- Horseshoes (horseshoe)
- Ice sledge hockey (puck)
- Javelin (javelin)
- Ringette (ring)
- Shuffleboard (discs)
- Ultimate Frisbee (flying disc)

Foot Fetishes

Miss Meghan's 10 Sexiest Sneakers

Meghan Cleary, shoe guru and author of The Perfect Fit: What Your Shoes Say About You, *has some interesting things to say about athletic footwear. Here, from her shoe-lover's blog, missmeghan.blogspot.com, is her list of the 10 sexiest sneakers:*

1. New Balance M992GL Heritage
2. Eighty Twenty Heather
3. Tretorn Nylite
4. Nike Air Jordan I
5. Puma Mostro
6. JB Classics J.B.Getlo
7. Pirelli Pzero Rosso
8. Vans Classic Slip On
9. Converse Chuck Taylor
10. Adidas Stan Smith

Football Originals

The Founding Teams Of The National Football League

Ohio, specifically The Ohio League, was the birthplace of pro football in the early 1900s. But with no official governing body for the sport, teams across the U.S. cannibalized each other, causing chaos. So, in 1920, representatives from four teams met at a Canton car dealership and created the American Professional Football Association, which a year later became the National Football League. Here are the 18 original NFL teams (and their years of birth):

- Akron Pros (1920)
- Buffalo All-Americans (1920)
- Canton Bulldogs (1920)
- Chicago Bears (1920)
- Chicago Cardinals (1920)
- Columbus Panhandles (1920)
- Dayton Triangles (1920)
- Evansville Crimson Giants (1921)
- Green Bay Packers (1921)
- Hammond (Indiana) Pros (1920)
- Louisville Brecks (1921)
- Oorang (Ohio) Indians (1922)
- Milwaukee Badgers (1922)
- Minneapolis Marines (1921)
- Racine (Wisconsin) Legion (1922)
- Rochester (New York) Jeffersons (1920)
- Rock Island (Illinois) Independents (1920)
- Toledo Maroons (1922)

Football Unoriginals

The Founding Teams Of The World Football League ...

The WFL was conceived by Don Regan and Gary L. Davidson (one of the guys behind two other upstart pro leagues in the 1960s and 1970s, the American Basketball Association and the World Hockey Association). Their modest dream? To compete with the NFL, much as the AFL had done a decade earlier. Alas, the dream lasted less than two seasons. Here are the 12 original teams:

EASTERN DIVISION	CENTRAL DIVISION	WESTERN DIVISION
Florida Blazers	Birmingham Americans	Hawaiians
Jacksonville Sharks[1]	Chicago Fire	Houston Texans[4]
N.Y. Stars[2]	Detroit Wheels[3]	Portland Storm
Philadelphia Bell	Memphis Southmen	Southern California Sun

Note: [1]Went bankrupt after 14 games, relaunched as Express the next year; [2]Moved to Charlotte after three months due to poor attendance and changed name to Hornets; [3]Went bankrupt after 14 games; [4]Moved to Shreveport because they couldn't afford Astrodome rent, and changed name to Steamer.

... and The Founding Teams Of The United States Football League

The basic idea behind the USFL was simple: exploit the NFL's offseason with games scheduled in the spring. Former ESPN president Chet Simmons was the first commissioner in 1983, and he struck a deal with his old network to televise two games a week for two years. But even a second TV deal with ABC couldn't steer the league clear of money troubles. With deep-pocketed owners, including Donald Trump of the New Jersey Generals, ignoring the payroll limit and driving up salaries, the USFL folded after three seasons. Here are the 12 original teams:

ATLANTIC DIVISION	CENTRAL DIVISION	PACIFIC DIVISION
Boston Breakers	Birmingham Stallions	Arizona Wranglers
New Jersey Generals	Chicago Blitz	Denver Gold
Philadelphia Stars	Michigan Panthers	Los Angeles Express
Washington Federals	Tampa Bay Bandits	Oakland Invaders

Fore Thoughts

The Original Rules Of Golf

Shortly before the Annual Challenge for the Edinburgh Silver Club in 1744, the Gentlemen Golfers of Leith—later known as the Honorable Company of Edinburgh Golfers—wrote the 13 original rules of the game.

1. You must tee your ball, within a club's length of the hole.

2. Your tee must be upon the Ground.

3. You are not to change the ball which you strike off the tee.

4. You are not to remove, stones, bones or any break club for the sake of playing your ball, except upon the fair green & that only within a club's length of your ball.

5. If your ball comes among watter, or any wattery filth, you are at liberty to take out your ball & bringing it behind the hazard and teeing it, you may play it with any club and allow your adversary a stroke for so getting out your ball.

6. If your balls be found anywhere touching one another, You are to lift the first ball, till you play the last.

7. At holling, you are to play your ball honestly for the hole, and, not to play upon your adversary's ball, not lying in your way to the hole.

8. If you should lose your ball, by its being taken up, or any other way, you are to go back to the spot, where you struck last & drop another ball, and allow your adversary a stroke for the misfortune.

9. No man at holling his ball, is to be allowed, to mark his way to the hole with his club or, any thing else.

10. If a ball be stopp'd by any person, horse, dog, or any thing else, the ball so stop'd must be played where it lyes.

11. If you draw your club, in order to strike & proceed so far in the stroke, as to be bringing down your club; if then, your club shall break, in, any way, it is to be accounted a stroke.

12. He, whose ball lyes farthest from the hole is obliged to play first.

13. Neither trench, ditch, or dyke, made for the preservation of the links, nor the scholar's holes or the soldier's lines, shall be accounted a hazard; but the ball is to be taken out/teed/ and play'd with any iron club.

Fowl Plays

Baseball Players Who Have Killed Birds During a Game

1981

In a game between Oregon rivals Eugene and Medford of the Class A Northwest League, future major leaguer Eric Davis of Eugene hit a ball that struck and killed a bird in flight. A Medford outfielder caught the ball for an out.

1983

In the fifth inning of a game between the Toronto Blue Jays and New York Yankees in Toronto, Yankee outfielder Dave Winfield fired a warm-up ball from center field and struck a seagull that was walking on the field. After the game, Winfield was briefly arrested for cruelty to animals.

1987

In the third inning of a game between the Atlanta Braves and New York Mets in New York, Braves outfielder Dion James hit a fly ball that killed a dove. James reached second base on a double.

1999

In the fifth inning of an International League playoff game between the Scranton/Wilkes-Barre Red Barons and the Charlotte Knights, the Barons' Pat Burrell lofted a fly ball to left that struck and killed a goatsucker. The ball (and the bird) dropped in front of leftfielder Tilson Brito for a single.

2001

In the seventh inning of an exhibition game between the Arizona Diamondbacks and the San Francisco Giants in Arizona, D-backs pitcher Randy Johnson threw a pitch that hit and killed a dove in front of home plate.

Fútbol Finales

World Cup Championship Games

1930 Uruguay 4, Argentina 2 (host country: Uruguay)

1934 Italy 2, Czechoslovakia 1 (Italy)

1938 Italy 4, Hungary 2 (France)

1950 Uruguay 2, Brazil 1 (Brazil)

1954 West Germany 3, Hungary 2 (Switzerland)

1958 Brazil 5, Sweden 2 (Sweden)

1962 Brazil 3, Czechoslovakia 1 (Chile)

1966 England 4, West Germany 2 (England)

1970 Brazil 4, Italy 1 (Mexico)

1974 West Germany 2, Netherlands 1 (West Germany)

1978 Argentina 3, Netherlands 1 (Argentina)

1982 Italy 3, West Germany 1 (Spain)

1986 Argentina 3, West Germany 2 (Mexico)

1990 West Germany 1, Argentina 0 (Italy)

1994 Brazil 0, Italy 0 (Brazil won on penalty kicks, 3-2) (USA)

1998 France 3, Brazil 0 (France)

2002 Brazil 2, Germany 0 (South Korea and Japan)

2006 Italy 1, France 1 (Italy won on penalty kicks, 5-3) (Germany)

Note: The 1942 and 1946 Cups were cancelled because of World War II.

A B C D E F G H I J K L M N O P Q R S T U V W X Y Z

Global
G
Ground

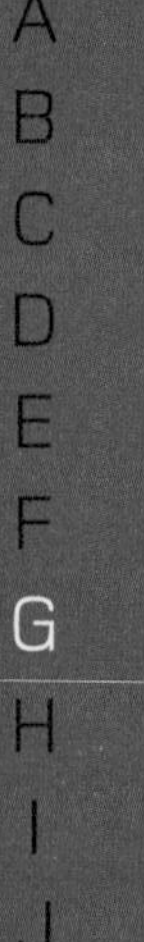

Global Game

International Firsts In The NBA

Argentina Ruben Wolkowyski (2000-01, Seattle SuperSonics); Juan "Pepe" Sanchez (2000-01, 76ers)

Australia Luc Longley (1991-92, Minnesota Timberwolves)

Bahamas Mychal Thompson (1978-79, Portland Trail Blazers)

Belize Milt Palacio (1999-2000, Vancouver Grizzlies)

Bosnia-Herzegovina Damir Markota (Milwaukee Bucks, 2006-07)

Brazil Rolando Ferreira (1988-89, Portland Trail Blazers)

Bulgaria Georgi Glouchkov (1985-86, Phoenix Suns)

Cameroon Ruben Boumtje Boumtje (2001-02, Portland Trail Blazers)

Canada Norm Baker (1946-47, Chicago Stags*)

China Wang Zhizhi (2000-01, Dallas Mavericks)

Congo (Zaire) Dikembe Mutombo (1991-92, Denver Nuggets)

Croatia Drazen Petrovic (1989-90, Portland Trail Blazers)

Cuba Andres Guibert (1993-94, Minnesota Timberwolves)

Czech Republic George Zidek (1995-96, Charlotte Hornets)

Denmark Lars Hansen (1978-79, Seattle SuperSonics)

Dominica Garth Joseph (2000-01, Toronto Raptors)

Dominican Republic Tito Horford (1988-89, Milwaukee Bucks)

Egypt Alaa Abdelnaby (1990-91, Portland Trail Blazers)

England Chris Harris (1955-56, St. Louis Hawks)

Estonia Martin Muursepp (1996-97, Miami Heat)

Finland Hanno Möttölä (2000-01, Atlanta Hawks)

France Tariq Abdul-Wahad (1997-98, Sacramento Kings)

Georgia Vladimir Stepania (1998-99, Seattle SuperSonics)

Germany Frido Frey (1946-47, New York Knicks*)

Greece Iakovos "Jake" Tsakalidis (2000-01, Phoenix Suns)

Guyana Rawle Marshall (Dallas Mavericks, 2005-06)

Haiti Yvon Joseph (1985-86, New Jersey Nets)

Hungary Kornel David (1998-89, Chicago Bulls)

Iceland Petur Gudmundsson (1981-82, Portland Trail Blazers)

Ireland Pat Burke (2002-03, Orlando Magic)

Italy Hank Biasatti (1946-47, Toronto Huskies*)

Jamaica Wayne Sappleton (1984-85, New Jersey Nets)

Japan Yuta Tabuse (2004-05, Phoenix Suns)

Latvia Gundars Vetra (1992-93, Minnesota Timberwolves)

Lebanon Rony Seikaly (1988-89, Miami Heat)

Lithuania Sarunas Marciulionis (1989-90, Golden State Warriors)

Luxembourg Alvin Jones (2001-02, Philadelphia 76ers)

Mali Soumaila Samake (2000-01, New Jersey Nets)

Mexico Horacio Llamas (1996-97, Phoenix Suns)

Montenegro Zarko Paspalj (1989-90, San Antonio Spurs)

Morocco Mike Flynn (1975-76, Indiana Pacers)

Netherlands Hank Beenders (1946-47, Providence Steamrollers*)

New Zealand Sean Marks (1998-99, Toronto Raptors)

Nigeria Hakeem Olajuwon (1984-85, Houston Rockets)

Norway Torgeir Bryn (1989-90, Los Angeles Clippers)

Panama Rolando Blackman (1981-82, Dallas Mavericks)

Panama Canal Zone Stuart Gray (1984-85, Indiana Pacers)

Poland Cezary Trybanski (2002-03, Memphis Grizzlies)

Puerto Rico Butch Lee (1978-79, Atlanta Hawks)

Romania Ernie Grunfeld (1977-78, Milwaukee Bucks)

Russia Thomas Meschery (1967-68, Seattle SuperSonics)

Scotland Robert Archibald (2002-03, Memphis Grizzlies)

Senegal Makhtar N'diaye (1998-99, Vancouver Grizzlies)

Serbia Vlade Divac (1989-90, Los Angeles Lakers)

South Korea Ha Seung-Jin (2004-05, Portland Trail Blazers)

Slovenia Marko Milic (1997-98, Phoenix Suns)

Spain Fernando Martin (1986-87, Portland Trail Blazers)

St. Vincent and the Grenadines Adonal Foyle (1997-98, Golden State Warriors)

Sudan Manute Bol (1985-86, Washington Bullets)

Sweden Miles Simon (1998-99, Orlando Magic)

Trinidad and Tobago Ken Charles (1973-74, Buffalo Braves)

Turkey Hidayet Turkoglu (2000-01, Sacramento Kings)

Ukraine Alexander Volkov (1989-90, Atlanta Hawks)

Uruguay Esteban Batista (2005-06, Atlanta Hawks)

U.S. Virgin Islands Tim Duncan (1997-98, San Antonio Spurs)

Venezuela Carl Herrera (1991-92, Houston Rockets)

* Basketball Association of America (BAA) team

A B C D E F G H I J K L M N O P Q R S T U V W X Y Z

Gotchas

THE OL' HIDDEN BALL TRICK

Defined by the Dickson Baseball Dictionary *as "a time-honored legal ruse in which a baseman conceals the ball in hopes that the baserunner believes it has been returned to the pitcher," the hidden ball trick was once so common that baseball added a rule in 1897 to discourage its use. The trick has now fallen into disuse. In the past 12 years, according to the web site Retrosheet and baseball historian Bill Deane, the play has been pulled off just six times.*

September 19, 1997 Cleveland Indians third baseman Matt Williams tagged Kansas City Royals second baseman Jed Hansen

April 25, 1998 Baltimore Orioles first baseman Rafael Palmeiro tagged Oakland A's left fielder Rickey Henderson

June 26, 1999 San Francisco Giants first baseman J.T. Snow tagged Los Angeles Dodgers pitcher Carlos Perez

September 15, 2004 Florida Marlins third baseman Mike Lowell tagged Montreal Expos catcher Brian Schneider

August 10, 2005 Florida Marlins third baseman Mike Lowell tagged Arizona Diamondbacks center fielder Luis Terrero

June 8, 2007 Boston Red Sox shortstop Julio Lugo tagged Arizona Diamond-backs infielder Alberto Callaspo

Grappling Poundages

WRESTLING WEIGHT CLASSES

There was only one weight class at the first modern Olympics in 1896. Today, there are seven international classes each for men and women. Here they are—identified by maximum weight.

OLYMPICS

Men (Greco-Roman and Freestyle):

55 kg/121 pounds
60 kg/132 pounds
66 kg/145.5 pounds
74 kg/163 pounds
84 kg/185 pounds
96 kg/211.5 pounds
120 kg/264.5 pounds

Women (Freestyle):

48kg/105.5 pounds
51 kg/112.25 pounds*
55 kg/121 pounds
59 kg/130 pounds*
63 kg/138.75 pounds
67 kg/147.5 pounds*
72 kg/158.5 pounds

Note: Governed by FILA (Fédération Internationale des Luttes Associées).
* These weight classes are for all international competitions except the Olympics.

Great Beginnings

23 Ways To Get To First Base

Determining the precise number of ways to reach first base is like filing a tax return. The numbers vary, depending on who does the counting. The Baseball Hall of Fame looked at the Official Rules and came up with 23 possibilities. For the record, just three—hit, walk and hit by pitch—officially extend a streak of reaching safely in consecutive games.

1. Hit
2. Fielder's choice[1]
3. Forceout at another base
4. Preceding runner put out allows batter to reach first base[2]
5. Sacrifice bunt fails to advance the runner[3]
6. Hit by pitch
7. Error
8. Walk
9. Intentional walk
10. Pinch-runner
11. Dropped third strike
12. Catcher interference[4]
13. Fair ball hits runner
14. Fair ball hits umpire
15. Sacrifice fly dropped
16. Obstruction of runner[5]
17. Fielder interference[6]
18. Spectator interference[7]
19. Fan obstruction[8]
20. Runner out on appeal[9]
21. Failure to deliver pitch within 20 seconds on a three-ball count
22. Four illegal pitches
23. Game suspended with runner on first; if he's traded prior to the makeup game, another player may take his place

Notes: [1]Example: runner on second base, ball hit to shortstop, shortstop throws to third base for tag; [2]Example: in previous scenario, shortstop tags runner; [3]Fielder's choice on a bunt; [4]Catcher impedes batter; [5]Example: second baseman obstructs base-runner on way to second on batted ball in play; [6]Example: pitcher obstructs batter on his way to first base; [7]Of the ball; [8]Of batter; [9]Example: runner on first base, ball hit to right field, runner misses second base on the way to third base and is called out on appeal; batter at first base is credited with an at-bat but not a hit.

Greek Goners

Discontinued Olympic Sports

SPORT	LAST GAMES
CRICKET	1900
CROQUET	1900
BASQUE PELOTA[1]	1900
GOLF	1904
ROQUE[2]	1904
LACROSSE	1908
JEU DE PAUME[3]	1908
RACKETS[4]	1908
WATER MOTOR SPORTS[5]	1908
TUG-OF-WAR	1920
RUGBY	1924
POLO	1936
BASEBALL	2008
SOFTBALL	2008

Note: [1]Like squash or racquetball, but instead of a racket the player uses a curved basket to propel the ball against a wall; [2]Variant of croquet, with hard rubber balls, shorter mallets, hard-surface courts, and boundary walls against which the balls can be hit; [3]Ancestor of tennis; [4]Similar to squash; [5]Motorboat races

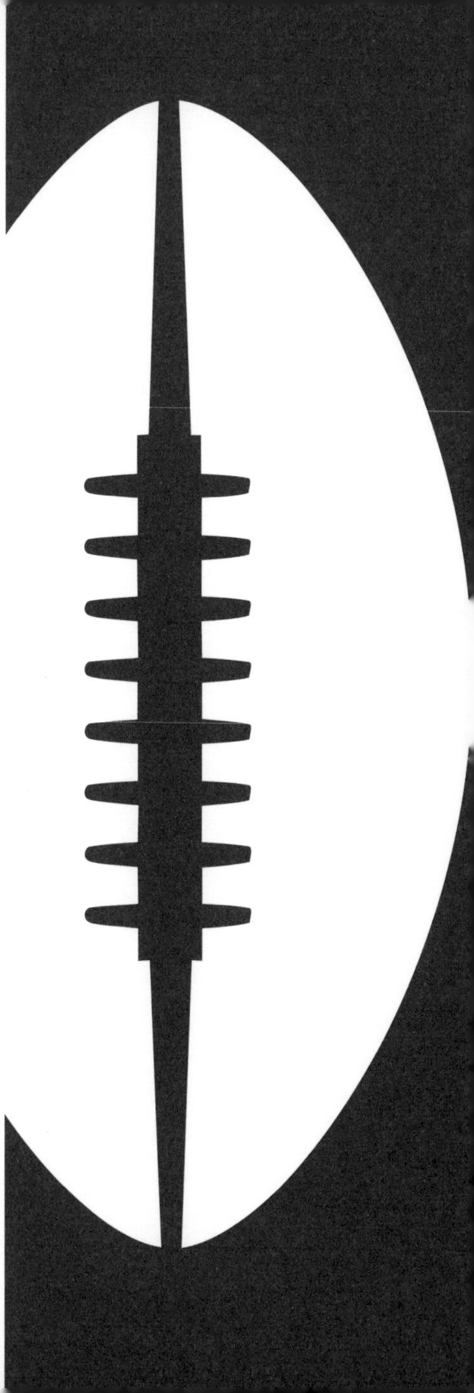

Green Bay Watch

Vince Lombardi's "Winning Isn't Everything ..." Speech

Like "Play it again, Sam" and "Elementary, my dear Watson"—phrases that were never actually uttered by those who were said to have said them—Vince Lombardi's last speech on June 21, 1970, didn't include the immortal phrase "winning isn't everything." You know who did say it? According to author David Maraniss in his Lombardi biography, When Pride Still Mattered, *it was either UCLA football coach Henry "Red" Sanders or a young actress in the John Wayne movie* Trouble Along the Way. *The coach's speech was still pretty good, though. Here it is:*

"Winning is not a sometime thing; it's an all the time thing. You don't win once in a while; you don't do things right once in a while; you do them right all the time. Winning is a habit. Unfortunately, so is losing.

There is no room for second place. There is only one place in my game, and that's first place. I have finished second twice in my time at Green Bay, and I don't ever want to finish second again. There is a second place bowl game, but it is a game for losers played by losers. It is and always has been an American zeal to be first in anything we do, and to win, and to win, and to win.

Every time a football player goes to ply his trade he's got to play from the ground up—from the soles of his feet right up to his head. Every inch of him has to play. Some guys play with their heads. That's okay. You've got to be smart to be number one in any business. But more importantly, you've got to play with your heart, with every fiber of your body. If you're lucky enough to find a guy with a lot of head and a lot of heart, he's never going to come off the field second.

Running a football team is no different than running any other kind of organization—an army, a political party or a business. The principles are the same. The object is to win—to beat the other guy. Maybe that sounds hard or cruel. I don't think it is.

It is a reality of life that men are competitive and the most competitive games draw the most competitive men. That's why they are there—to compete. To know the rules and objectives when they get in the game. The object is to win fairly, squarely, by the rules—but to win.

And in truth, I've never known a man worth his salt who, in the long run, deep down in his heart, didn't appreciate the grind, the discipline. There is something in good men that really yearns for discipline and the harsh reality of head-to-head combat.

I don't say these things because I believe in the "brute" nature of man or that men must be brutalized to be combative. I believe in God, and I believe in human decency. But I firmly believe that any man's finest hour, the greatest fulfillment of all that he holds dear, is that moment when he has worked his heart out in a good cause and lies exhausted on the field of battle—victorious."

Gridiron Maidens

Official Names Of NFL Cheerleading Squads

Arizona Cardinals: Cardinals Cheerleaders
Atlanta Falcons: Atlanta Falcons Cheerleaders
Baltimore Ravens: Ravens Cheerleaders
Buffalo Bills: Buffalo Jills
Carolina Panthers: TopCats
Cincinnati Bengals: Ben-Gals
Dallas Cowboys: Dallas Cowboys Cheerleaders
Denver Broncos: Broncos Cheerleaders
Houston Texans: Houston Texans Cheerleaders
Indianapolis Colts: Indianapolis Colts Cheerleaders
Jacksonville Jaguars: The Roar
Kansas City Chiefs: Kansas City Chiefs Cheerleaders
Miami Dolphins: Miami Dolphins Cheerleaders
Minnesota Vikings: Minnesota Vikings Cheerleaders
New England Patriots: Patriots Cheerleaders
New Orleans Saints: Saintsations
Oakland Raiders: Raiderettes
Philadelphia Eagles: Philadelphia Eagles Cheerleaders
St. Louis Rams: St. Louis Rams Cheerleaders
San Diego Chargers: Charger Girls
San Francisco 49ers: Gold Rush
Seattle Seahawks: Sea Gals
Tampa Bay Buccaneers: Buccaneers Cheerleaders
Tennessee Titans: Titans Cheerleaders
Washington Redskins: Washington Redskins Cheerleaders

Note: Chicago Bears, Cleveland Browns, Detroit Lions, Green Bay Packers, New York Giants, New York Jets, and Pittsburgh Steelers do not have cheerleaders.

Ground Rules

Olympic Sport Criteria

The question has been debated forever: What makes a sport a sport? Well, here's the answer. At least according to Chapter 5 of the Olympic Charter.

1. Olympic Sports included in the Programme of the Olympic Games:

To be included in the programme of the Olympic Games, an Olympic sport must conform to the following criteria:

1.1 Only sports widely practised by men in at least seventy-five countries and on four continents, and by women in at least forty countries and on three continents, may be included in the programme of the Games of the Olympiad;

1.2 Only sports widely practised in at least twenty-five countries and on three continents may be included in the programme of the Olympic Winter Games;

1.3 Only sports that adopt and implement the World Anti-Doping Code can be included and remain in the programme of the Olympic Games;

1.4 Sports are admitted to the programme of the Olympic Games at least seven years before specific Olympic Games in respect of which no change shall thereafter be permitted ...

Hands-On

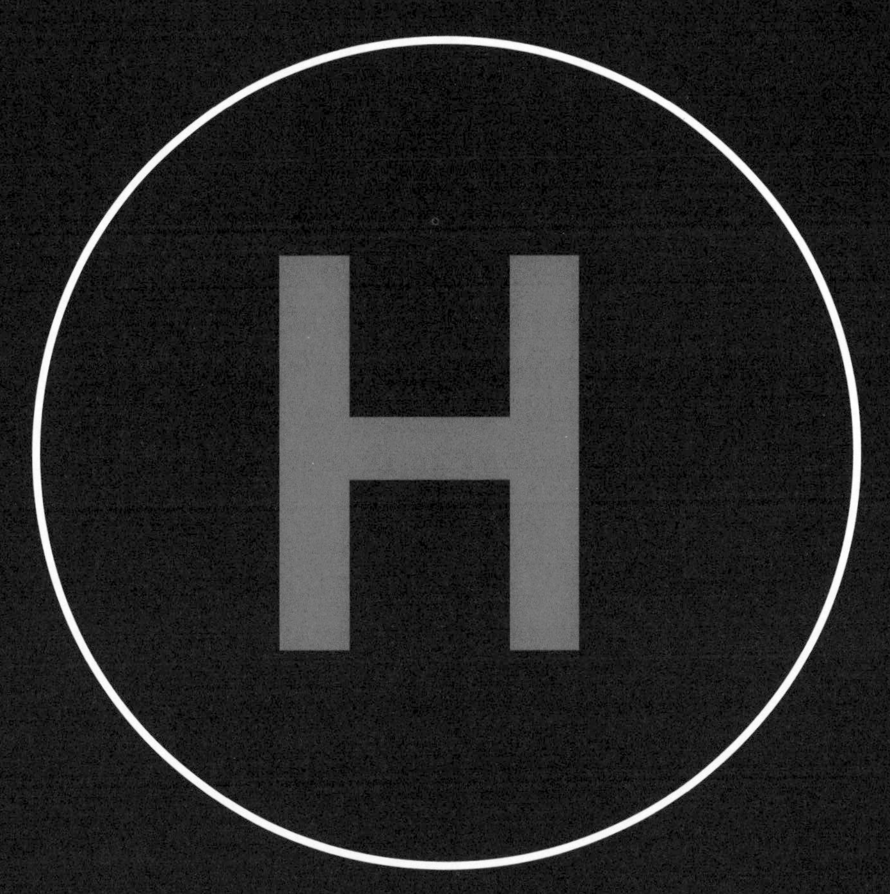

Huge

Hands-On Management

The Responsibility Code Of The World Rock Paper Scissors Society

To some, Rock Paper Scissors is a kids' game. To others it's a way of life. Here are some rules to live by, as codified by the sport's governing body, the World RPS Society.

1. Safety first! Always ensure that all players have removed sharp jewelry and watches.
2. Ensure agreement, before the first round, on priming conventions (we recommend the standard 3 prime shoot).
3. Always establish what is to be decided or whether the match is to be played for honour.
4. Pre-determine the number of rounds required to win the match (remember, odd numbers only).
5. Encourage novice development by explaining blunders in judgment with a mind toward being helpful. Don't berate.
6. Think twice before using RPS for life-threatening decisions.
7. Always respect foreign cultures. When abroad, consider yourself an ambassador of the World RPS Society.

Hardwood Regulations

The Original Rules Of Basketball

The first organized basketball game was played in December 1891 at the International Training School at the YMCA in Springfield, Massachusetts. The game was invented as a way for students there to get some exercise during the cold winter months. Basketball's creator—James Naismith, a second-year student and instructor—codified his new game on paper the morning of the first game.

1. The ball may be thrown in any direction with one or both hands.
2. The ball may be batted in any direction with one or both hands, but never with the fist.
3. A player cannot run with the ball. The player must throw it from the spot on which he catches it, allowance to be made for a man running at a good speed if he tries to stop.
4. The ball must be held in or between the hands. The arms or body must not be used for holding it.
5. No shouldering, holding, pushing, tripping, or striking in any way the person of an opponent shall be allowed. The first infringement of this rule by any person shall count as a foul; the second shall disqualify him until the next goal is made or, if there was evident intent to injure the person, for the whole of the game.

6. No substitute shall be allowed.
7. A foul is striking at the ball with the fist, violations of Rules 3 and 4, and such as described in Rule 5.
8. If either side makes three consecutive fouls, it shall count a goal for the opponents (consecutive means without the opponents in the meantime making a foul).
9. A goal shall be made when the ball is thrown or batted from the grounds into the basket and stays there, providing those defending the goal do not touch or disturb the goal. If the ball rests on the edge and the opponent moves the basket, it shall count as a goal.
10. When the ball goes out of bounds, it shall be thrown into the field and played by the person first touching it. In case of a dispute, the umpire shall throw it straight into the field. The thrower-in is allowed five seconds. If he holds it longer, it shall go to the opponent. If any side persists in delaying the game, the umpire shall call a foul on that side.
11. The umpire shall be judge of the men and shall note the fouls and notify the referee when three consecutive fouls have been made. He shall have the power to disqualify men according to Rule 5.
12. The referee shall be the judge of the ball and shall decide when the ball is in play, in bounds, to which side it belongs, and shall keep the time. He shall decide when a goal has been made and keep account of the goals with any other duties that are usually performed by a referee.
13. The time shall be two 15-minute halves with five minutes' rest between.
14. The side making the most goals in that time shall be declared the winners. In case of a draw, the game may, by agreement of the captains, be continued until another goal is made.

Hit Parade

A Single By Many Other Names

- Bagger
- Baltimore chop
- Banjo hit
- Base hit
- Base knock
- Base rap
- Bingle
- Bloop
- Broken-bat single
- Chink
- Daisy hit
- Dink
- Drooper
- Duck snort
- Dunker
- Dying quail
- Flare
- Gork
- Grenade
- In-betweener
- Jam Shot
- Knock
- Lollipop
- Looper
- One-bagger
- One-base hit
- One-sacker
- Parachute
- Plunker
- Poke
- Safe hit
- Safety
- Scratch
- Seeing-eye single
- Squib
- Texas Leaguer
- Tweener

Hockey Originals

Founding Teams Of The National Hockey League

When the National Hockey League's first modern expansion occurred in 1967, the existing teams—Boston Bruins, Chicago Black Hawks, Detroit Red Wings, Montreal Canadiens, New York Rangers, and Toronto Maple Leafs—were known as the Original Six. If only it were that simple. The real story goes back a half a century earlier. With many young men off to fight World War I, Canada's National Hockey Association suspended operations on November 10, 1917. That was the official line, anyway. The true reason behind the stoppage was to create a new league without Toronto Arenas owner Eddie Livingstone, whose constant tirades had made him unpopular with other owners. And so, on November 26, 1917, the NHL was formed, with a new Toronto franchise. Here are the five original NHL teams (and, years of birth):

- **Montreal Canadiens (1909)**
- **Montreal Wanderers[1] (1903)**
- **Ottawa Senators[2] (1901)**
- **Quebec Bulldogs[3] (1917)**
- **Toronto Arenas (1917)**

Note: [1]Only played in six games because their arena burned to the ground; [2]Not connected with current franchise of same name; [3]Owner chose not to operate team until the 1919-20 season.

Hockey Unoriginals

Founding Teams Of The World Hockey Association

When the WHA was formed in 1971, it was given little chance to succeed, as much because its two founders—Gary Davidson and Dennis Murphy—had no hockey experience as because of the dominance of the NHL. But when talented netminder Bernie Parent signed on, other stars followed, including the great, if aging, Bobby Hull. The carpetbaggers got enough people to notice that, following the 1977-78 season, four WHA teams (Edmonton Oilers, New England Whalers, Quebec Nordiques, Winnipeg Jets) were absorbed by the NHL before the others folded. Here are the original 12 WHA teams:

EASTERN DIVISION

Cleveland Crusaders
New England Whalers[1]
New York Raiders
Ottawa Nationals
Philadelphia Blazers
Quebec Nordiques[2]

WESTERN DIVISION

Alberta Oilers[3]
Chicago Cougars
Houston Aeros
Los Angeles Sharks
Minnesota Fighting Saints
Winnipeg Jets[4]

Note: [1]Now Carolina Hurricanes; [2]Now Colorado Avalanche; [3]Now Edmonton Oilers; [4]Now Phoenix Coyotes

A B C D E F G H I J K L M N O P Q R S T U V W X Y Z

Hold 'em Honchos

World Series of Poker Main Event Champions

1970 Johnny Moss (awarded by player vote; pot was winner take all)
1971 Johnny Moss ($30,000 winner's share)
1972 Amarillo Slim Preston ($80,000)
1973 Puggy Pearson ($130,000)
1974 Johnny Moss ($160,000)
1975 Sailor Roberts ($210,000)
1976 Doyle Brunson ($220,000)
1977 Doyle Brunson ($340,000)
1978 Bobby Baldwin ($210,000)
1979 Hal Fowler ($270,000)
1980 Stu Ungar ($385,000)
1981 Stu Ungar ($375,000)
1982 Jack Strauss ($520,000)
1983 Tom McEvoy ($580,000)
1984 Jack Keller ($660,000)
1985 Bill Smith ($700,000)
1986 Berry Johnston ($570,000)
1987 Johnny Chan ($625,000)
1988 Johnny Chan ($700,000)
1989 Phil Hellmuth Jr. ($755,000)
1990 Mansour Matloubi ($895,000)
1991 Brad Daugherty ($1,000,000)
1992 Hamid Dastmalchi ($1,000,000)
1993 Jim Bechtel ($1,000,000)
1994 Russ Hamilton ($1,000,000)
1995 Dan Harrington ($1,000,000)
1996 Huck Seed ($1,000,000)
1997 Stu Ungar ($1,000,000)
1998 Scotty Nguyen ($1,000,000)
1999 J.J. "Noel" Furlong ($1,000,000)
2000 Chris Ferguson ($1,500,000)
2001 Carlos Mortensen ($1,500,000)
2002 Robert Varkonyi ($2,000,000)
2003 Chris Moneymaker ($2,500,000)
2004 Greg Raymer ($5,000,000)
2005 Joseph Hachem ($7,500,000)
2006 Jamie Gold ($12,000,000)
2007 Jerry Yang ($8,250,000)

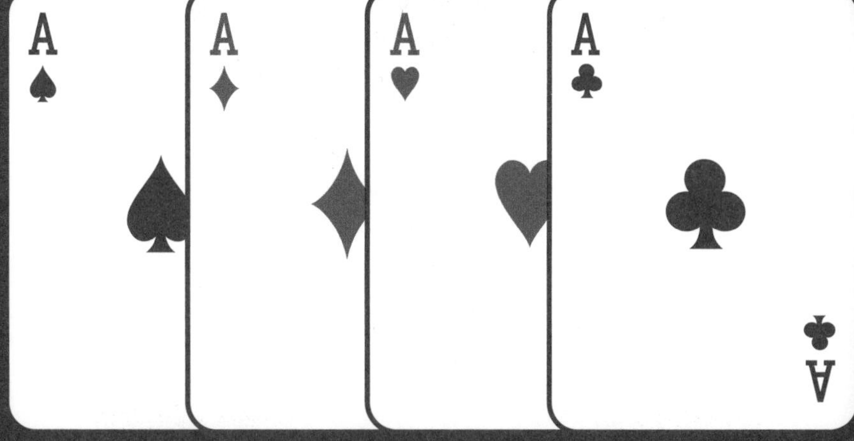

Hoop Hellraisers

Official Names of NBA Cheer and Dance Squads

Atlanta Hawks: A-Town Dancers
Boston Celtics: Celtics Dancers
Charlotte Bobcats: Charlotte Bobcats Dance Team
Chicago Bulls: Chicago Luvabulls
Cleveland Cavaliers: Cavalier Girls
Dallas Mavericks: Dallas Mavericks Dancers
Denver Nuggets: Nuggets Dancers
Detroit Pistons: Automotion
Golden State Warriors: Warrior Girls
Houston Rockets: Rockets Power Dancers
Indiana Pacers: Pacemates
Los Angeles Clippers: Clippers Spirit Dance Team
Los Angeles Lakers: Laker Girls
Memphis Grizzlies: Grizzlies Dance Team
Miami Heat: HEAT Dancers
Milwaukee Bucks: Energee!
Minnesota Timberwolves: Timberwolves Dance Team
New Jersey Nets: Nets Dancers
New Orleans Hornets: Honeybees
New York Knicks: Knicks City Dancers
Orlando Magic: Orlando Magic Dancers
Philadelphia 76ers: Sixers Dancers
Phoenix Suns: Suns Dancers
Portland Trail Blazers: BlazerDancers
Sacramento Kings: Kings Royal Court Dancers
San Antonio Spurs: Silver Dancers
Seattle Sonics: Sonics Dance Team
Toronto Raptors: Dance Pak
Utah Jazz: Nu Skin Jazz Dancers
Washington Wizards: Wizards Dancers

Hoops Originals

The Founding Teams Of The National Basketball Association

Once, there was the Basketball Association of America, founded in 1946. But the BAA wasn't the only pro game around; it battled with the National Basketball League for dominance in the late 1940s. The BAA was in the bigger cities, but the NBL had better players. Then, before the 1948-49 season, the NBL's four best teams—Fort Wayne, Rochester, Indianapolis, and Minneapolis—merged with the BAA. Overnight, the best players, biggest arenas, and largest media markets were united. A year later, the six surviving NBL teams were absorbed into the BAA and the league was renamed the National Basketball Association. Here are the original NBA franchises:

EASTERN DIVISION

Baltimore Bullets
Boston Celtics
New York Knickerbockers
Philadelphia Warriors[1]
Syracuse Nationals[2]
Washington Capitols

CENTRAL DIVISION

Chicago Stags
Fort Wayne Zollner Pistons[3]
Minneapolis Lakers[4]
Rochester (New York) Royals[5]
St. Louis Bombers

WESTERN DIVISION

Anderson (Indiana) Duffey Packers
Denver Nuggets[6]
Indianapolis Olympians
Sheboygan (Wisconsin) Redskins
Tri-Cities Blackhawks[7, 8]
Waterloo (Iowa) Hawks

Notes: [1]Now Golden State Warriors; [2]Now Philadelphia 76ers; [3]Now Detroit Pistons; [4]Now Los Angeles Lakers; [5]Now Sacramento Kings; [6]Not associated with current Nuggets; [7]Played in Moline, Illinois, but were called Tri-Cities for the Moline and Rock Island, Illinois, and Davenport, Iowa, metro area; [8] Now Atlanta Hawks

Horse Play

Famous Thoroughbred Match Races

Iron Mask vs. Pan Zareta
1914, Juarez (Mexico)
Iron Mask defeated the future Hall of Famer by five lengths.

Hourless vs. Omar Khayyam
1917, Laurel Park (Maryland)
Belmont winner Hourless pulled ahead at the eighth pole to beat the foreign-bred Kentucky Derby winner.

Man o' War vs. Sir Barton
1920, Kenilworth Park (Windsor, Ontario)
The younger of the two legends routed Sir Barton by seven lengths.

Zev vs. Papyrus
1923, Belmont Park (New York)
Kentucky Derby winner Zev defeated the English Derby winner by five lengths on a muddy track.

Clang vs. Myrtlewood
1935, Hawthorne (Illinois) and Coney Island (Ohio)
The three-year-olds met twice in three weeks, with each horse winning by a nose.

Seabiscuit vs. War Admiral
1938, Pimlico Race Course (Baltimore)
Seabiscuit pulled away down the stretch for a four-length victory over the 1937 Triple Crown winner.

Alsab vs. Whirlaway
1942, Narragansett Park (Rhode Island)
Kentucky Derby runner-up Alsab managed to hang on by a nose and defeat the favorite (and 1941 Triple Crown winner).

Capot vs. Coaltown
1949, Pimlico Race Course
Eventual Horse of the Year Capot coasted to a 12-length victory in Coaltown's final race.

Nashua vs. Swaps
1955, Washington Park (Chicago)
Eddie Arcaro's handling and a quick start propelled Nashua to a six-and-a-half-length victory over the injured Derby winner.

Ruffian vs. Foolish Pleasure
1975, Belmont Park
Ruffian suffered a broken leg after jumping out to an early lead, handing Derby winner Foolish Pleasure the victory. Ruffian was put down the next morning.

Hot Commodities

Athletes Drafted In More Than One Sport

Danny Ainge: MLB (Toronto Blue Jays, 1977), NBA (Boston Celtics, 1981)

Cedric Benson: MLB (Los Angeles Dodgers, 2001), NFL (Chicago Bears, 2005)

Josh Booty: MLB (Florida Marlins, 1994), NFL (Seattle Seahawks, 2001)

Tom Brady: MLB (Montreal Expos, 1995), NFL (New England Patriots, 2000)

Jim Brown: NFL (Cleveland Browns, 1957), NBA (Syracuse Nationals, 1957)

Bobby Bryant: MLB (New York Yankees, 1966; Boston Red Sox, 1967), NFL (Minnesota Vikings, 1967)

Scott Burrell: MLB (Seattle Mariners, 1989), NBA (Charlotte Hornets, 1993)

Kerry Collins: MLB (Detroit Tigers, 1990; Toronto Blue Jays, 1994), NFL (Carolina Panthers, 1995)

Daunte Culpepper: MLB (New York Yankees, 1995), NFL (Minnesota Vikings, 1999)

John Elway: MLB (Kansas City Royals, 1979; New York Yankees, 1983), NFL (Baltimore Colts, 1983)

Kirk Gibson: MLB (Detroit Tigers, 1978), NFL (St. Louis Cardinals, 1979)

Tom Glavine: MLB (Atlanta Braves, 1984), NHL (Los Angeles Kings, 1984)

Tony Gwynn: NBA (San Diego Clippers, 1981), MLB (San Diego Padres, 1981)

Drew Henson: MLB (New York Yankees, 1998), NFL (Houston Texans, 2003)

Bo Jackson: NFL (Tampa Bay Buccaneers, 1986), MLB (Kansas City Royals, 1986)

Kevin Johnson: MLB (Oakland A's, 1986), NBA (Cleveland Cavaliers, 1987)

Rob Johnson: MLB (Minnesota Twins, 1991), NFL (Jacksonville Jaguars, 1995)

Brian Jordan: MLB (St. Louis Cardinals, 1988), NFL (Buffalo Bills, 1989)

Trajan Langdon: MLB (San Diego Padres, 1994), NBA (Cleveland Cavaliers, 1999)

Dan Marino: MLB (Kansas City Royals, 1979), NFL (Miami Dolphins, 1983)

Rodney Peete: MLB (Toronto Blue Jays, 1984; Oakland A's, 1988, 1989; Detroit Tigers, 1990), NFL (Detroit Lions, 1989)

Mike Prior: MLB (Baltimore Orioles, 1984; Los Angeles Dodgers, 1985; Houston Astros, 1986), NFL (Tampa Bay Buccaneers, 1985)

Pat Riley: NBA (San Diego Rockets, 1967), NFL (Dallas Cowboys, 1967)

Deion Sanders: MLB (Kansas City Royals, 1985; New York Yankees, 1988), NFL (Atlanta Falcons, 1989)

Otto Schnellbacher: NFL (Chicago Cardinals, 1947), NBA (Providence Steam Rollers, 1948)

Michael Vick: MLB (Colorado Rockies, 2000), NFL (Atlanta Falcons, 2001)

Charlie Ward: MLB (Milwaukee Brewers, 1993; New York Yankees, 1994), NBA (New York Knicks, 1994)

Chris Weinke: MLB (Toronto Blue Jays, 1990), NFL (Carolina Panthers, 2001)

Ricky Williams: MLB (Philadelphia Phillies, 1995), NFL (New Orleans Saints, 1995)

Dave Winfield: MLB (San Diego Padres, 1973), NBA (Atlanta Hawks, 1973), ABA (Utah Stars, 1973), NFL (Minnesota Vikings, 1973)

Huddle Parties

Famous Football Units

Four Horsemen: Notre Dame backfield, circa 1924 (QB Harry Stuhldreher, HBs Jim Crowley and Don Miller, FB Elmer Layden)

Fearsome Foursome: Los Angeles Rams defensive line, 1960s (DE Lamar Lundy, DT Rosey Grier, DT Merlin Olsen, DE Deacon Jones)

Purple People Eaters: Minnesota Vikings defensive line, 1960s-70s (DE Jim Marshall, DT Carl Eller, DT Gary Larsen, DE Alan Page)

Electric Company: Buffalo Bills offensive line, 1970s (OT Dave Foley, OG Reggie McKenzie, C Mike Montler, LG Joe DeLamielleure, OT Donnie Green, TE Paul Seymour)

Doomsday Defense: Dallas Cowboys defense, 1970s (DE Pat Toomay, DT Bob Lilly, DT Jethro Pugh, DE Larry Cole, LB Chuck Howley, LB Lee Roy Jordan, LB Dave Edwards, CB Herb Adderley, CB Mel Renfro, SS Cornell Green, FS Cliff Harris)

No-name Defense: Miami Dolphins defense, early 1970s (DE Vern Den Herder, DT Manny Fernandez, DT Bob Heinz, DE Bill Stanfill, LB Doug Swift, LB Nick Buoniconti, LB Mike Kolen, CB Tim Foley, CB Curtis Johnson, SS Jake Scott, FS Dick Anderson)

Steel Curtain: Pittsburgh Steelers defense, 1970s (DE L.C. Greenwood, DT Joe Greene, DT Ernie Holmes, DE Dwight White, LB Jack Ham, LB Jack Lambert, LB Andy Russell, CB J.T. Thomas, CB Mel Blount, SS Mike Wagner, FS Glen Edwards)

Orange Crush: Denver Broncos defense, 1970s (DL Rubin Carter, DL Barney Chavous, DL Lyle Alzado, LB Randy Gradishar, LB Tom Jackson, LB Bob Swenson, LB Joe Rizzo, CB Billy Thompson, CB Louis Wright, FS Steve Foley, SS Bernard Jackson)

Sack Exchange: New York Jets defensive line, 1980s (DE Mark Gastineau, DT Marty Lyons, DT Abdul Salaam, DE Joe Klecko)

The Hogs: Washington Redskins offensive line, 1980s (OT Joe Jacoby, OG Russ Grimm, OT George Starke, OG Mark May, TE Don Warren, TE Rick Walker)

The Smurfs: Washington Redskins wide receivers, 1980s (Alvin Garrett, Charlie Brown, Virgil Seay)

Huge Affronts

Mandatory Positions In International Bodybuilding Competitions

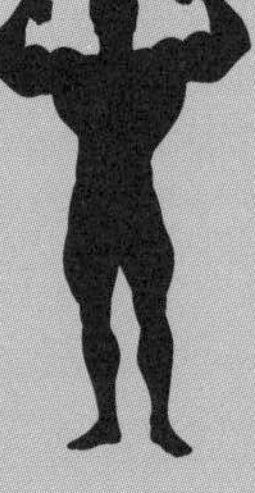

- **Front double biceps**
- **Front lat spread (men only)**
- **Side chest pose**
- **Side triceps pose**
- **Back lat spread (men only)**
- **Back double biceps**
- **Abdominals and thighs**

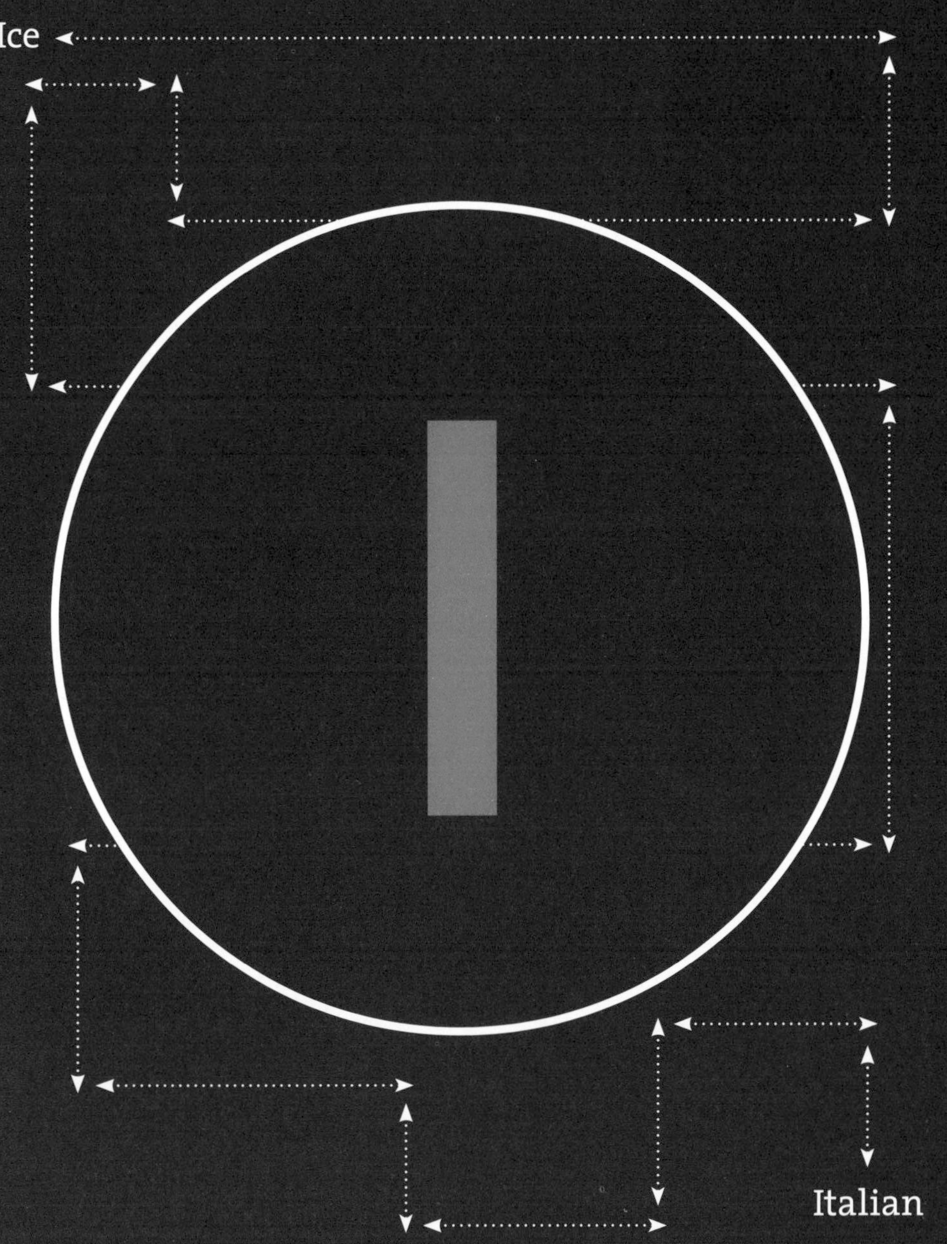
Ice
Italian

Ice Guys

Famous NHL Lines

Dynamite Line: Boston Bruins, 1920s-30s (LW Dutch Gainor, C Cooney Weiland, RW Dit Clapper)

Kid Line: Toronto Maple Leafs, 1930s (LW Busher Jackson, C Joe Primeau, RW Charlie Conacher)

Kraut Line: Boston Bruins, 1930s-40s (LW Woody Dumart, C Milt Schmidt, RW Bobby Bauer)

Pony Line: Chicago Black Hawks, 1940s (LW Doug Bentley, C Max Bentley, RW Bill Mosienko)

Punch Line: Montreal Canadiens, 1940s (LW Toe Blake, C Elmer Lach, RW Maurice Richard)

Production Line: Detroit Red Wings, 1940s-50s (LW Ted Lindsay, C Sid Abel, RW Gordie Howe; later, LW Frank Mahovlich, C Alex Delvecchio, Howe)

Scooter Line: Chicago Black Hawks, 1960s (LW Doug Mohns, C Stan Mikita, RW Ken Wharram; later, LW Ab McDonald, Mikita, Wharram)

Uke Line: Boston Bruins, 1960s (LW Johnny Bucyk, C Bronco Horvath, RW Vic Stasiuk)

Goal a Game (GAG) Line: New York Rangers, 1960s-70s (LW Rod Gilbert, C Jean Ratelle, RW Vic Hadfield)

French Connection: Buffalo Sabres, 1970s (LW Rick Martin, C Gilbert Perreault, RW Rene Robert)

Triple Crown Line: Los Angeles Kings, 1970s-80s (LW Charlie Simmer, C Marcel Dionne, RW Dave Taylor)

Legion of Doom: Philadelphia Flyers, 1990s (LW John LeClair, C Eric Lindros, RW Mikael Renberg)

Crash Line: New Jersey Devils, 1990s (LW Mike Peluso, C Bobby Holik, RW Randy McKay)

Grind Line: Detroit Red Wings, 2000s (LW Kirk Maltby, C Kris Draper, RW Darren McCarty)

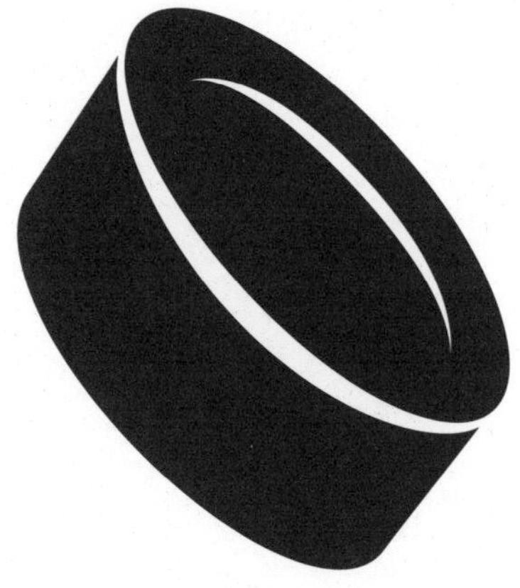

Ice Sculptures

NHL Awards And Trophies

Stanley Cup
(NHL champion)
Hart Memorial Trophy
(Most valuable player)
Vezina Trophy
(Best goalie)
James Norris Memorial Trophy
(Best defenseman)
Frank J. Selke Trophy
(Top defensive forward)
Lady Byng Memorial Trophy
(Sportsmanship and gentlemanly conduct)
Calder Memorial Trophy
(Rookie of the year)
Bill Masterton Memorial Trophy
(Perseverance and dedication to hockey)
Jack Adams Award
(Coach of the year)
Conn Smythe Trophy
(Playoffs MVP)
Art Ross Trophy
(Points leader)
Maurice Richard Trophy
(Top goal scorer)
William M. Jennings Trophy
(Goalie with fewest goals scored against)
Presidents' Trophy
(Best overall record)
Clarence S. Campbell Bowl
(Western Conference champion)
Prince Of Wales Trophy
(Eastern Conference champion)
King Clancy Memorial Trophy
(Leadership and humanitarian contribution)
Lester B. Pearson Award
(MVP, awarded by players)
Lester Patrick Trophy
(Outstanding service to hockey in the U.S.)

Ideal Ideas

The Fundamental Principles Of Olympism

The Olympics are more than just games—at least according to the Olympics. Here are the "Fundamental Principles of Olympism" from the official Olympic Charter.

1. Olympism is a philosophy of life, exalting and combining in a balanced whole the qualities of body, will, and mind. Blending sport with culture and education, Olympism seeks to create a way of life based on the joy of effort, the educational value of good examples, and respect for universal fundamental ethical principles.
2. The goal of Olympism is to place sport at the service of the harmonious development of man, with a view to promoting a peaceful society concerned with preservation of human dignity.
3. The Olympic Movement is the concerted, organised, universal, and permanent action, carried out under the supreme authority of the IOC, of all individuals and entities who are inspired by the values of Olympism. It covers the five continents. It reaches its peak with the bringing together of the world's athletes at the great sports festival, the Olympic Games. Its symbol is five interlaced rings.
4. The practice of sport is a human right. Every individual must have the possibility of practising sport, without discrimination of any kind and in the Olympic spirit, which requires mutual understanding with a spirit of friendship, solidarity, and fair play. The organisation, administration, and management of sport must be controlled by independent sports organisations.
5. Any form of discrimination with regard to a country or a person on grounds of race, religion, politics, gender, or otherwise is incompatible with belonging to the Olympic Movement.
6. Belonging to the Olympic Movement requires compliance with the Olympic Charter and recognition by the IOC.

Indoor Originals

Founding Teams Of The Arena Football League

Jim Foster, a former NFL marketing executive, attended an indoor soccer game at Madison Square Garden in 1981 and decided that pro football could thrive in such a setting as well. The Arena Football League was launched in 1987 and has been sending wide receivers careening into walls ever since. Its success has even spawned a developmental league (af2), which debuted in 2000. Here are the founding teams of the AFL:

- **Chicago Bruisers**
- **Denver Dynamite**
- **Pittsburgh Gladiators**

Integration Firsts

African-American Milestones In Major Sports

First NFL Players (modern era)
Kenny Washington and Woody Strode, Los Angeles Rams, 1946

First Pro Football Head Coach
Fritz Pollard, Akron Pros, 1921

First NFL Head Coach (modern era)
Art Shell, Oakland Raiders, 1989

First MLB player
Jackie Robinson, Brooklyn Dodgers, 1947

First MLB Manager
Frank Robinson, Cleveland Indians, 1974

First NBA Player
Earl Lloyd, Washington Capitols, 1950

First NBA Head Coach
Bill Russell, Boston Celtics, 1967

First NHL Player
Willie O'Ree, Boston Bruins, 1958

First Inductee Into Baseball Hall of Fame
Jackie Robinson, 1962

First Negro League Inductee Into Baseball Hall of Fame
Satchel Paige, Birmingham Black Barons, Baltimore Black Sox, Cleveland Cubs, Pittsburgh Crawfords, Kansas City Monarchs, Santo Domingo All-Stars, Newark Eagles, Satchel Paige's All-Stars, New York Black Yankees, Memphis Red Sox, Philadelphia Stars, Cleveland Indians, St. Louis Browns, Chicago American Giants, Kansas City A's, 1971

First Inductee in Pro Football Hall of Fame
Emlen Tunnell, New York Giants, Green Bay Packers, 1967

First Inductee Into Basketball Hall of Fame
Robert "Bob" Douglas, founder and coach of Harlem Renaissance, 1972

First Inductee Into Hockey Hall of Fame
Grant Fuhr, Edmonton Oilers, Toronto Maple Leafs, Buffalo Sabres, Los Angeles Kings, St. Louis Blues, Calgary Flames, 2003

A B C D E F G H I J K L M N O P Q R S T U V W X Y Z

Intermission Statements

Sports Stoppages Through History

MLB

1972, Lockout
Games missed: 86
Issue: pensions

1973, Lockout
Games missed: 0
Issue: salary arbitration

1976, Lockout
Games missed: 0
Issue: free agency

1980, Strike
Games missed: 0
Issue: free-agent compensation

1981, Strike
Games missed: 712
Issue: free-agent compensation

1985, Strike
Games missed: 0
Issue: salary arbitration

1990, Lockout
Games missed: 0
Issues: salary arbitration; salary cap

1994–95, Strike
Games missed: 920
Issues: salary cap; revenue sharing

NFL

1968, Lockout/Strike
Games missed: 0
Issue: pensions

1974, Strike
Games missed: 0
Issue: free agency

1980, Lockout/Strike
Games missed: 0
Issue: various

1982, Strike
Games missed: 196
Issue: compensation

1987, Strike
Games missed: 14
Issue: free agency

NHL

1992, Strike
Games missed: 0
Issue: marketing compensation

1994, Lockout
Games missed: 468
Issue: compensation rollback

2004, Lockout
Games missed: 2,460
Issue: salaries

NBA

1998, Strike
Games missed: 928
Issue: salaries

Iowa Corn

Terence Mann's "People Will Come" Speech From *Field Of Dreams*

Released in 1989, Field of Dreams *tells the story of Ray Kinsella (Kevin Costner), who builds a baseball diamond on his struggling Iowa farm. Among the many people Ray meets on his quixotic journey is reclusive author Terence Mann (James Earl Jones), who convinces Kinsella to chase his dreams when his brother-in-law, Mark, pressures him to sell the farm.*

MANN: Ray, people will come, Ray. They'll come to Iowa for reasons they can't even fathom. They'll turn into the driveway, not knowing for sure why they're doing it. They'll arrive at your door as innocent as children, longing for the past. "Of course we won't mind if you have a look around," you'll say. "It's only twenty dollars per person." They'll pass over the money without even thinking about it; for it is money they have and peace they lack.
MARK: Ray, just sign the papers.
MANN: And they'll walk out to the bleachers, sit in shirt-sleeves on a perfect afternoon. They'll find they have reserved seats somewhere along one of the baselines, where they sat when they were children and cheered their heroes. And they'll watch the game, and it'll be as if they had dipped themselves in magic waters. The memories will be so thick they'll have to brush them away from their faces.
MARK: Ray, when the bank opens in the morning, they'll foreclose.
MANN: People will come, Ray.
MARK: You're broke, Ray. Ya, sell now or you'll lose everything.
MANN: The one constant through all the years, Ray, has been baseball. America has rolled by like an army of steamrollers; it has been erased like a blackboard, rebuilt, and erased again. But baseball has marked the time. This field, this game, is a part of our past, Ray. It reminds us of all that once was good, and it could be again. Ohhhh, people will come, Ray. People will most definitely come.

Italian Battalion

Rocky Balboa's Career Bouts

OPPONENT	OUTCOME
Spider Rico *(Rocky)*	Win by knockout, Round 2
Apollo Creed *(Rocky)*	Loss, split decision
Apollo Creed *(Rocky II)*	Win by knockout, Round 15
Thunderlips *(Rocky III)*	Draw (charity match)
Clubber Lang *(Rocky III)*	Loss by knockout, Round 2
Clubber Lang *(Rocky III)*	Win by knockout, Round 3
Ivan Drago *(Rocky IV)*	Win by knockout, Round 15
Tommy Gunn *(Rocky V)*	Win by knockout, street fight
Mason Dixon *(Rocky Balboa)*	Loss, split decision

Jacks

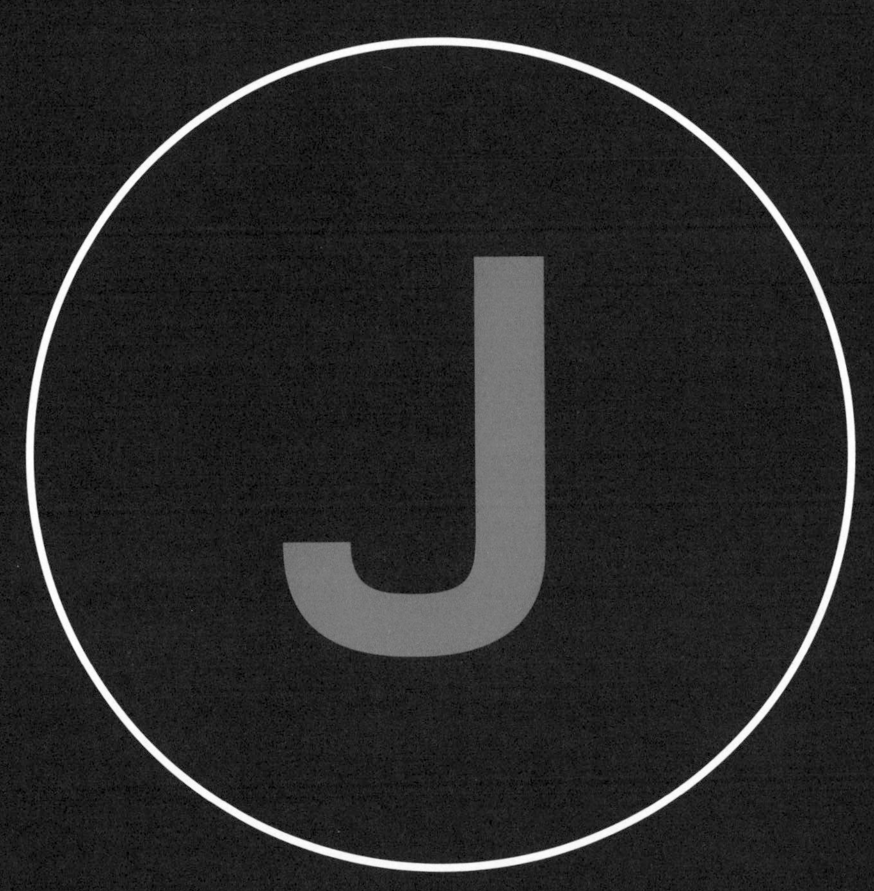

Just

A B C D E F G H I J K L M N O P Q R S T U V W X Y Z

Jacks Of All Trades

Winners Of The Original *Superstars* Competition

Brainchild of figure skating legend Dick Button, Superstars first aired on ABC in 1973, running uninterrupted for 21 more years (it was revived in 1998). Ten athletes from various sports were matched in a 10-event competition, with the participants receiving not only prize money but also plots of land in Rotonda, Florida. (An athlete chose seven of 10 events in which to participate, but could not compete in an event related to his sport.) Those 10 events? Tennis, swimming, weight lifting, bowling, golf (nine holes), table tennis, 100-yard dash, hitting a baseball, half-mile run, and bicycle racing. (The infamous obstacle course replaced table tennis in 1974.) Here are the winners and their day jobs.

1973 Bob Seagren (pole vault)
1974 Kyle Rote Jr. (soccer)
1975 O.J. Simpson (NFL)
1976 Kyle Rote Jr. (soccer)
1977 Kyle Rote Jr. (soccer)
1978 Wayne Grimditch (water skiing)
1979 Greg Pruitt (NFL)
1980 Charles White (NFL)
1981 Renaldo Nehemiah (hurdles)
1982 Renaldo Nehemiah (hurdles, NFL)
1983 Renaldo Nehemiah (hurdles, NFL)
1984 Tom Petranoff (javelin)
1985 Mark Gastineau (NFL)
1986 Renaldo Nehemiah (hurdles)
1987 Herschel Walker (NFL)
1988 Herschel Walker (NFL)
1989 Willie Gault (NFL)
1990 Willie Gault (NFL)
1991 Kelly Gruber (MLB)
1992 Mike Powell (long jump)
1993 Dave Johnson (decathlon)
1994 Dave Johnson (decathlon)

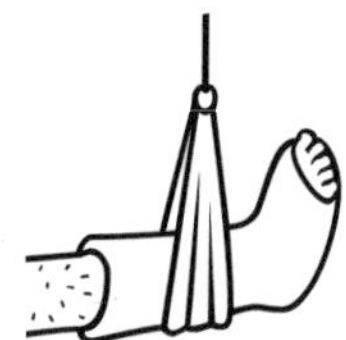

Jinx Alerts

Common Sports Superstitions

AUTO RACING

It's good luck to ...

Find a heads-up penny ... eat a specific pre-race meal.

It's bad luck to ...

Wear green ... encounter the number 13 ... eat peanuts.

BASEBALL

It's good luck to ...

Spit in your hand before picking up the bat ... stick a wad of gum on your hat brim ... sleep with your bat if you're in a slump ... step on a base before running off the field at the end of an inning.

It's bad luck to ...

See a dog walk across the diamond before the first pitch ... lend your bat to a fellow player ... speak to a pitcher in the dugout if he's throwing a no-hitter or a perfect game.

BASKETBALL
It's good luck to ...
Be the last person to shoot a basket during the warm-up ... wipe the soles of your sneakers.

It's bad luck to ...
Forget to bounce the ball before taking a foul shot.

BOWLING
It's good luck to ...
Have the number 300 on your license plate ... carry charms in your bowling bag.

It's bad luck to ...
Change clothes during a winning streak.

FISHING
It's good luck to ...
Spit on your bait before casting your rod ... throw back your first catch.

It's bad luck to ...
Keep fishing after a barefoot woman passes you on the way to the dock ... change rods ... talk about how many fish you've caught until you're done.

FOOTBALL
It's good luck to ...
Wear double numbers (88, for example) on your uniform.

It's bad luck to ...
Take a new number when you're traded to another team.

GOLF
It's good luck to ...
Carry coins in your pocket ... start play with an odd-numbered club.

It's bad luck to ...
Use a ball with a number on it that's higher than 4.

HOCKEY
It's good luck to ...
Tap the goalie on his pads before a game.

It's bad luck to ...
Let hockey sticks lie across each other ... say "shutout" in the locker room before a game.

RODEO
It's good luck to ...
Shave before a competition.

It's bad luck to ...
Put your left foot in the stirrup first ... wear yellow.

TENNIS
It's good luck to ...
Walk around the outside of the court when switching sides.

It's bad luck to ...
Hold more than two balls at a time when serving ... wear yellow.

Jockey Sorts

Racing Silks Guidelines

A horse of a different color may fly in some areas, but in thoroughbred racing, there are some definite rules for racing silks. Here are The Jockey Club's design guidelines:

1. Front and back of silks must be identical, except for seam design.

2. Colors must be registered in the name of one person only; not a stable name or Mr. & Mrs. (example: Mary E. Jones).

3. Designs are limited to those listed in guideline no. 7.

4. Navy blue is not an available color.

5. A maximum of two colors is allowed on the jacket and two on the sleeves, for a maximum of four colors.

6. These colors will be renewable on December 31st of the year they are registered.

7. You may have an acceptable emblem or up to three initials on the ball, yoke, circle, or braces design. You may have one initial on the opposite shoulder of the sash design, the box frame, or the diamond.

Jump Master

EVEL KNIEVEL'S *WIDE WORLD OF SPORTS* APPEARANCES

Legendary daredevil Evel Knievel was inextricably connected to ABC*'s equally legendary* Wide World of Sports, *which used his motorcycle exploits to boost its ratings in the 1970s. Here are Knievel's* WWOS *jumps and results:*

DATE	LOCATION	JUMP	RESULT
November 10, 1973	Los Angeles Coliseum	50 stacked cars	Successful
February 17, 1974	North Richmond Hill, Texas	11 Mack trucks	Successful
August 31, 1974	Canadian National Exhibition, Toronto	13 Mack trucks	Successful
September 8, 1974	Snake River Canyon, Idaho	Canyon	Crashed
May 31, 1975	Wembley Stadium, London	13 double-decker buses	Crashed
October 25, 1975	King's Island, Cincinnati	14 Greyhound buses	Successful
October 30, 1976	Kingdome, Seattle	7 Greyhound buses	Successful

Note: On New Year's Day, 1968, Evel Knievel attempted to jump 151 feet over the fountains at Caesars Palace. He cleared the gap, but his crash on the landing put him in a coma for 30 days. In 1989, his son Robbie successfully completed the feat.

A B C D E F G H I J K L M N O P Q R S T U V W X Y Z

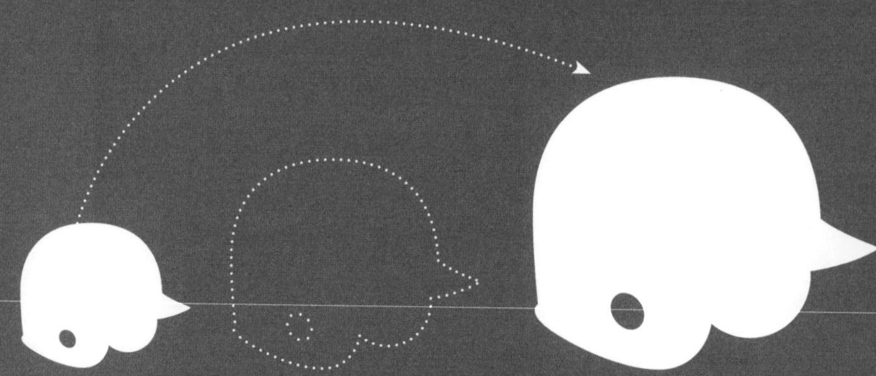

Jumping The Line

Drafted Baseball Players Who Skipped The Minor Leagues

Since the inception of Major League Baseball's draft in 1965, only these 20 players managed to go directly to the big leagues:

1967 Mike Adamson, P: USC to Baltimore Orioles

1969 Steve Dunning, P: Stanford University to Cleveland Indians

1971 Burt Hooton, P: University of Texas to Chicago Cubs

1971 Rob Ellis, INF: Michigan State to Milwaukee Brewers

1971 Pete Broberg, P: Dartmouth to Washington Senators

1972 Dave Roberts, INF: University of Oregon to San Diego Padres

1973 Dick Ruthven, P: Fresno State to Philadelphia Phillies

1973 Eddie Bane, P: Arizona State to Minnesota Twins

1973 David Clyde, P: Westchester H.S. (Texas) to Texas Rangers

1973 Dave Winfield, OF: University of Minnesota to San Diego Padres

1978 Mike Morgan, P: Valley H.S. (Nevada) to Oakland A's

1978 Tim Conroy, P: Gateway H.S. (Pennsylvania) to Oakland A's

1978 Brian Milner, C: Southwest H.S. (Texas) to Toronto Blue Jays

1978 Bob Horner, INF: Arizona State to Atlanta Braves

1985 Pete Incaviglia, OF: Oklahoma State to Montreal Expos

1988 Jim Abbott, P: University of Michigan to California Angels

1989 John Olerud, INF: Washington State to Toronto Blue Jays

1993 Darren Dreifort, P: Wichita State to Los Angeles Dodgers

1995 Ariel Prieto, P: Fajardo University (Cuba) to Oakland A's

2000 Xavier Nady, OF: University of California-Berkeley to San Diego Padres

Jumps For Joy

Types Of Sport Parachuting Competitions

ACCURACY LANDING: Oldest event in competitive parachuting. Competitors attempt to land as close to a small target as possible.

FREEFALL STYLE: Competitors execute various quick and accurate mandatory maneuvers during freefall, before deploying chute.

FREESTYLE: Individual freefall with choreographed maneuvers, executed as part of a team for points.

FREEFLYING: Unrestricted freefall in which maneuvers are controlled by wind direction.

FORMATION SKYDIVING: Teams of two or more freefallers shape sequences of geometric formations.

CANOPY FORMATION: Teams of two or more skydivers with chutes open connect to make formations with their canopies during descent.

SKYSURFING: Freefall using a specially rigged board, or rigid panel, attached to skydiver's feet, to perform flips or spins during descent.

Just For Kicks

Different Words For Athletic Shoes

From Charlie's Sneaker Pages (sneakers.pair.com) comes this list of names for sneakers and other athletic shoes:

Aerobic Shoes ... Basketball boots ... Boat shoes ... Bobos (Boston) ... Boots (England) ... Bumper boots (England) ... Cleats ... Cross-trainers ... Daps (Wales) ... Deck shoes ... Drug shoes ... Felony shoes ... Fishheads (cheap sneakers; Pittsburgh, Baltimore in late '60s) ... Football boots (England) ... Go-fasters ... Gym shoes ... Grapplers ... High-tops ... Hoop shoes ... Keds (India) ... Kicks ... Plimsolls (England) ... Outing shoes (beach shoes; U.S.A.) ... Runners... Sabogs (*A Clockwork Orange*) ... Shoeclacks (French Canada) ... Sneaks ... Sneakers ... Soccer boots (U.S.A.) ... Speed shoes... Tackies (South Africa, Ireland) ... Tennie-runners ... Tennies ... Tennis shoes ... Track shoes ... Trainers (England)

Keepsakes

Known

Keepsakes

College Football Rivalry Trophies

Administaff Bayou Bucket: University of Houston vs. Rice University

Apple Cup: University of Washington vs. Washington State University

Black Diamond Trophy: Virginia Tech University vs. West Virginia University

Brice-Cowell Musket: University of Maine vs. University of New Hampshire

Bronze Boot: University of Wyoming vs. Colorado State University

Commander in Chief's Trophy: U.S. Military Academy vs. U.S. Naval Academy

Commonwealth Cup: Virginia Tech University vs. University of Virginia

Cy-Hawk Trophy: University of Iowa vs. Iowa State University

Floyd of Rosedale: University of Minnesota vs. University of Iowa

Fremont Cannon: University of Nevada-Las Vegas vs. University of Nevada-Reno

Golden Boot: University of Arkansas vs. Louisiana State University

Golden Egg Trophy: University of Mississippi vs. Mississippi State University

Golden Hat Trophy/Governor's Cup: University of Texas vs. University of Oklahoma

Governor's Cup: University of Kansas vs. Kansas State University

Governor's Victory Bell: University of Minnesota vs. Penn State University

Illibuck: University of Illinois vs. Ohio State University

Ireland Trophy: Notre Dame vs. Boston College

Iron Skillet: Southern Methodist University vs. Texas Christian University

Jeweled Shillelagh: Notre Dame vs. USC

Land Grant Trophy: Penn State University vs. Michigan State University

Little Brown Jug: University of Michigan vs. University of Minnesota

Maloof Trophy: University of New Mexico vs. New Mexico State University

Marching Band Drum: University of Kansas vs. University of Missouri

Megaphone Trophy: Michigan State University vs. Notre Dame

Missouri–Nebraska Bell: University of Missouri vs. University of Nebraska

ODK–Foy Sportsmanship Trophy: Auburn University vs. University of Alabama

Old Brass Spittoon: University of Indiana vs. Michigan State University

Old Oaken Bucket: University of Indiana vs. Purdue University

Paul Bunyan's Axe: University of Minnesota vs. University of Wisconsin

Paul Bunyan Trophy: University of Michigan vs. Michigan State University

Peace Pipe: Bowling Green University vs. University of Toledo

Purdue Cannon: Purdue University vs. University of Illinois

River Bell Trophy: Marshall University vs. Ohio University

Shillelagh Trophy: Notre Dame vs. Purdue University

Silver Spade and the Brass Spittoon: University of Texas-El Paso vs. University of New Mexico State

Sweet Sioux Tomahawk: University of Illinois vs. Northwestern University

Telephone Trophy: Iowa State University vs. University of Missouri

Territorial Cup: University of Arizona vs. Arizona State University

Textile Bowl Trophy: Clemson University vs. North Carolina State University

The Heartland Trophy: University of Iowa vs. University of Wisconsin

The Stanford Axe: Stanford University vs. University of California

The Tiger Rag: Louisiana State University vs. Tulane University

Victory Bell: University of Cincinnati vs. Miami University (Ohio)

Victory Bell: UCLA vs. USC

War Canoe Trophy: University of Florida vs. University of Miami

A B C D E F G H I J K L M N O P Q R S T U V W X Y Z

A B C D E F G H I J K L M N O P Q R S T U V W X Y Z

Kennel Club Champs

Best-In-Show Winners By Breed At The Westminster Kennel Club Dog Show

Fox Terrier (17; 1907-10, 1915-17, 1920, 1926, 1928, 1930-31, 1934, 1937, 1946, 1966, 1992)
Scottish Terrier (7; 1911, 1945, 1950, 1965, 1967, 1985, 1995)
English Springer Spaniel (6; 1963, 1971-72, 1993, 2000, 2007)
Airedale Terrier (4; 1912, 1919, 1922, 1933)
Boxer (4; 1947, 1949, 1951, 1970)
Cocker Spaniel (4; 1921, 1940-41, 1954)
Doberman Pinscher (4; 1939, 1952-53, 1989)
Sealyham Terrier (4; 1924, 1927, 1936, 1977)
Standard Poodle (4; 1935, 1958, 1973, 1991)
Miniature Poodle (3; 1943, 1959, 2002)
Pekingese (3; 1960, 1982, 1990)
Pointer (3; 1925, 1932, 1986)
Afghan Hound (2; 1957, 1983)
Bull Terrier (2; 1918, 2006)
Bulldog (2; 1913, 1955)
German Shorthaired Pointer (2; 1974, 2005)
Lakeland Terrier (2; 1968, 1976)
Newfoundland (2; 1984, 2004)
Norwich Terrier (2; 1994, 1998)
Old English Sheepdog (2; 1914,1975)
Toy Poodle (2; 1956, 1961)
West Highland White Terrier (2; 1942, 1962)
Bedlington Terrier (1; 1948)
Bichon Frisé (1; 2001)
Clumber Spaniel (1; 1996)
Collie (1; 1929)
English Settler (1; 1938)
German Shepherd (1; 1987)
Irish Water Spaniel (1; 1979)
Kerry Blue Terrier (1; 2003)
Papillon (1; 1999)
Pomeranian (1; 1988)
Pug (1; 1981)
Siberian Husky (1; 1980)
Skye Terrier (1; 1969)
Standard Schnauzer (1; 1997)
Welsh Terrier (1; 1944)
Whippet (1; 1964)
Yorkshire Terrier (1; 1978)
Beagle (1; 2008)

Note: Best in Show was not awarded in 1923.

Kickoff Calamity

The Announcer's Call Of The Stanford Band Kick-return Play

1982. Stanford leads California with four seconds to play. Here's the call by Cal announcer Joe Starkey, of one of the most memorable plays in college football history:

"All right, here we go with the kickoff. Harmon will probably try to squib it … and he does. Ball comes loose and the Bears have to get out of bounds. Rogers along the sideline, another one ... they're still in deep trouble at midfield, they tried to do a couple of ... the ball is still loose as they get it to Rogers. They get it back to the 30, they're down to the 20 ... Oh, the band is out on the field! He's gonna go into the end zone! He got into the end zone! Will it count? The Bears have scored but the bands are out on the field. There were flags all over the place. Wait and see what happens—we don't know who won the game. There are flags on the field. We have to see whether or not the flags are against Stanford or Cal. The Bears may have made some illegal laterals. It could be that it won't count. The Bears, believe it or not, took it all the way into the end zone. If the penalty is against Stanford, California would win the game. If it is not, the game is over and Stanford has won. We've heard no decision yet. Everybody is milling around on the field. AND THE BEARS … THE BEARS HAVE WON!! THE BEARS HAVE WON!! OH MY GOD, THE MOST AMAZING, SENSATIONAL, TRAUMATIC, HEART-RENDING ... EXCITING, THRILLING FINISH IN THE HISTORY OF COLLEGE FOOTBALL! California has won the Big Game over Stanford. Oh, excuse me for my voice, but I have never, never seen anything like it in the history of … I have ever seen any game in my life! The Bears have won it! There will be no extra point! [Color analyst Jan Hutchins interjects: "Hold it right here, don't anybody go away ... After just about everybody on the kickoff team handled the ball, Kevin Moen finally did it. And he ran through 15 members of the Stanford band, nobody tackled him. The fools!"] ... Len Shapiro, our statistician, has just held up a card and it says the truth. The Stanford band just cost their team that ball game. The Stanford band ran out on the field, it left all the defenders in an impossible situation to get to the Bears carrying the ball. They couldn't tackle 'em. The band, in effect, served as extra blockers. The official had no choice but to let the play go as was. The Bears have scored on the kickoff, brought it all the way back. At least five men handled the ball on one lateral after another. I thought Rogers was dead at one point. He got rid of the ball … I believe it was Kevin Moen that Jan said that scored the winning touchdown as the kickoff came from the 25-yard line. This place is like it has never been, ever. Stanford can't believe it."

A B C D E F G H I J K L M N O P Q R S T U V W X Y Z

Known Aliases

Sports Moments Or Events That Have Earned Nicknames

MERKLE'S BONER

September 23, 1908. New York Giants rookie Fred Merkle singles in the bottom of the ninth inning with a runner on first, two outs, and the score tied. The next batter hits a single, and as Merkle sees the runner ahead of him score, he heads to the Giants' dugout, assuming the game is over. Chicago Cubs second baseman Johnny Evers notices Merkle never touched second base, so he appeals to the umpire, who rules the play a force out, the final out, and the game a tie. The Cubs and Giants finish the season tied in the standings and play a one-game playoff to see who will advance to the World Series. The Cubs win.

THE LONG COUNT

September 22, 1927. Fifty seconds into the seventh round, Jack Dempsey knocks down heavyweight champ Gene Tunney. The referee not only tells Dempsey to go to his corner, but follows him there. When the ref returns to count out Tunney, he ignores the timekeeper's count of five and starts at one. At nine, Tunney gets up. He later resumes control of the fight and wins by decision.

THE SHOT HEARD 'ROUND THE WORLD

October 3, 1951. In the ninth inning of the final game of a three-game playoff between the New York Giants and the Brooklyn Dodgers, Giants outfielder Bobby Thomson hits a three-run home run that gives his team a come-from-behind 5-4 win against their archrivals, and the pennant.

THE GREATEST GAME EVER PLAYED

December 28, 1958. In the first sudden-death overtime game in NFL history, Baltimore Colts running back Alan Ameche's one-yard touchdown gives the Colts a 23-17 win over the New York Giants.

THE ICE BOWL

December 31, 1967. It's 13 degrees below zero with a wind chill of -46 at Lambeau Field in Wisconsin. With 13 seconds remaining in the NFL Championship Game against the Dallas Cowboys, Green Bay Packers quarterback Bart Starr sneaks across the goal line for the winning score.

THE HEIDI GAME

November 17, 1968. When a nationally televised game between the New York Jets and the Oakland Raiders runs late, NBC cuts away from the game to show the movie *Heidi*. Fans bombard the network's phone lines but miss the two touchdowns the Raiders score in the final minute to win the game.

THE IMMACULATE RECEPTION

December 23, 1972. With 22 seconds left at their own 40-yard line, the Pittsburgh Steelers trail the Oakland Raiders 7-6 in a playoff game. On fourth and 10, quarterback Terry Bradshaw throws a desperation pass downfield that deflects off Raiders safety Jack Tatum and is scooped up by running back Franco Harris, who takes it in for the winning touchdown.

THE HOLY ROLLER

September 10, 1978. With 10 seconds left and no timeouts remaining, the Oakland Raiders are on the San Diego Chargers' 14-yard line. They trail 20-14. Raiders quarterback Ken Stabler rolls to his right and, just before he is about to be sacked by linebacker Woody Lowe, he underhands the ball forward. Knowing that anything less than a touchdown ends the game, running back Pete Banaszak kicks and pushes the ball ahead on the ground to Raiders tight end Dave Casper, who stumbles with and kicks the ball into the end zone, where he falls on it for the game winner.

THE MIRACLE ON ICE

February 22, 1980. In the semifinal game of the 1980 Winter Olympics in Lake Placid, New York, the U.S. hockey team upsets the heavily favored Soviets 4-3 on Mike Eruzione's third-period goal. The team then beats Finland for the gold medal.

THE CATCH

January 10, 1982. In the NFC Championship game, Joe Montana scrambles and flings a six-yard touchdown pass to Dwight Clark with 51 seconds left to give the San Francisco 49ers a 28-27 win over the Dallas Cowboys.

THE HAND OF GOD GOAL

June 22, 1986. In a quarterfinal game in soccer's World Cup, Diego Maradona scores a goal for Argentina against England on an uncalled handball he later credits to "the hand of God."

THE DRIVE

January 11, 1987. Trailing the Cleveland Browns 20-13 with 5:32 to play and a trip to the Super Bowl on the line, Denver Broncos quarterback John Elway drives his team 98 yards in 15 plays for a touchdown. The Broncos win in overtime on a Rich Karlis field goal.

THE SHOT

May 7, 1989. With his Chicago Bulls trailing by one in the deciding fifth game of a first-round playoff series in Cleveland, Michael Jordan takes an inbounds pass and hits an 18-footer at the buzzer over the Cavaliers' Craig Ehlo to win the game and the series.

THE COMEBACK

January 3, 1993. Trailing the Houston Oilers 35-3 early in the third quarter, Buffalo Bills back-up quarterback Frank Reich leads his team to a 41-38 overtime playoff win, the biggest comeback in NFL history.

THE MUSIC CITY MIRACLE

January 8, 2000. With 16 seconds left on the clock and the Buffalo Bills leading the Tennessee Titans 16-15 in a first-round playoff game, the Bills kick off to Lorenzo Neal, who hands it to Frank Wycheck, who throws a controversial lateral across the field to Kevin Dyson, who runs uncontested down the sideline for the winning touchdown.

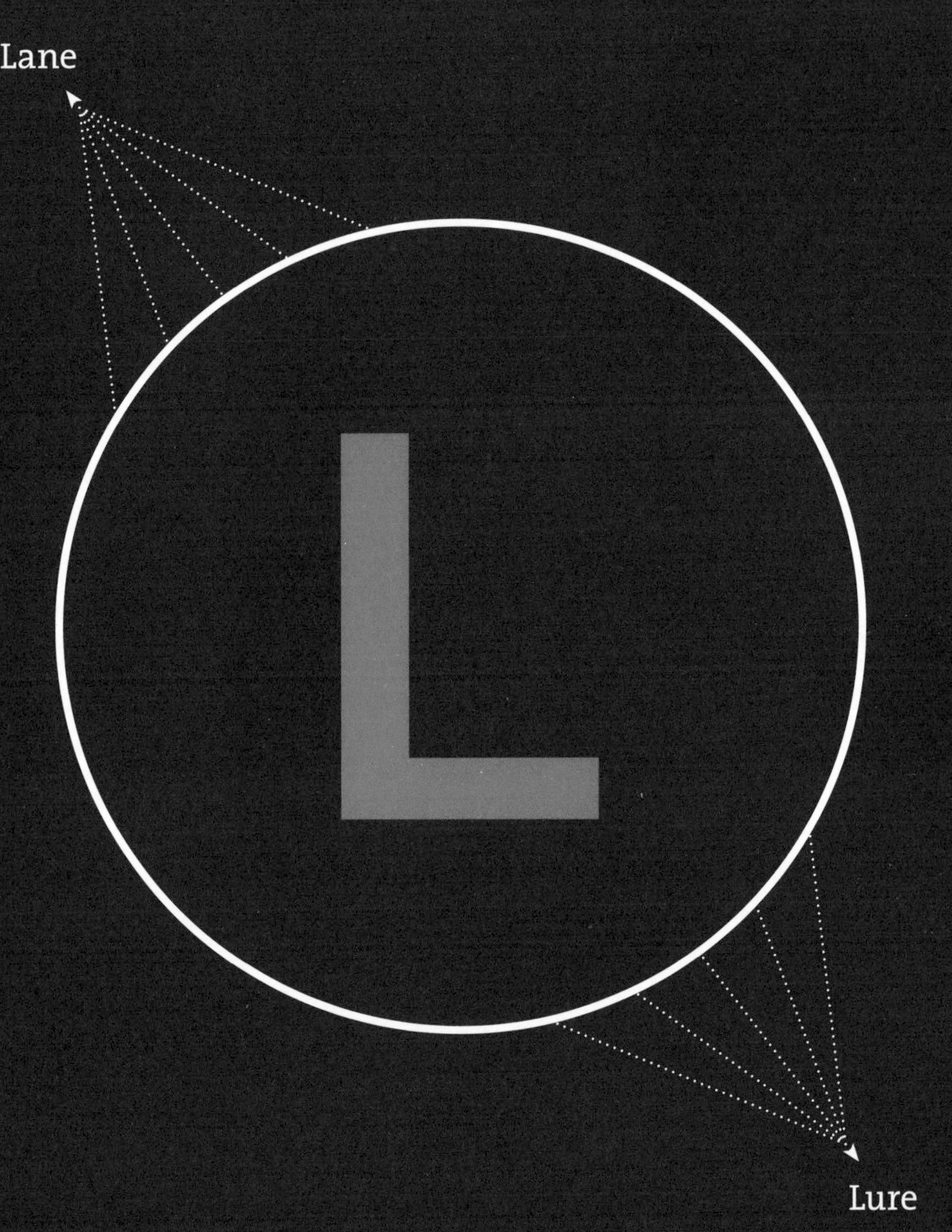
Lane
L
Lure

A B C D E F G H I J K L M N O P Q R S T U V W X Y Z

Lane Change

NASCAR Champions And Their Earnings

From 1949 to 1970, stock car racing's main series was known as the Grand National Championship. In 1971, it became the Winston Cup, and in 2004, the Nextel Cup. Here are the champs:

YEAR	DRIVER	CAR	EARNINGS
1949	Red Byron	Oldsmobile	$5,800
1950	Bill Rexford	Oldsmobile	$6,175
1951	Herb Thomas	Hudson	$18,200
1952	Tim Flock	Hudson	$20,210
1953	Herb Thomas	Hudson	$27,300
1954	Lee Petty	Chrysler	$26,706
1955	Tim Flock	Chrysler	$33,750
1956	Buck Baker	Chrysler	$29,790
1957	Buck Baker	Chevrolet	$24,712
1958	Lee Petty	Oldsmobile	$20,600
1959	Lee Petty	Plymouth	$45,570
1960	Rex White	Chevrolet	$45,260
1961	Ned Jarrett	Chevrolet	$27,285
1962	Joe Weatherly	Pontiac	$56,110
1963	Joe Weatherly	Pontiac	$58,110
1964	Richard Petty	Plymouth	$98,810
1965	Ned Jarrett	Ford	$77,966
1966	David Pearson	Dodge	$59,205
1967	Richard Petty	Plymouth	$130,275
1968	David Pearson	Ford	$118,842
1969	David Pearson	Ford	$183,700
1970	Bobby Isaac	Dodge	$121,470
1971	Richard Petty	Plymouth	$309,225
1972	Richard Petty	Plymouth	$227,015
1973	Benny Parsons	Chevrolet	$114,345
1974	Richard Petty	Dodge	$299,175
1975	Richard Petty	Dodge	$284,980
1976	Cale Yarborough	Chevrolet	$294,591
1977	Cale Yarborough	Chevrolet	$385,576
1978	Cale Yarborough	Oldsmobile	$422,980
1979	Richard Petty	Chevrolet	$416,650

YEAR	DRIVER	CAR	EARNINGS
1980	Dale Earnhardt	Chevrolet	$451,360
1981	Darrell Waltrip	Buick	$539,050
1982	Darrell Waltrip	Buick	$682,085
1983	Bobby Allison	Buick	$613,700
1984	Terry Labonte	Chevrolet	$417,293
1985	Darrell Waltrip	Chevrolet	$702,298
1986	Dale Earnhardt	Chevrolet	$868,100
1987	Dale Earnhardt	Chevrolet	$1,041,120
1988	Bill Elliott	Ford	$812,775
1989	Rusty Wallace	Pontiac	$860,990
1990	Dale Earnhardt	Chevrolet	$1,307,830
1991	Dale Earnhardt	Chevrolet	$1,029,060
1992	Alan Kulwicki	Ford	$907,510
1993	Dale Earnhardt	Chevrolet	$1,326,240
1994	Dale Earnhardt	Chevrolet	$1,465,890
1995	Jeff Gordon	Chevrolet	$2,088,460
1996	Terry Labonte	Chevrolet	$4,030,648
1997	Jeff Gordon	Chevrolet	$4,201,227
1998	Jeff Gordon	Chevrolet	$6,175,867
1999	Dale Jarrett	Ford	$3,608,829
2000	Bobby Labonte	Pontiac	$4,041,750
2001	Jeff Gordon	Chevrolet	$6,649,080
2002	Tony Stewart	Pontiac	$4,695,150
2003	Matt Kenseth	Ford	$4,038,120
2004	Kurt Busch	Ford	$4,200,330
2005	Tony Stewart	Chevrolet	$6,987,530
2006	Jimmie Johnson	Chevrolet	$8,909,140
2007	Jimmie Johnson	Chevrolet	$7,646,421

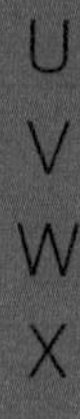

League Of Nations

INTERNATIONAL FIRSTS IN THE NFL

American Samoa Tuufuli Uperesa (1971, Philadelphia Eagles)

Argentina Bob Breitenstein (1965, Denver Broncos)

Armenia Mike Gulian (1923, Buffalo All-Americans)

Australia Colin Ridgway (1965, Dallas Cowboys)

Austria-Hungary Bullets Walson (Charles Wolosin) (1921, Washington Senators)

Bahamas Ed Smith (1973, Denver Broncos)

Barbados Roger Farmer (1979, New York Jets)

Belgium George Jakowenko (1974, Oakland Raiders)

Belize Bill Gutteron (1926, Los Angeles Buccaneers)

Bermuda Rocky Thompson (1971, New York Giants)

Bolivia Wilson Alvarez (1981, Seattle Seahawks)

Cameroon Roman Oben (1996, New York Giants)

Canada Tommy Hughitt (1920, Buffalo All-Americans)

Colombia Jairo Penaranda (1981, Los Angeles Rams)

Croatia Visco Grgich (1946, San Francisco 49ers)

Cuba Lou Molinet (1927, Frankford Yellow Jackets)

Cyprus Garo Yepremian (1966, Detroit Lions)

Czechoslovakia Mirro Roder (1973, Chicago Bears)

Denmark Carl Jorgensen (1934, Green Bay Packers)

El Salvador Jose Cortez (1999, New York Giants)

England Larry Green (1920, Canton Bulldogs)

Estonia Michael Roos (2005, Tennessee Titans)

France Charles Romes (1977, Buffalo Bills)

Germany Phil Nesser (1920, Columbus Panhandles)

Ghana Ebenezer Ekuban (1999, Dallas Cowboys)

Greece Gust Zarnas (1938, Chicago Bears)

Guam Troy Andrew (2001, Miami Dolphins)

Guatemala Ted Hendricks (1969, Baltimore Colts)

Honduras Steve Van Buren (1944, Philadelphia Eagles)

Hungary Pete Gogolak (1964, Buffalo Bills)

Ireland Birdie Maher (1920, Detroit Heralds)

Italy Ping Bodie (1921, Chicago Cardinals)

Ivory Coast Amos Zereoue (1999, Pittsburgh Steelers)

Jamaica Craig Bingham (1982, Pittsburgh Steelers)

Japan John Arnold (1979, Detroit Lions); Rick Berns (1979, Tampa Bay Buccaneers)

Latvia Vilnis Ezerins (1968, Los Angeles Rams)

Lebanon Jimmy Jemail (1921, New York Giants)

Liberia Bhawoh Jue (2001, Green Bay Packers)

Libya Tony Cherry (1986, San Francisco 49ers)

Marshall Islands Todd Lyght (1991, Los Angeles Rams)

Mexico Aldo Richins (1935, Detroit Lions)

The Netherlands Case Debruijn (1982, Kansas City Chiefs)

New Zealand Riki Ellison (1983, San Francisco 49ers)

Nigeria Obed Ariri (1984, Tampa Bay Buccaneers)

Norway Einar Irgens (1921, Minneapolis Marines)

Panama Jim Schuber (1930, Brooklyn Dodgers)

Paraguay Benny Ricardo (1976, Buffalo Bills)

Philippines Mike Corgan (1943, Detroit Lions)

Poland Jack Grossman (1932, Brooklyn Dodgers)

Puerto Rico Ken Amato (2003, Tennessee Titans)

Romania Harry Seidelson (1925, Frankford Yellow Jackets)

Russia Al Greene (1922, Milwaukee Badgers)

Scotland Chick Lang (1927, Duluth Eskimos)

Serbia Filip Filipovic (2002, Dallas Cowboys)

Sierra Leone B.J. Tucker (2005, San Francisco 49ers)

Slovenia Joe Kodba[1] (1947, Baltimore Colts)

South Africa Gary Anderson (1982, Pittsburgh Steelers)

South Korea John Lee (1986, St. Louis Cardinals)

Spain Jess Rodriguez (1929, Buffalo Bisons)

St. Kitts and Nevis Erasmus James (2005, Minnesota Vikings)

Sweden Frank Johnson (1920, Akron Pros)

Taiwan Tony Daykin (1977, Detroit Lions)

Thailand Tony Brown (1992, Houston Oilers)

Tonga Vai Sikahema (1986, St. Louis Cardinals)

Trinidad & Tobago Sankar Montoute (1987, Tampa Bay Buccaneers)

Turkey Tunch Ilkin (1980, Pittsburgh Steelers)

Uganda Kato Serwanga (1998, New England Patriots)

Ukraine Igor Olshansky (2004, San Diego Chargers)

U.S. Virgin Islands Jeff Faulkner (1987, Kansas City Chiefs)

Venezuela Alan Pringle (1975, Detroit Lions)

Yugoslavia Novo Bojovic (1985, St. Louis Cardinals)

Wales Allen Watson (1970, Pittsburgh Steelers)

Western Samoa Jesse Sapolu (1983, San Francisco 49ers)

Zaire Tim Biakabutuka (1996, Carolina Panthers)

Note: [1]Played for the Colts when they were in the AAFC, a league that merged with the NFL in 1950.

A B C D E F G H I J K L M N O P Q R S T U V W X Y Z

Links Language

Golf Scoring Names

Ace: A hole in one
Par: Number of strokes a player is meant to take on a given hole
Birdie: One stroke under par
Eagle: Two under par
Albatross (also double eagle): Three under par
Condor* (also triple eagle): Four under par (hole-in-one on a par-five)
Bogey: One over par
Snowman*: Any score of eight

*Slang, not regarded as official terminology by the PGA.

Little Giants

Roster Of The Bad News Bears

Released in 1976, The Bad News Bears *tells the story of an inept California Little League team and its alcoholic manager, Morris Buttermaker (Walter Matthau), who, with the help of his ex-girlfriend's rocket-armed daughter, Amanda Whurlitzer (Tatum O'Neal), turns the Bears into winners. Here, courtesy of Chico's Bail Bonds, is the full roster.*

C Mike Engleberg
1B Toby Whitewood
2B Jimmy Feldman
3B Regi Tower
SS Tanner Boyle
OF Ahmad Abdul Rahim
OF Kelly Leak
OF Rudi Stein
P Amanda Whurlitzer

BENCH: Jose Agilar, Miguel Agilar, Timmy Lupus, Alfred Ogilvie

Long Runs

The World's Oldest Continual Sporting Events

1361 Annual Kirkpinar Oil Wrestling Championship (Turkey)
1644 Palio of Siena (Italy; horse racing)
1673 The Ancient Scorton Silver Arrow (England; archery)
1776 St. Leger Stakes (England; horse racing)
1780 Epsom Derby (England; horse racing)
1805 Eton-Harrow (England; cricket)
1826 The Royal St. John's Regatta (Canada; sailing)
1829 Oxford and Cambridge Boat Race (England; rowing)
1839 Henley Royal Regatta (England; rowing)
1851 America's Cup (U.S.; sailing)
1852 Harvard-Yale Regatta (U.S.; rowing)
1860 The Open Championship (Scotland; golf)
1867 Belmont Stakes (U.S.; horse racing)
1867 Champagne Stakes (U.S.; horse racing)
1868 Harvard University-Yale University (U.S; baseball)
1870 Dixie Handicap (U.S.; horse racing)
1873 Preakness Stakes (U.S.; horse racing)
1873 Princeton University-Yale University (U.S.; football)
1875 Kentucky Derby (U.S.; horse racing)
1875 Harvard University-Yale University (U.S.; football)
1877 Westminster Kennel Club Dog Show (U.S.)
1877 Wimbledon (England; tennis)
1881 U.S. Championships (now U.S. Open; tennis)
1882 The Ashes (England; cricket)
1884 Lafayette University-Lehigh University (U.S.; football)
1884 Williams College-Amherst College (U.S.; football)
1888 University of Miami (Ohio)-University of Cincinnati (U.S.; football)
1890 Army-Navy (U.S.; football)
1890 University of Wisconsin-University of Minnesota (U.S.; football)
1895 Penn Relays (U.S.; track & field)
1896 Modern Olympic Games (Athens)
1896 Paris Marathon (France)
1896 University of Mississippi-Louisiana State University (U.S.; football)
1897 Ohio State University-University of Michigan (U.S.; football)
1897 University of Minnesota-University of Michigan (U.S.; football)
1897 Boston Marathon (U.S.)
1898 Michigan State University-University of Michigan (U.S., football)
1902 Rose Bowl (U.S.; football)
1903 Tour de France (France; cycling)
1903 World Series (U.S.; baseball)
1908 Millrose Games (U.S.; track & field)

Lure Language

Basic Fly Part Descriptions

So much to know about fly-fishing, so little time to learn it. To get started, here is a primer on tying the perfect fly by Terry Hellekson, from *Fish Flies: The Encyclopedia of the Fly Tier's Art:*

Head: That portion of the fly immediately behind the eye of the hook. It normally consists of tying threads; however, dubbed heads and beads are not uncommon.

Shoulder: This is normally a feather, which is tied in as a background for the cheeks on Atlantic salmon flies. In any case, it is always a portion of the wing which never extends more than two-thirds the length of the wing.

Cheeks: A small feather, most often jungle cock or a suitable substitute, which is tied at each side of the wing. In most cases the cheeks will be tied parallel to the wing and seldom the body.

Underwing: Any portion of the wing that has wing materials tied over it. Some wings can have more than one underwing.

Overwing: This is the uppermost part of the wing when the wing has two or more parts.

Topping: This is the final top of the wing and is only there for decorative purposes. This is not to be confused with the term horns as found on some Atlantic salmon fly patterns.

Tail: Material, normally barbs from a feather, extending out the rear of the fly body. The tail is generally the second material tied onto a hook, right after the tip of the fly. On a few patterns, the butt will be tied in first and the tail tied over it, but this is specified with the individual patterns.

Tip: This consists of either tinsel, floss, or other threadlike materials. It is the first material to be wrapped to the rear of the hook. Tips can be tied in one or more parts; two parts is usually the norm when there is more than one material.

Tag: A tag is a short piece of material tied in over the tail that is always loose on one end. Some fly-fishing writers, such as French author Charles Gaidy, agree fully with this definition. Other works tend to get the tag and tip mixed up. The tag is a different part of the fly than the tip.

Butt: Located at the extreme rear of the body. Material will normally be chenille, peacock herl, ostrich herl, or dubbing, and it occupies a portion of the body area.

Aft Body: The rear portion of the body, which can consist of any portion located past the center of the body.

Center Joint: This is material centered on the body, with materials located on either side.

Trailer: Material tied into the body in the style of a long tag. This is normally tied into the center of the body at either the top or the bottom and trails back.

Ribbing: Material that is wrapped spirally over the body material with space left over between each wrap.

Hackle: Any feather that is wrapped spirally over any portion of the fly whose barbs project away from the body to some degree. Also, any hairs or other fibers tied in at the throat of the fly or spun on as a collar.

Maiden

M

Musical

A B C D E F G H I J K L M N O P Q R S T U V W X Y Z

Maiden Voyages

Baseball Skippers Who Never Played Professionally

There are countless football and basketball coaches who never played their games as pros. But in the history of Major League Baseball, only six men since 1900 managed to manage in the big leagues without playing at the professional level.

MANAGER	RECORD
Ed Barrow (Detroit Tigers, 1903-04; Boston Red Sox, 1918-20)	310-320
Hugo Bezdek (Pittsburgh Pirates, 1917-1919)	166-187
Judge Fuchs (Boston Braves, 1929)[1]	56- 98
Ted Turner (Atlanta Braves, 1977)[1]	0-1
John Boles (Florida Marlins, 1996-2001)	205-241
Carlos Tosca (Toronto Blue Jays, 2002-2004)	191-191

Note: [1]Owned the team, hired himself.

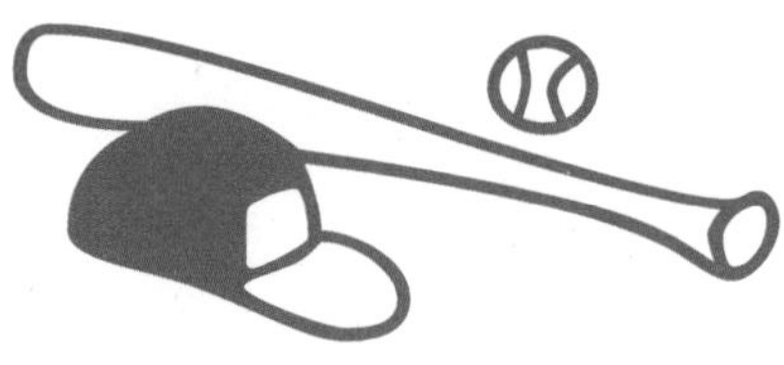

Mailed-In Monuments

Sports Figures On U.S. Postage Stamps

- Arthur Ashe (tennis; issued 2005)
- Bear Bryant (college football; 1997)
- Walter Camp (college football; 2003)
- Roy Campanella (MLB; 2006)
- Roberto Clemente (MLB; 1984, 2000)
- Ty Cobb (MLB; 2000)
- Mickey Cochrane (MLB; 2000)
- Eddie Collins (MLB; 2000)
- Dizzy Dean (MLB; 2000)
- Jack Dempsey (boxing; 1998)
- Eddie Eagan (bobsled, boxing; 1990)
- Ray Ewry (track; 1990)
- Jimmie Foxx (MLB; 2000)
- Lou Gehrig (MLB; 1989, 2000)
- Josh Gibson (Negro Leagues baseball; 2000)
- Red Grange (college football; 2003)

- Hank Greenberg (MLB; 2006)
- Lefty Grove (MLB; 2000)
- George Halas (NFL; 1997)
- Rogers Hornsby (MLB; 2000)
- Walter Johnson (MLB; 2000)
- Bobby Jones (golf; 1981, 1998)
- Duke Kahanamoku (surfing; 2002)
- Vince Lombardi (NFL; 1990, 1997)
- Joe Louis (boxing; 1993)
- Helene Madison (swimming; 1990)
- Mickey Mantle (MLB; 2006)
- Rocky Marciano (boxing; 1999)
- Roger Maris (MLB; 1999)
- Christy Mathewson (MLB; 2000)
- Bronko Nagurski (college football; 2003)
- James Naismith (basketball; 1961)
- Ernie Nevers (college football; 2003)
- Notre Dame's Four Horsemen (college football; 1998)
- Mel Ott (MLB; 2006)
- Francis Ouimet (golf; 1988)
- Jesse Owens (track; 1990, 1998)
- Satchel Paige (Negro Leagues baseball; 2000)
- Jackie Robinson (MLB; 1982, 1997, 2000)
- Knute Rockne (college football; 1988)
- Sugar Ray Robinson (boxing; 2006)
- Wilma Rudolph (track; 2004)
- Babe Ruth (MLB; 1983, 2000)
- San Francisco 49ers (NFL; 2000)
- Secretariat (horse racing; 1999)
- George Sisler (MLB; 2000)
- Tris Speaker (MLB; 2000)
- Jim Thorpe (various; 1984)
- Pie Traynor (MLB; 2000)
- Honus Wagner (MLB; 2000)
- Pop Warner (college football; 1997)
- Hazel Wightman (tennis; 1990)
- Cy Young (MLB; 2000)
- Babe Didrikson Zaharias (golf; 1981)

Maple Leaf Croon

Official Lyrics Of "O Canada!"

ENGLISH

O Canada!
Our home and native land!
True patriot love in all thy sons command.
With glowing hearts we see thee rise,
The True North strong and free!
From far and wide, O Canada, we stand on guard for thee.
God keep our land glorious and free!
O Canada, we stand on guard for thee.
O Canada, we stand on guard for thee.

FRENCH

O Canada! Terre de nos aïeux,
Ton front est ceint de fleurons glorieux!
Car ton bras sait porter l'épée,
Il sait porter la croix!
Ton histoire est une épopée
Des plus brillants exploits.
Et ta valeur, de foi trempée,
Protégera nos foyers et nos droits.
Protégera nos foyers et nos droits.

ENGLISH TRANSLATION OF THE FRENCH TRANSLATION

O Canada! Land of our forefathers
Thy brow is wreathed with a glorious garland of flowers.
As in thy arm ready to wield the sword,
So also is it ready to carry the cross.
Thy history is an epic of the most brilliant exploits.
Thy valour steeped in faith
Will protect our homes and our rights
Will protect our homes and our rights.

A B C D E F G H I J K L **M** N O P Q R S T U V W X Y Z

A B C D E F G H I J K L M N O P Q R S T U V W X Y Z

Medal Pushers

Other Olympic Games

AAU JUNIOR OLYMPICS

Annual. United States participants must be 20 or under. (Table tennis age is under 22.) Events include many in the Olympics, along with jump roping, dance/drill, baton twirling, and more.

BEER OLYMPICS

Annual. Held in Wauwatosa, Wisconsin, all participants must be over 21. Events include chugging relay, keg toss, loose case race, and dizzy relay.

CALIFORNIA FIREFIGHTER'S OLYMPICS

Annual. Participants must be full-time paid firefighters in California. Events include bass fishing, 3-on-3 basketball, darts, flag football, horseshoes, hockey, volleyball, water skiing, and Texas Hold 'Em.

CHAP OLYMPICS

Annual. Held in England and sponsored by *The Chap* magazine, events include cucumber sandwich discus, quill throwing, and relating of anecdotes.

DEAF OLYMPICS

Quadrennial. Participants in this international event must be deaf. Events are similar to those in the Summer and Winter Olympics.

CONNECTICUT POLICE K-9 OLYMPICS

Annual. Competition is open to full-time law enforcement and correctional officers and their dogs. Events include obedience, tactical range, criminal apprehension, and obstacles. One of many such games throughout the United States.

INTERNATIONAL MATH OLYMPICS

Annual. Students in grades K-12 from around the world compete in addition and multiplication and are judged on accuracy and speed. There are individual events and class-average events.

PARALYMPICS

Quadrennial. International athletes compete in six disability groups: amputee, cerebral palsy, visual impairment, spinal cord injury, intellectual disability, and a group that includes all those who do not fit into the aforementioned groups. Sports include Summer and Winter Olympic events, as well as wheelchair events such as fencing, basketball, rugby, tennis, and curling.

SCIENCE OLYMPICS

Annual. Students in grades K-12 from around the world compete in a variety of theoretical and practical events.

SENIOR OLYMPICS

Bi-annual. Competitors, who must be over the age of 50, compete in many of the same events held in the Summer Olympics.

SPECIAL OLYMPICS
Bi-annual. Children and adults with intellectual disabilities from around the world compete in Olympic-style events.

Memorable Lanes

Bowlers Who Have Rolled 900s

According to the United States Bowling Congress, only 11 bowlers have ever thrown a perfect 900 three-game series.

Jeremy Sonnenfeld, Lincoln, Nebraska; February 2, 1997
Tony Roventini, Greenfield, Wisconsin; November 9, 1998
Vince Wood, Moreno Valley, California; September 29, 1999
Robby Portalatin, Jackson, Michigan; December 28, 2000
James Hylton, Salem, Oregon; May 2, 2001
Jeff Campbell II, New Castle, Pennsylvania; June 12, 2004
Darren Pomije, New Prague, Minnesota; December 9, 2004
Robert Mushtare, Fort Drum, New York; December 3, 2005
Lonnie Billiter Jr., Fairfield, Ohio; February 13, 2006
Robert Mushtare, Fort Drum, New York; February 19, 2006
Mark Wukoman, Greenfield, Wisconsin; April 22, 2006

Monday Best

Announcers On *Monday Night Football*

1970: Keith Jackson, Howard Cosell, Don Meredith
1971–73: Frank Gifford, Howard Cosell, Don Meredith
1974: Frank Gifford, Howard Cosell, Alex Karras, Fred Williamson
1975–76: Frank Gifford, Howard Cosell, Alex Karras
1977–78: Frank Gifford, Howard Cosell, Don Meredith
1979–82: Frank Gifford, Howard Cosell, Don Meredith, Fran Tarkenton
1983: Frank Gifford, Howard Cosell, Don Meredith, O.J. Simpson
1984: Frank Gifford, Don Meredith, O.J. Simpson
1985: Frank Gifford, O.J. Simpson, Joe Namath
1986: Al Michaels, Frank Gifford
1987–97: Al Michaels, Frank Gifford, Dan Dierdorf
1998: Al Michaels, Dan Dierdorf, Boomer Esiason
1999: Al Michaels, Boomer Esiason
2000–01: Al Michaels, Dan Fouts, Dennis Miller
2002–2005: Al Michaels, John Madden
2006: Mike Tirico, Joe Theismann, Tony Kornheiser

Moving Picks

No. 1 Selections In The NBA Draft

The NBA draft began in 1947, when the league was called the Basketball Association of America. The initial rules allowed teams to forfeit their first-round picks to select a player from their immediate vicinity. This "territorial" system helped to spur interest at a time when teams struggled to build fan bases. That practice was dropped in 1967, when the league agreed to let a coin flip between the last-place finishers in its two divisions determine which would get the top pick, then assigned draft slots to the remaining teams based on win-loss records. In 1985, to avoid the temptation to lose games to get a higher choice, the NBA began a lottery system.

1947 Clifton McNeely, G; Pittsburgh Ironmen from Texas Western University

1948 Andy Tonkovich, G; Providence Steamrollers from Marshall University

1949 Howie Shannon, G; Providence Steamrollers from Kansas State University

1950 Charlie Share, C; Boston Celtics from Bowling Green University

1951 Gene Melchiorre, G; Baltimore Bullets from Bradley University

1952 Mark Workman, F; Milwaukee Hawks from West Virginia University

1953 Ernie Beck, G/F; Philadelphia Warriors from University of Pennsylvania

1954 Frank Selvy, G/F; Baltimore Bullets from Furman University

1955 Dick Ricketts, F; Milwaukee Hawks from Duquesne University

1956 Sihugo Green, G/F; Rochester Royals from Duquesne University

1957 Rod Hundley, G; Cincinnati Royals from West Virginia University

1958 Elgin Baylor, F; Minneapolis Lakers from Seattle University

1959 Bob Boozer, F; Cincinnati Royals from Kansas State University

1960 Oscar Robertson, G; Cincinnati Royals from University of Cincinnati

1961 Walt Bellamy, C; Chicago Packers from Indiana University

1962 Bill McGill, F; Chicago Packers from University of Utah

1963 Art Heyman, F; New York Knicks from Duke University

1964 Jim Barnes, F; New York Knicks from Texas Western University

1965 Fred Hetzel, F; San Francisco Warriors from Davidson College

1966 Cazzie Russell, F; New York Knicks from University of Michigan

1967 Jimmy Walker, G; Detroit Pistons from Providence College

1968 Elvin Hayes, F; San Diego Rockets from University of Houston

1969 Lew Alcindor, C; Milwaukee Bucks

from UCLA

1970 Bob Lanier, C; Detroit Pistons from St. Bonaventure University

1971 Austin Carr, G; Cleveland Cavaliers from University of Notre Dame

1972 LaRue Martin, C; Portland Trail Blazers from Loyola University (Chicago)

1973 Doug Collins, F; Philadelphia 76ers from Illinois State University

1974 Bill Walton, C; Portland Trail Blazers from UCLA

1975 David Thompson; G, Atlanta Hawks from North Carolina State University

1976 John Lucas, G; Houston Rockets from University of Maryland

1977 Kent Benson, F; Milwaukee Bucks from Indiana University

1978 Mychal Thompson, C; Portland Trail Blazers from University of Minnesota

1979 Earvin Johnson, G; Los Angeles Lakers from Michigan State University

1980 Joe Barry Carroll, C; Golden State Warriors from Purdue University

1981 Mark Aguirre, F; Dallas Mavericks from DePaul University

1982 James Worthy, F; Los Angeles Lakers from University of North Carolina

1983 Ralph Sampson, C; Houston Rockets from University of Virginia

1984 Akeem Olajuwon, C; Houston Rockets from University of Houston

1985 Patrick Ewing, C; New York Knicks from Georgetown University

1986 Brad Daugherty, C; Cleveland Cavaliers from University of North Carolina

1987 David Robinson, C; San Antonio Spurs from Navy

1988 Danny Manning, F; Los Angeles Clippers from University of Kansas

1989 Pervis Ellison, C; Sacramento Kings from University of Louisville

1990 Derrick Coleman; F; New Jersey Nets from Syracuse University

1991 Larry Johnson, F; Charlotte Hornets from University of Nevada, Las Vegas

1992 Shaquille O'Neal; C; Orlando Magic from Louisiana State University

1993 Chris Webber, F; Orlando Magic from University of Michigan

1994 Glenn Robinson, F; Milwaukee Bucks from Purdue University

1995 Joe Smith, F; Golden State Warriors from University of Maryland

1996 Allen Iverson, G; Philadelphia 76ers from Georgetown University

1997 Tim Duncan, F; San Antonio Spurs from Wake Forest University

1998 Michael Olowokandi, C; Los Angeles Clippers from Pacific University

1999 Elton Brand, F; Chicago Bulls from Duke University

2000 Kenyon Martin, F; New Jersey Nets from University of Cincinnati

2001 Kwame Brown, F; Washington Wizards from Glynn Academy (Georgia)

2002 Yao Ming, C; Houston Rockets from Shanghai Sharks, China

2003 LeBron James, F; Cleveland Cavaliers from St. Vincent-St. Mary H.S. (Ohio)

2004 Dwight Howard, F; Orlando Magic from S.W. Atlanta Christian Academy (Georgia)

2005 Andrew Bogut, C; Milwaukee Bucks from University of Utah

2006 Andrea Bargnani, F; Toronto Raptors from Benetton Treviso, Italy

2007 Greg Oden, C; Portland Trailblazers from Ohio State University

2008 Derrick Rose, F; Chicago Bulls from University of Memphis

A B C D E F G H I J K L M N O P Q R S T U V W X Y Z

Moving Targets

Habitually Relocated Pro Teams

A'S (MLB)
Philadelphia: Athletics (1901-54)
Kansas City: Athletics (1955-67)
Oakland: Athletics (1968-present)

BRAVES (MLB)
Boston: Red Stockings (1871-82), Beaneaters (1883-1906), Doves (1907-10), Rustlers (1911), Braves (1912-35), Bees (1936-40), Braves (1941-52)
Milwaukee: Braves (1953-65)
Atlanta: Braves (1966-present)

CARDINALS (NFL)
Chicago: Morgan Athletic Club (1898), Normals (1899-1900), Racine Cardinals (1901-06, re-formed 1913-18, 1918-21), Cardinals (1922-43), Card-Pitt (1944)[1], Chicago Cardinals (1945-59)
St. Louis: Cardinals (1960-1987)
Arizona: Cardinals (1988-present)[2]

CLIPPERS (NBA)
Buffalo: Braves (1970-78)
San Diego: Clippers (1978-84)
Los Angeles: (1984-present)

DEVILS (NHL)
Kansas City: Scouts (1974-76)
Colorado (Denver): Rockies (1976-82)
New Jersey (East Rutherford): Devils (1982-present)

HAWKS (NBA)
Tri-Cities (Illinois): Blackhawks (1946-51)
Milwaukee: Hawks (1951-55)
St. Louis: Hawks (1955-68)
Atlanta: Hawks (1968-present)

KINGS (NBA)
Rochester (New York): Royals (1948-57)
Cincinnati: Royals (1957-72)
Kansas City: Kings (1972-85)[3]
Sacramento: Kings (1985-present)

LAKERS (NBA)
Detroit: Gems (1946-47)
Minneapolis: Lakers (1947-60)
Los Angeles: Lakers (1960-present)

ORIOLES (MLB)
Milwaukee: Brewers (1901)
St. Louis: Browns (1902-53)
Baltimore: Orioles (1954-present)

RAIDERS (NFL)
Oakland: Raiders (1960-81)
Los Angeles: Raiders (1982-94)
Oakland: Raiders (1995-present)

Note: [1]Wartime merger with Pittsburgh; [2]Known as Phoenix Cardinals from 1988-93; [3]Known as Kansas City-Omaha Kings from 1972-1975

Musical Lineup

Players Named In Terry Cashman's "Talkin' Baseball"

- Hank Aaron
- Grover Cleveland Alexander
- Yogi Berra
- Vida Blue
- Bobby Bonds
- George Brett
- Roy Campanella
- Rod Carew
- Bob Feller
- Eddie Gaedel
- Steve Garvey
- Reggie Jackson
- Ralph Kiner
- Ted Kluszewski
- Sal "The Barber" Maglie
- Mickey Mantle
- Willie Mays
- Stan "The Man" Musial
- Don "The Newc" Newcombe
- Mel Parnell
- Gaylord Perry
- Dan Quisenberry
- Phil "Scooter" Rizzuto
- Frank Robinson
- Jackie Robinson
- Pete Rose
- Mike Schmidt
- Tom Seaver
- Duke Snider
- Rusty Staub
- Casey Stengel
- Bobby Thomson
- Ted "Thumper" Williams

Named
N
Numerical

Named Games

OTHER "SUPER BOWLS"

- **The Super Bowl of Street Legal Drag Racing[1]**
- **The Souper Bowl of Caring[2]**
- **The Illinois Valley Super Bowl[3]**
- **Super Bowl Noodle House[4]**
- **Boyesen Super Bowl[5]**
- **Libbey Glassware 45.5 oz. Super Bowl[6]**
- **Super Bowl Portable Restrooms[7]**
- **The Dancesport Super Bowl[8]**
- **Super Bowl Speedway[9]**
- **Indiana Academic Super Bowl[10]**

[1]Chicago racing series; [2]Religious fund-raiser; [3]Bowling center; [4]Seattle restaurant; [5]Motorcycle fuel tank ("Curved interior turns fuel inward to eliminate splashing, foaming, bogging"); [6]Giant drink glass; [7]"A Family Owned Colorado Tradition for Over 30 Years"; [8]National dance competition; [9]Texas racetrack; [10]Scholarly showdown

NASCAR Talk

A GLOSSARY OF RACING SLANG

Back marker: Car running off the pace near the rear of the field

Bear grease: Any patching material used to fill cracks and holes or smooth bumps on a track's surface

Bite: Traction

Cats: The favored term for drivers when addressing one another

Deck lid: Trunk lid of a race car

Dirty air: Air used and discarded by the lead car

Esses: A series of acute left and right hand turns on a road course

Factory: The Big Three auto manufacturers (General Motors, Ford, and Chrysler)

Flat out: Racing a car as fast as possible under given weather and track conditions

Grinders: Brakes

Groove: Best route around a racetrack

Happy hour: Last official practice session before a race

Hauler: Eighteen-wheel tractor-trailer rig used to transport two race cars, engines, tools, and support equipment to the racetracks

Hot rod: Favorite term for the car

Marbles: Bits of rubber, dirt, and gravel on a track

One of them racing deals: Term used when drivers refer to an accident or on-track incident without placing blame on a specific driver

Round: To use a car's springs to make chassis adjustments

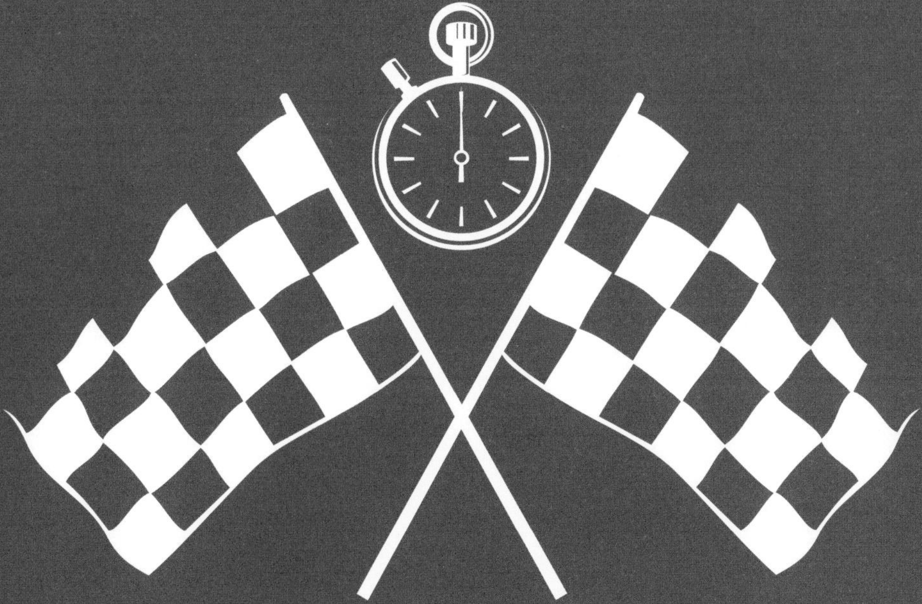

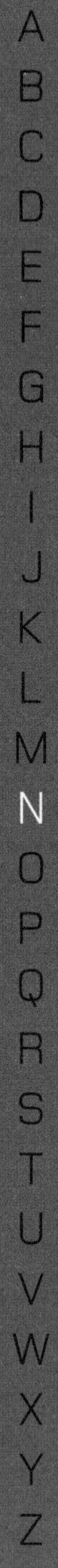

Rubbing is racing: Phrase used to acknowledge that stock car racing is a contact sport

Running on rails: Used to describe a car that is handling perfectly

Scuffs: Used tires

Setup: Tuning and adjustments made to a car's suspension before and during a race

Silly season: Period that begins during the latter part of a current season, when teams announce driver, crew, or sponsor changes

Slick: Track condition in which it is hard for tires to adhere to the surface or get a good bite

Splash and go: Pit stop in which crew fills car with gas, without changing the tires or making any other major adjustments

Stick: Traction

Stickers: New tires

Stop 'n' go: Penalty, usually assessed for speeding on pit road or for unsafe driving. The driver must stop at team's pit for a timed penalty

Stroking: Going easy early in a race so equipment doesn't wear down before the end

That's racing: Term used when describing an accident or mechanical problem

Tight: When the front wheels of a car lose traction before the rear wheels do

Trading paint: Aggressive driving involving a lot of bumping and rubbing

A B C D E F G H I J K L M N O P Q R S T U V W X Y Z

Net Gains

Goals By NHL Goaltenders

Before the 1960s, NHL goalies rarely left the crease, and pulling a goalie to add a skater simply wasn't done. It wasn't until 1979 that Billy Smith became the first netminder to score a goal, and he got credit for it only because he was the last New York Islander to touch the puck before a rival player knocked it into his own goal. In 1987, Ron Hextall became the first goaltender to shoot and score. Like all those that followed, it was into an empty net.

REGULAR SEASON

Billy Smith, New York Islanders (November 28, 1979 vs. Colorado Rockies)

Ron Hextall, Philadelphia Flyers (December 8, 1987 vs. Boston Bruins)

Chris Osgood, Detroit Red Wings (March 6, 1996 vs. Hartford Whalers)

Damian Rhodes, Ottawa Senators (January 2, 1999 vs. New Jersey Devils)

Martin Brodeur, New Jersey Devils (February 15, 2000 vs. Philadelphia Flyers)

Jose Theodore, Montreal Canadiens (January 2, 2001 vs. New York Islanders)

Evgeni Nabokov, San Jose Sharks (March 10, 2002 vs. Vancouver Canucks)

Mika Noronen, Buffalo Sabres (February 14, 2004 vs. Toronto Maple Leafs)

Chris Mason, Nashville Predators (April 15, 2006 vs. Phoenix Coyotes)

PLAYOFFS

Ron Hextall, Philadelphia Flyers (April 11, 1989 vs. Washington Capitals)

Martin Brodeur, New Jersey Devils (April 17, 1997 vs. Montreal Canadiens)

Net Originals

Founding Teams Of The American Basketball Association

The ABA, which began play in 1967, was the brainchild of Dennis Murphy and Gary Davidson, the duo behind the WHA and (in Davidson's case) WFL. With only 10 teams in the NBA in 1966, Murphy saw room for competition in pro hoops (not to mention room for a red-white-and-blue ball). But while the ABA had its drawing points—the acrobatic play of Julius "Dr. J" Erving chief among them—many teams struggled financially. So when the NBA offered a merger deal in 1976, the ABA owners accepted. Here are the 11 original ABA teams:

- Anaheim Amigos
- Dallas Chaparrals
- Denver Rockets
- Houston Mavericks
- Indiana Pacers
- Kentucky Colonels
- Minnesota Muskies
- New Jersey Americans
- New Orleans Buccaneers
- Oakland Oaks
- Pittsburgh Pipers

23 42 99 92

Never Agains

PLAYERS WITH NUMBERS RETIRED BY MORE THAN ONE TEAM

NBA

Kareem Abdul-Jabbar: Milwaukee Bucks, Los Angeles Lakers (No. 33)

Charles Barkley: Philadelphia 76ers, Phoenix Suns (34)

Wilt Chamberlain: Philadelphia 76ers, Los Angeles Lakers, Golden State Warriors (13)

Clyde Drexler: Portland Trail Blazers, Houston Rockets (22)

Julius Erving: New Jersey Nets (32), Philadelphia 76ers (6)

Michael Jordan: Chicago Bulls, Miami Heat (honorary) (23)

Bob Lanier: Milwaukee Bucks, Detroit Pistons (16)

Oscar Robertson: Milwaukee Bucks (1), Sacramento Kings (14)

Nate Thurmond: Golden State Warriors, Cleveland Cavaliers (42)

MLB

Hank Aaron: Atlanta Braves, Milwaukee Brewers (44)

Rod Carew: California Angels, Minnesota Twins (29)

Rollie Fingers: Oakland A's, Milwaukee Brewers (34)

Carlton Fisk: Boston Red Sox (27), Chicago White Sox (72)

Reggie Jackson: New York Yankees (44), Oakland A's (9)

Frank Robinson: Cincinnati Reds, Baltimore Orioles (20)

Nolan Ryan: Houston Astros, Texas Rangers (34), California Angels (30)

Jackie Robinson: All, MLB mandated (42)

NHL

Ray Bourque: Boston Bruins, Colorado Avalanche (77)

Wayne Gretzky: All, NHL mandated (99)

Tim Horton: Buffalo Sabres (2), Toronto Maple Leafs (7)

Mark Messier: New York Rangers, Edmonton Oilers (11)

NFL

Reggie White: Philadelphia Eagles, Green Bay Packers (92)

Nifty Fifty

THE NBA'S 50 GREATEST PLAYERS

In 1996, the unveiling of this list—chosen by a panel of sports journalists, former players and coaches, current and former general managers, and team executives—tipped off the league's season-long-NBA at 50-celebration. Here it is, in alphabetical order:

1. Kareem Abdul-Jabbar
2. Nate Archibald
3. Paul Arizin
4. Charles Barkley
5. Rick Barry
6. Elgin Baylor
7. Dave Bing
8. Larry Bird
9. Wilt Chamberlain
10. Bob Cousy
11. Dave Cowens
12. Billy Cunningham
13. Dave DeBusschere
14. Clyde Drexler
15. Julius Erving
16. Patrick Ewing
17. Walt Frazier
18. George Gervin
19. Hal Greer
20. John Havlicek
21. Elvin Hayes
22. Magic Johnson
23. Sam Jones
24. Michael Jordan
25. Jerry Lucas
26. Karl Malone
27. Moses Malone
28. Pete Maravich
29. Kevin McHale
30. George Mikan
31. Earl Monroe
32. Hakeem Olajuwon
33. Shaquille O'Neal
34. Robert Parish
35. Bob Pettit
36. Scottie Pippen
37. Willis Reed
38. Oscar Robertson
39. David Robinson
40. Bill Russell
41. Dolph Schayes
42. Bill Sharman
43. John Stockton
44. Isiah Thomas
45. Nate Thurmond
46. Wes Unseld
47. Bill Walton
48. Jerry West
49. Lenny Wilkens
50. James Worthy

Nine East

JAPANESE BASEBALL LEAGUE TEAMS

CENTRAL LEAGUE

Chunichi Dragons
Hanshin Tigers
Hiroshima Toyo Carp
Tokyo Yakult Swallows
Yokohama BayStars
Yomiuri Giants

PACIFIC LEAGUE

Chiba Lotte Marines
Fukuoka SoftBank Hawks
Hokkaido Nippon Ham Fighters
Orix Buffaloes
Seibu Lions
Tohoku Rakuten Golden Eagles

No Cigars

Triple Crown Near Misses In Thoroughbred Racing History

Eighteen horses have won the Kentucky Derby and the Preakness Stakes, only to have their Triple Crown hopes dashed in the Belmont Stakes. Here they are, with their Belmont finish and the horse who won:

1944 Pensive (2nd; Bounding Home)
1958 Tim Tam (2nd; Cavan)
1961 Carry Back (7th; Sherluck)
1964 Northern Dancer (3rd; Quadrangle)
1966 Kauai King (4th; Amberoid)
1968 Forward Pass (2nd; Stage Door Johnny)
1969 Majestic Prince (2nd; Arts and Letters)
1971 Canonero II (4th; Pass Catcher)
1979 Spectacular Bid (3rd; Coastal)
1981 Pleasant Colony (3rd; Summing)
1987 Alysheba (4th; Bet Twice)
1989 Sunday Silence (2nd; Easy Goer)
1997 Silver Charm (2nd; Touch Gold)
1998 Real Quiet (2nd; Victory Gallop)
1999 Charismatic (3rd; Lemon Drop Kid)
2002 War Emblem (8th; Sarava)
2003 Funny Cide (3rd; Empire Maker)
2004 Smarty Jones (2nd; Birdstone)
2008 Big Brown (9th; Da' Tara)

Note: Burgoo King (1932) and Bold Venture (1936) did not start in the Belmont because of injuries.

A B C D E F G H I J K L M N O P Q R S T U V W X Y Z

No-Loss Leaders

Notable Winning Streaks

151 high school football games: De La Salle, Concord, California. (1992-2003)

132 years of America's Cup yachting victories: United States (1851-1983)

112 400M hurdles races: Edwin Moses (1977-1987)

88 college basketball games: UCLA (1971-74)

74 tennis matches: Martina Navratilova (1984)

49 boxing matches: Rocky Marciano (1947-55)

33 NBA games: Los Angeles Lakers (1971-72)

27 World Chess Championships: Emanuel Lasker (1894-1920)

27 NCAA Division III swimming and diving national championships: Kenyon College (1980-present)

26 MLB games: New York Giants (1916)

18 NFL games: New England Patriots (2003-04)

17 NHL games: Pittsburgh Penguins (1993)

17 women's golf tournaments: Babe Didrikson Zaharias (1944-47)

17 World Checkers Championships: Marion Tinsley (1975-1991)

11 men's golf tournaments: Byron Nelson (1945)

10 NASCAR races: Richard Petty (1967)

9 NCAA women's soccer national championships: North Carolina (1986-94)

9 NCAA men's wrestling national championships: Iowa (1978-86)

7 F1 races: Michael Schumacher (2004)

7 Tour de France bicycle races: Lance Armstrong (1999-2005)

Number Ones

First Picks In The NFL Draft

The brainchild of commissioner Bert Bell, the draft was created to bring parity to the league. Before its implementation in 1936, collegiate players could sign with any team, giving stronger teams an unfair advantage. But Bell's design had teams select in inverse order of their previous season's finish, with the league champ picking last.

1936 Jay Berwanger, HB; Philadelphia Eagles from University of Chicago

1937 Sam Francis, FB; Philadelphia Eagles from University of Nebraska

1938 Corbett Davis, FB; Cleveland Rams from Indiana University

1939 Ki Aldrich, C; Chicago Cardinals from Texas Christian University

1940 George Cafego, HB; Chicago Cardinals from University of Tennessee

1941 Tom Harmon, HB; Chicago Bears from University of Michigan

1942 Bill Dudley, HB; Pittsburgh Steelers from University of Virginia

1943 Frank Sinkwich, HB; Detroit Lions from University of Georgia

1944 Angelo Bertelli, QB; Boston Yanks from Notre Dame

1945 Charley Trippi, HB; Chicago Cardinals from University of Georgia

1946 Frank Dancewicz, QB; Boston Yanks from Notre Dame

1947 Bob Fenimore, HB; Chicago Bears from Oklahoma State University

1948 Harry Gilmer, QB; Washington Redskins from University of Alabama

1949 Chuck Bednarik, C/LB; Philadelphia Eagles from University of Pennsylvania

1950 Leon Hart, OE/DE; Detroit Lions from Notre Dame

1951 Kyle Rote, HB; New York Giants from Southern Methodist University

1952 Bill Wade, QB; Los Angeles Rams from Vanderbilt University

1953 Harry Babcock, OE/DE; San Francisco 49ers from University of Georgia

1954 Bobby Garrett, QB; Cleveland Browns from Stanford University

1955 George Shaw, QB; Baltimore Colts from University of Oregon

1956 Gary Glick, DB; Pittsburgh Steelers from Colorado A&M University

1957 Paul Hornung, HB; Green Bay Packers from Notre Dame

1958 King Hill, QB; Chicago Cardinals from Rice University

1959 Randy Duncan, QB; Green Bay Packers from University of Iowa

1960 Billy Cannon, RB; Los Angeles Rams from Louisiana State University

1961 Tommy Mason, RB; Minnesota Vikings from Tulane University

1961 [AFL] Ken Rice, G; Buffalo Bills from Auburn University

1962 Ernie Davis, RB; Washington Redskins from Syracuse University

1962 [AFL] Roman Gabriel, QB; Oakland Raiders from North Carolina State University

1963 Terry Baker, QB; Los Angeles Rams from Oregon State University

1963 [AFL] Buck Buchanan, DT; Dallas Texans from Grambling State University

1964 Dave Parks, WR; San Francisco 49ers from Texas Tech University

1964 [AFL] Jack Concannon, QB; Boston Patriots from Boston College

1965 Tucker Frederickson, RB; New York Giants from Auburn University

1965 [AFL] Lawrence Elkins, WR; Houston Oilers from Baylor University

1966 Tommy Nobis, LB; Atlanta Falcons from University of Texas

1966 [AFL] Jim Grabowski, RB; Miami Dolphins from University of Illinois

1967 Bubba Smith, DE; Baltimore Colts from Michigan State University

1968 Ron Yary, OT; Minnesota Vikings from USC **1969** O.J. Simpson, RB; Buffalo Bills from USC

1970 Terry Bradshaw, QB; Pittsburgh Steelers from Louisiana Tech University

A B C D E F G H I J K L M N O P Q R S T U V W X Y Z

Number Ones, continued from page 155

1971 Jim Plunkett, QB; New England Patriots from Stanford University

1972 Walt Patulski, DT; Buffalo Bills from Notre Dame

1973 John Matuszak, DE; Houston Oilers from University of Tampa

1974 Ed Jones, DE; Dallas Cowboys from Tennessee State University

1975 Steve Bartkowski, QB; Atlanta Falcons from University of California

1976 Lee Roy Selmon, DE; Tampa Bay Buccaneers from University of Oklahoma

1977 Ricky Bell, RB; Tampa Bay Buccaneers from USC

1978 Earl Campbell, RB; Houston Oilers from University of Texas

1979 Tom Cousineau, LB; Buffalo Bills from Ohio State University

1980 Billy Sims, RB; Detroit Lions from University of Oklahoma

1981 George Rogers, RB; New Orleans Saints from University of South Carolina

1982 Kenneth Sims, DT; New England Patriots from University of Texas

1983 John Elway, QB; Baltimore Colts from Stanford University

1984 Irving Fryar, WR; New England Patriots from University of Nebraska

1985 Bruce Smith, DE; Buffalo Bills from Virginia Tech University

1986 Bo Jackson, RB; Tampa Bay Buccaneers from Auburn University

1987 Vinny Testaverde, QB; Tampa Bay Buccaneers from University of Miami

1988 Aundray Bruce, LB; Atlanta Falcons from Auburn University

1989 Troy Aikman, QB; Dallas Cowboys from UCLA

1990 Jeff George, QB; Indianapolis Colts from University of Illinois

1991 Russell Maryland, DT; Dallas Cowboys from University of Miami

1992 Steve Emtman, DT; Indianapolis Colts from University of Washington

1993 Drew Bledsoe, QB; New England Patriots from Washington State University

1994 Dan Wilkinson, DT; Cincinnati Bengals from Ohio State University

1995 Ki-Jana Carter, RB; Cincinnati Bengals from Penn State University

1996 Keyshawn Johnson, WR; New York Jets from USC

1997 Orlando Pace, OT; St. Louis Rams from Ohio State University

1998 Peyton Manning, QB; Indianapolis Colts from University of Tennessee

1999 Tim Couch, QB; Cleveland Browns from University of Kentucky

2000 Courtney Brown, DE; Cleveland Browns from Penn State University

2001 Michael Vick, QB; Atlanta Falcons from Virginia Tech University

2002 David Carr, QB; Houston Texans from Fresno State University

2003 Carson Palmer, QB; Cincinnati Bengals from USC

2004 Eli Manning, QB; San Diego Chargers from University of Mississippi

2005 Alex Smith, QB; San Francisco 49ers from University of Utah

2006 Mario Williams, DE; Houston Texans from North Carolina State University

2007 JaMarcus Russell, QB; Oakland Raiders from LSU

2008 Jake Long, OT; Miami Dolphins from University of Michigan

HELLO, MY NAME IS

7525707

A B C D E F G H I J K L M N O P Q R S T U V W X Y Z

Numerical Nomenclature

North American Pro And College Team Names With Numbers In Them

14ers: Colorado (Broomfield, Colorado; NBA Development League)

Colt 45's: Houston (MLB)[1]

49ers: Long Beach State University; San Francisco (NFL); University of North Carolina at Charlotte; Yuba College (Marysville, California.)

51s: Las Vegas (Pacific Coast League baseball)

66ers: Inland Empire (San Bernadino, California; California League Baseball); Tulsa (NBA Development League)

67's: Ottawa (Ontario Hockey League)

76ers: Philadelphia (NBA)

89ers: Oklahoma City (Pacific Coast League baseball)[2]

97s: Danville (Virginia) (Carolina League Baseball)[3]

1836: Houston (MLS)[4]

Note: [1]Now Astros; [2]Now RedHawks; [3]Now Myrtle Beach Pelicans; [4]Now Dynamo

Obsessed

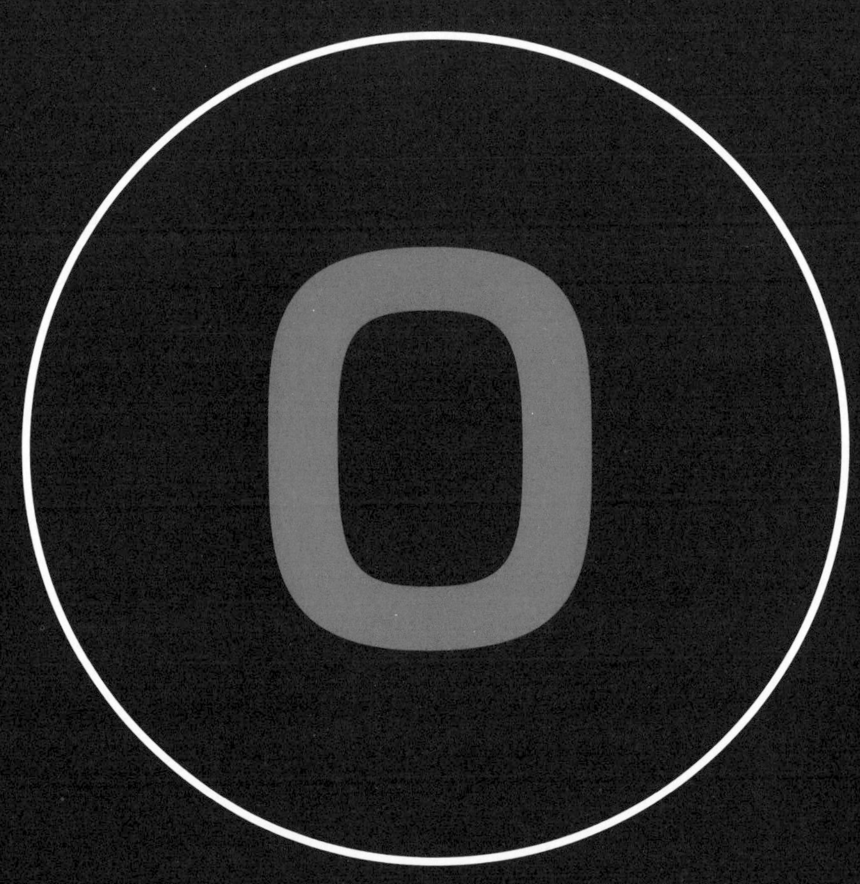

Oval

Obsessed Aquatics

English Channel Milestones

1872 First official attempt to swim the Channel
J. B. Johnson (England); abandoned after one hour and three minutes

1875 First man to swim the Channel, England to France
Matthew Webb (England); time: 21:45

1923 First man to swim the Channel, France to England
Enrico Tiraboschi (Italy); 16:33

1926 First woman to swim the Channel, France to England
Gertrude Ederle (U.S.); 14:39

1961 First man to swim the Channel both ways, non-stop
Antonio Abertondo (Argentina); 43:10

1962 First man to swim the Channel underwater
Fred Baldasare (U.S.); in a frogman suit; 19:01

1978 Fastest crossing by a woman, England to France
Penny Lee Dean (U.S.); 17:40

1981 First nonstop three-way crossing
Jon Erikson (U.S.); 38:27

1983 Youngest female to cross the Channel
Samantha Druce (England); 12 years, 118 days; 15:28

1988 Fastest crossing by a man, France to England
Richard Davey (England); 8:05

1988 Youngest male to cross the Channel
Thomas Gregory (England); 11 years, 11 months; 11:54

1989 Fastest crossing by a woman, France to England
Alison Streeter (England); 8:48

1999 Oldest woman to cross the Channel
Carol Sing (U.S.); 57 years; 12:32

2004 Oldest man to cross the Channel
George Burnstad (U.S.); 70 years, 4 days; 15:59

2004 Fastest crossing of the Channel by man, England to France
Christof Wandsratch (Germany); 7:03:52

Most crossings of the Channel by woman
Alison Streeter (England); 43

Most crossings of the Channel by man
Kevin Murphy (England); 33

Open Roads

Athletes Nicknamed Dusty

Bob "Dusty" Rhoads
(MLB pitcher; 1902-1909)

Charlie "Dusty" Rhodes
(MLB pitcher; 1906-1909)

Gordon "Dusty" Rhodes
(MLB pitcher; 1929-1936)

James Lamar "Dusty" Rhodes
(MLB outfielder; 1952-1959)

Virgil "Dusty Rhodes" Runnels Jr.
(pro wrestler; 1970s-80s)

Damian "Dusty" Rhodes
(NHL goalie; 1990-2002)

Oscar Might

Sports Movies Nominated For Best Picture

The Champ (boxing; 1931)
Here Comes Mr. Jordan (boxing; 1941)
The Pride of the Yankees (baseball; 1942)
The Hustler (billiards; 1961)
Rocky (boxing; 1976)*
Heaven Can Wait (football; 1978)
Breaking Away (cycling; 1979)
Raging Bull (boxing; 1980)
Chariots of Fire (track; 1981)*
Field of Dreams (baseball; 1989)
Jerry Maguire (football; 1996)
Seabiscuit (horse racing; 2003)
Million Dollar Baby (boxing; 2004)*

Note: *Won Academy Award

Oval Office Politics

Baseball As A Presidential Talking Point

George W. Bush (2001–2009)

"One of the great things about living here [the White House] is that you don't have to sign up for a baseball fantasy camp to meet your heroes. It turns out, they come here."

George H.W. Bush (1989–93)

"The game seems to move along pretty good ... but I don't even mind when it drags."

Ronald Reagan (1981–89)

"Our national pastime, that is if you discount political campaigning."

Jimmy Carter (1977–81)

"I was on the varsity basketball team in high school, and, when I was in submarines, I was the pitcher on our baseball team. I learned there, obviously, that you have to be mutually dependent to achieve an identifiable goal, and you have to learn how to accept either defeat or victory with some degree of equanimity and look to the next contest with hope and anticipation. I think you have to yield sometimes your own selfish aspirations for the common good and be able to deal with one another in an open, sometimes competitive way, but not a personally antagonistic way. I think those are some of the lessons that you learn from team sports and I hope that I remember them."

Gerald Ford (1974–77)
"Whenever I can, I always watch the Detroit Tigers on the radio."

Richard Nixon (1969–74)
"I don't know a lot about politics, but I do know a lot about baseball."

Lyndon Johnson (1963–69)
"They booed Ted Williams too, remember? They'll say about me I knocked the ball over the fence, but they don't like the way he stands at the plate."

John F. Kennedy (1961–63)
"Last year, more Americans went to symphonies than went to baseball games. This may be viewed as an alarming statistic, but I think that both baseball and the country will endure."

Dwight Eisenhower (1953–61)
"You cannot hit a home run by bunting. You have to step up there and take a cut at the ball. Never be more scared of the enemy than you think he is of you."

Harry Truman (1945–53)
"I couldn't see well enough to play when I was a boy, so they gave me a special job—they made me an umpire."

Franklin D. Roosevelt (1933–45)
"You know how I really feel? I feel like a baseball team going into the ninth inning with only eight men left to play."

Herbert Hoover (1929–33)
"Next to religion, baseball has furnished a greater impact on American life than any other institution."

Calvin Coolidge (1923–29)
"They are a great band, these armored knights of the bat and ball. They are held up in a high standard of honor on the field, which they have seldom betrayed. While baseball remains our national game, our national tastes will be on a higher level and our national ideals on a finer foundation."

Warren G. Harding (1921–23)
"I never saw a game without taking sides and never want to see one. There is the soul of the game."

William Howard Taft (1909–13)
"The game of baseball is a clean, straight game, and it summons to its presence everybody who enjoys clean, straight athletics. It furnishes amusement to the thousands and thousands."

Grover Cleveland (1885–89, 1893–97)
"What do you imagine the American people would think of me if I wasted my time going to the ball game?"

Chester A. Arthur (1881–85)
"Good ballplayers make good citizens."

Pass-Happy
P
Pounds

A B C D E F G H I J K L M N O P Q R S T U V W X Y Z

Pass-Happy Originals

Founding Teams Of The American Football League

In 1958, Lamar Hunt tried to purchase the NFL's Chicago Cardinals. Told to take a hike, he decided to start his own league instead. The AFL never equaled the NFL in revenue, but its strategy of outbidding the senior league for marquee college stars (most notably Joe Namath) and showcasing wide-open passing attacks got it noticed. In 1970, three years after the first Super Bowl between the leagues, the NFL and AFL formally merged. There's no better evidence of the strength of the AFL than the fact that all eight of the original teams were absorbed into the senior league.

EASTERN DIVISION

Boston Patriots[1]
Buffalo Bills
Houston Oilers[2]
New York Titans[3]

WESTERN DIVISION

Dallas Texans[4]
Denver Broncos
Los Angeles Chargers[5]
Oakland Raiders

Notes: [1]Now New England Patriots; [2]Now Tennessee Titans; [3]Now New York Jets; [4]Now Kansas City Chiefs; [5]Now San Diego Chargers.

Peach Pitfalls

Ty Cobb's Batting Fundamentals

In 1938, a rookie baseball player named Sam Chapman wrote a letter to baseball great Ty Cobb, requesting advice on hitting right-handed. A legendary grump, Cobb was nonetheless willing to share his wisdom. Unfortunately, it didn't translate; Chapman finished his career with a lifetime average of .266.

1. DON'T GRIP YOUR BAT AT THE VERY END; leave, say, an inch or two. ALSO, LEAVE AT LEAST AN INCH OR MORE SPACE BETWEEN YOUR HANDS; that gives you balance and control of bat, and also keeps hands from interfering with each other during swing.

2. Take position at plate, especially against right-hand pitchers, BACK OF PLATE, and against a man with a real curve, YOU CAN STAY ON BACK LINE OF BATTING BOX. Now try to hit to right-center. I don't mean you should place the ball in any one spot, but start now practicing to hit your right-handers to the opposite field. An inside ball from a right-hand pitcher you will naturally pull, say, to left-center.

3. DON'T SLUG AT FULL SPEED; LEARN TO MEET THEM FIRMLY, and you will be surprised at the results.

4. Now, to hit as I ask, to right-center or center. YOU STAND AWAY FROM PLATE the distance you can see with mind's eye that you can hit the ball that curves on inside corner, to center. This distance away from the plate will allow you to hit the outside ball to right. In other words, you protect the plate both on inside pitches and outside.

5. Remember, THE PLATE IS THE PITCHER'S OBJECTIVE AND HE HAS TO COME TO IT. I use "back of plate" expression to mean towards the catcher, away from plate to denote distance from plate towards outside of box. Now, USE A SLIGHTLY CLOSED STANCE, AND KEEP A LITTLE MORE WEIGHT ON YOUR FRONT FOOT THAN BACK. That gives you balance and won't pull you away from curves. You are always in position to give maximum drive.

6. DON'T PULL A CURVE BALL FROM A RIGHT-HANDER. The ball is revolving away from you. Hit with the revolution and to right field.

7. KEEP YOUR LEFT ELBOW COCKED ON LEVEL WITH YOUR HANDS OR EVEN HIGHER. Never let the elbows down below the hands, and keep your hands always well away from the body—keep pushing them out, even with your body or back.

8. KEEP YOUR BACK LEG STRAIGHT. Of course, if you put your weight more on the front leg, then the back leg will be straight.

9. IF HIGH FAST BALLS INSIDE REALLY BOTHER YOU: crouch over from waist and pass them up. Don't bite, in other words. In crouching, you make the pitcher throw lower, which forces him away from the position that bothers you. But I think with the instructions I have given, you will hit them wherever they pitch.

10. AGAINST A SPEEDY LEFT-HANDER DON'T PULL. Use same stance I have given you, and when he throws you his curve, knock him down with it or you will naturally pull it, as the ball is breaking in to you. BUT AGAINST A LEFT-HANDER OF FAIR SPEED: Move up in the box, also closer to the plate, and PULL THIS STYLE OF PITCHING.

A B C D E F G H I J K L M N O P Q R S T U V W X Y Z

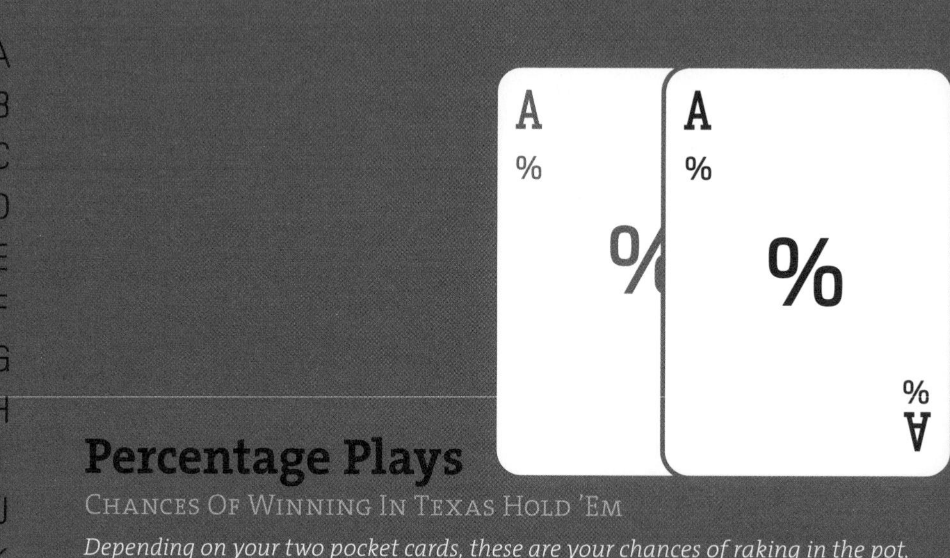

Percentage Plays

Chances Of Winning In Texas Hold 'Em

Depending on your two pocket cards, these are your chances of raking in the pot.

A–A 31.00%
A–K (s) 20.19%
A–Q (s) 18.66%
A–J (s) 17.47%
A–10 (s) 16.63%
A–9 (s) 14.60%
A–8 (s) 13.89%
A–7 (s) 13.35%
A–6 (s) 12.97%
A–5 (s) 13.43%
A–4 (s) 13.17%
A–3 (s) 13.07%
A 2 (s) 12.69%
A–K 16.67%
A–Q 14.87%
A–J 13.45%
A–10 12.43%
A–9 10.20%
A–8 9.42%
A–7 8.83%
A–6 8.39%
A–5 8.92%
A–4 8.72%
A–3 8.50%
A–2 8.18%
K–K 26.02%
K–Q (s) 18.08%
K–J (s) 17.05%
K–10 (s) 16.14%
K–9 (s) 14.15%
K–8 (s) 12.77%
K–7 (s) 12.23%
K–6 (s) 11.84%
K–5 (s) 11.57%
K–4 (s) 11.40%
K–3 (s) 11.26%
K–2 (s) 11.27%
K–Q 14.43%
K–J 13.18%
K–10 12.23%
K–9 9.93%
K–8 8.45%
K–7 7.86%
K–6 7.46%
K–5 7.13%
K–4 6.95%
K–3 6.87%
K–2 6.76%
Q–Q 22.03%
Q–J (s) 16.58%
Q–10 (s) 15.84%
Q–9 (s) 13.82%
Q–8 (s) 12.42%
Q–7 (s) 11.20%
Q–6 (s) 10.85%
Q–5 (s) 10.55%
Q–4 (s) 10.43%
Q–3 (s) 10.42%
Q–2 (s) 10.28%
Q–J 12.89%
Q–10 11.99%
Q–9 9.81%
Q–8 8.28%
Q–7 6.97%
Q–6 6.58%
Q–5 6.26%
Q–4 6.13%
Q–3 6.05%
Q–2 5.95%
J–J 19.09%
J–10 (s) 15.78%
J–9 (s) 13.80%
J–8 (s) 12.47%
J–7 (s) 11.12%
J–6 (s) 10.10%
J–5 (s) 9.86%
J–4 (s) 9.73%
J–3 (s) 9.57%
J–2 (s) 9.50%
J–10 12.13%
J–9 9.99%
J–8 8.50%
J–7 7.10%
J–6 5.94%
J–5 5.63%
J–4 5.50%
J–3 5.41%
J–2 5.33%
10–10 16.83%
10–9 (s) 14.07%
10–8 (s) 12.73%
10–7 (s) 11.47%

10-6 (s) 10.31%
10-5 (s) 9.23%
10-4 (s) 9.11%
10-3 (s) 9.06%
10-2 (s) 8.97%
10-9 10.38%
10-8 8.93%
10-7 7.53%
10-6 6.28%
10-5 5.22%
10-4 5.04%
10-3 4.95%
10-2 4.88%
9-9 15.29%
9-8 (s) 12.63%
9-7 (s) 11.74%
9-6 (s) 10.65%
9-5 (s) 9.56%
9-4 (s) 8.70%
9-3 (s) 8.53%
9-2 (s) 8.46%
9-8 8.97%
9-7 7.96%
9-6 6.77%
9-5 5.60%
9-4 4.65%
9-3 4.51%
9-2 4.47%
8-8 14.16%
8-7 (s) 12.02%
8-6 (s) 11.16%
8-5 (s) 10.12%
8-4 (s) 9.14%
8-3 (s) 8.23%
8-2 (s) 8.11%
8-7 8.36%
8-6 7.40%
8-5 6.30%
8-4 5.25%
8-3 4.33%
8-2 4.20%
7-7 13.36%
7-6 (s) 11.47%
7-5 (s) 10.69%
7-4 (s) 9.74%
7-3 (s) 8.75%
7-2 (s) 7.91%
7-6 7.88%
7-5 7.01%
7-4 5.96%
7-3 4.94%
7-2 4.04%
6-6 12.77%
6-5 (s) 11.13%
6-4 (s) 10.44%
6-3 (s) 9.49%
6-2 (s) 8.48%
6-5 7.57%
6-4 6.75%
6-3 5.73%
6-2 4.72%
5-5 12.15%
5-4 (s) 10.90%
5-3 (s) 10.18%
5-2 (s) 9.25%
5-4 7.36%
5-3 6.57%
5-2 5.56%
4-4 11.94%
4-3 (s) 9.81%
4-2 (s) 9.02%
4-3 6.17%
4-2 5.40%
3-3 11.93%
3-2 (s) 8.70%
3-2 5.02%
2-2 11.86%

Note: (s) cards of the same suit.

Pinch Hitters

The Founding Teams Of The All-american Girls Professional Baseball League

During World War II, quite a few minor league baseball teams disbanded because so many men had been drafted. Fearing the draft would have the same effect on the major leagues, Chicago Cubs owner Philip Wrigley created a committee to keep the national pastime alive. The result was the All-American Girls Softball League, which began in the spring of 1943. Early in the first season, the league's name was changed to the All-American Girls Professional Baseball League (the game incorporated elements of both softball and baseball), a fictionalized version of which was the subject of the 1992 movie A League of Their Own. *The AAGPL folded in 1954. Here are the four original teams:*

- Kenosha (Wisconsin) Comets
- Racine (Wisconsin) Belles
- Rockford (Illinois) Peaches
- South Bend (Indiana) Blue Sox

A B C D E F G H I J K L M N O P Q R S T U V W X Y Z

Place Holders

Official Olympic Abbreviations Of Participating Countries

Afghanistan AFG ... Albania ALB ... Algeria ALG ... American Samoa ASA ... Andorra AND... Angola ANG ...Antigua and Barbuda ANT ... Argentina ARG ... Armenia ARM ... Aruba ARU ... Australia AUS ... Austria AUT ... Azerbaijan AZE ... Bahamas BAH ... Bahrain BRN ... Bangladesh BAN... Barbados BAR ... Belarus BLR ... Belgium BEL ... Belize BIZ ... Benin BEN ... Bermuda BER ... Bhutan BHU ... Bolivia BOL ... Bosnia and Herzegovina BIH ... Botswana BOT ... Brazil BRA ... British Virgin Islands IVB ... Brunei Darussalam BRU ... Bulgaria BUL ... Burkina Faso BUR ... Burundi BDI ... Cambodia CAM ... Cameroon CMR ... Canada CAN ... Cape Verde CPV ... Cayman Islands CAY ... Central African Republic CAF ... Chad CHA ... Chile CHI ... China CHN ... Chinese Taipei TPE ... Colombia COL ... Comoros COM ... Congo CGO ... Cook Islands COK ... Costa Rica CRC ... Cote d'Ivoire CIV ... Croatia CRO ... Cuba CUB ... Cyprus CYP ... Czech Republic CZE ... Democratic Republic of the Congo COD ... Denmark DEN ... Djibouti DJI ... Dominica DMA ... Dominican Republic DOM ... Ecuador ECU ... Egypt EGY ... El Salvador ESA ... Equatorial Guinea GEQ ... Eritrea ERI ... Estonia EST ... Ethiopia ETH ... Federated States of Micronesia FSM ... Fiji FIJ ... Finland FIN ... France FRA ... Gabon GAB ... Gambia GAM ... Georgia GEO ... Germany GER ... Ghana GHA ... Greece GRE ... Grenada GRN ... Guam GUM ... Guatemala GUA ... Guinea GUI ... Guinea-Bissau GBS ... Guyana GUY ... Haiti HAI ... Honduras HON ... Hong Kong HKG ... Hungary HUN ... Iceland ISL ... India IND... Indonesia INA ... Iran IRI ... Iraq IRQ ... Ireland IRL ... Israel ISR ... Italy ITA ... Jamaica JAM ... Japan JPN ... Jordan JOR ... Kazakhstan KAZ ... Kenya KEN ... Kiribati KIR ... Korea KOR ... Kuwait KUW ... Kyrgyzstan KGZ ... Laos LAO ... Latvia LAT ... Lebanon LIB ... Lesotho LES ... Liberia LBR ... Libya LBA ... Liechtenstein LIE ... Lithuania LTU ... Luxembourg LUX ... Macedonia MKD ... Madagascar MAD ... Malawi MAW ... Malaysia MAS ... Maldives MDV ... Mali MLI ... Malta MLT ... Marshall Islands MHL ... Mauritania MTN ... Mauritius MRI ... Mexico MEX ... Moldova MDA ... Monaco MON ... Mongolia MGL ... Morocco MAR ... Mozambique MOZ ... Myanmar MYA ... Namibia NAM ... Nauru NRU ... Nepal NEP ... Netherlands NED ... Netherlands Antilles AHO ... New Zealand NZL ... Nicaragua NCA ... Niger NGR ... Nigeria NGA ... North Korea PRK ... Norway NOR ... Oman OMA ... Pakistan PAK ... Palau PLW ... Palestine PLE ... Panama PAN ... Papua New Guinea PNG ... Paraguay PAR ... Peru PER ... Philippines PHI ... Poland POL ... Portugal POR ... Puerto Rico PUR ... Qatar QAT ... Romania ROM ... Russia RUS ... Rwanda RWA ... Saint Kitts and Nevis SKN ... Saint Lucia LCA ... Saint Vincent and the Grenadines VIN ... Samoa SAM ... San Marino SMR ... Sao Tome and Principe STP ... Saudi Arabia KSA ... Senegal SEN ... Serbia SRB ... Seychelles SEY ... Sierra Leone SLE ... Singapore SIN ... Slovakia SVK ... Slovenia SLO ... Solomon Islands SOL ... Somalia SOM ... South Africa RSA ... Spain ESP ... Sri Lanka SRI

... Sudan SUD ... Suriname SUR ... Swaziland SWZ ... Sweden SWE ... Switzerland SUI ... Syria SYR ... Tadjikistan TJK ... Tanzania TAN ... Thailand THA ... Timor-Leste TLS ... Togo TOG ... Tonga TGA ... Trinidad and Tobago TRI ... Tunisia TUN ... Turkey TUR ... Turkmenistan TKM ... Uganda UGA ... Ukraine UKR ... United Arab Emirates UAE ... United Kingdom (Great Britain) GBR ... United States USA ... Uruguay URU ... Uzbekistan UZB ... Vanuatu VAN ... Venezuela VEN ... Vietnam VIE ... Virgin Islands ISV ... Yemen YEM ... Zambia ZAM ... Zimbabwe ZIM

Play Times

Lengths Of Various Sports

FULL CONTEST

5 days: Cricket test match
1 day: One-day cricket
90 minutes: Soccer; bandy
80 minutes: Rugby; Australian rules football
70 minutes: Field hockey
60 minutes: Lacrosse; team handball; American and Canadian professional football; college football; ice hockey; netball; korfball
56 minutes: Polo
48 minutes: NBA basketball; roller hockey
40 minutes: College basketball; WNBA basketball; international basketball; roller derby
30 minutes: Bicycle polo
28 minutes: Water polo
5 minutes: Olympic judo (men's)
4 minutes: Olympic judo (women's)

IN-CONTEST PERIODS

45 minutes: Soccer half; bandy half
40 minutes: Rugby half
35 minutes: Field hockey half
30 minutes: Team handball half; korfball half
20 minutes: College basketball half; Australian Rules football quarter; ice hockey period
15 minutes: Lacrosse quarter; professional football quarter; college football quarter; netball quarter
12 minutes: NBA basketball quarter; roller hockey quarter
10 minutes: WNBA basketball quarter; international basketball period
7:30 minutes: Bicycle polo quarter
7 minutes: Polo chukka; water polo quarter
4:30 minutes: Figure skating, long program (men's)
4 minutes: Figure skating, long program (ladies); ice dancing, free dance
3 minutes: First round, college wrestling; boxing round
2:50 minutes: Figure skating, short program
2:30 minutes: Ice dancing, original dance
2 minutes: Second and third rounds, college wrestling
Up to 60 seconds: Steer dogging (clock stops when the steer is roped)
40 seconds: Time to shoot 20 shots from 10 meters in modern pentathlon
30 seconds: Final Jeopardy!
8 seconds: Bull/steer riding, rough stock rodeo

A B C D E F G H I J K L M N O P Q R S T U V W X Y Z

Poetic Injustice

THE WORDS OF "CASEY AT THE BAT"

The outlook wasn't brilliant for the
Mudville nine that day,
The score stood four to two, with but one
inning more to play.
And then when Cooney died at first, and
Barrows did the same,
A sickly silence fell upon the patrons of
the game.

A straggling few got up to go in deep
despair. The rest
Clung to that hope which springs eternal
in the human breast;
They thought, if only Casey could get but a
whack at that—
We'd put up even money, now, with Casey
at the bat.

But Flynn preceded Casey, as did also
Jimmy Blake,
And the former was a lulu and the latter
was a cake;
So upon that stricken multitude grim
melancholy sat,
For there seemed but little chance of
Casey's getting to the bat.

But Flynn let drive a single, to the
wonderment of all,
And Blake, the much despis-ed, tore the
cover off the ball;
And when the dust had lifted, and the men
saw what had occurred,
There was Jimmy safe at second and Flynn
a-hugging third.

Then from five thousand throats and more
there rose a lusty yell;
It rumbled through the valley, it rattled in
the dell;
It knocked upon the mountain and recoiled
upon the flat,
For Casey, mighty Casey, was advancing to
the bat.

There was ease in Casey's manner as he
stepped into his place;
There was pride in Casey's bearing and a
smile on Casey's face.
And when, responding to the cheers, he
lightly doffed his hat,
No stranger in the crowd could doubt
'twas Casey at the bat.

Ten thousand eyes were on him as he
rubbed his hands with dirt;
Five thousand tongues applauded when he
wiped them on his shirt.
Then while the writhing pitcher ground the
ball into his hip,
Defiance gleamed in Casey's eye, a sneer
curled Casey's lip.

And now the leather-covered sphere came
hurtling through the air,
And Casey stood a-watching it in haughty
grandeur there.
Close by the sturdy batsman the ball
unheeded sped—
"That ain't my style," said Casey. "Strike
one," the umpire said.

From the benches, black with people,
there went up a muffled roar,
Like the beating of the storm-waves on a
stern and distant shore.

"Kill him! Kill the umpire!" shouted someone
on the stand;
And it's likely they'd a-killed him had not
Casey raised his hand.

With a smile of Christian charity great
Casey's visage shone;
He stilled the rising tumult; he bade the
game go on;
He signaled to the pitcher, and once more
the spheroid flew;
But Casey still ignored it, and the umpire
said, "Strike two."

"Fraud!" cried the maddened thousands,
and echo answered fraud;
But one scornful look from Casey and the
audience was awed.
They saw his face grow stern and cold,
they saw his muscles strain,
And they knew that Casey wouldn't let
that ball go by again.
The sneer is gone from Casey's lip, his
teeth are clenched in hate;
He pounds with cruel violence his bat upon
the plate.
And now the pitcher holds the ball, and
now he lets it go,
And now the air is shattered by the force
of Casey's blow.

Oh, somewhere in this favored land the
sun is shining bright;
The band is playing somewhere, and
somewhere hearts are light,
And somewhere men are laughing, and
somewhere children shout;
But there is no joy in Mudville—mighty
Casey has struck out.

Note: There are several versions of "Casey." This is the one first published by Ernest Lawrence Thayer (writing as "Phin") in San Francisco's *Daily Examiner* on June 3, 1888.

Points Taken

Scoring Values In Various Sports

1: **Archery** *(hit on outer white part of target)*; **Australian rules football** *(behind)*; **badminton, croquet, curling, handball, horseshoes, jai alai, lawn bowling, paddle ball, pétanque, racquetball, squash, table tennis, volleyball, wrestling** *(point)*; **bandy, bicycle polo, field hockey, ice hockey, korfball, lacrosse, netball, polo, soccer, water polo** *(goal)*; **baseball, cricket, kickball, softball** *(run)*; **basketball** *(free throw)*; **bowling** *(single pin knockdown)*; **football** *(kicked extra point)*; **Canadian football** *(rouge)*; **golf** *(stroke)*; **rugby league** *(drop kick)*

2: **Archery** *(hit on inner white)*; **basketball** *(field goal)*; **football** *(safety; two-point conversion)*; **horseshoes** *(two shoes closer than opponent's)*; **rugby league** *(penalty kick/goal kick)*; **rugby union** *(try conversion)*; **wrestling** *(takedown, reversal, near fall)*

3: **Archery** *(hit on outer black)*; **basketball** *(field goal behind 3-point line)*; **football** *(field goal)*; **horseshoes** *(ringer)*; **rugby union** *(drop kick, penalty kick)*; **wrestling** *(near fall)*

4: **Archery** *(hit on inner black)*; **cricket** *(ball crosses boundary)*; **horseshoes** *(one ringer and next-closest shoe)*; **rugby league** *(try)*; **wrestling** *(near fall)*

5: **Archery** *(hit on outer blue)*; **rugby union** *(try)*

6: **Archery** *(hit on inner blue)*; **Australian rules football** *(goal)*; **cricket** *(ball crosses boundary on fly)*; **football** *(touchdown)*; **horseshoes** *(two ringers)*

7: **Archery** *(hit on outer red)*; **shuffleboard** *(landing in third tier)*

8: **Archery** *(hit on inner red)*; **shuffleboard** *(landing in second tier)*

9: **Archery** *(hit on outer yellow)*

10: **Archery** *(hit on inner yellow)*; **bowling** *(strike)*; **boxing, gymnastics, diving, synchronized swimming** *(perfect score)*; **shuffleboard** *(landing in the tip)*

15: **Tennis** *(first point)*

30: **Tennis** *(second point)*

40: **Tennis** *(third point)*

100: **Rodeo** *(perfect score)*

300: **Bowling** *(perfect score, 12 strikes)*

Posers

Heisman Trophy Winners

1935: Jay Berwanger, RB, University of Chicago
1936: Larry Kelley, E, Yale University
1937: Clint Frank, QB, Yale University
1938: Davey O'Brien, QB, Texas Christian University
1939: Nile Kinnick, HB, Iowa University
1940: Tom Harmon, HB, University of Michigan
1941: Bruce Smith, HB, University of Minnesota
1942: Frank Sinkwich, HB, University of Georgia
1943: Angelo Bertelli, QB, Notre Dame
1944: Les Horvath, QB, Ohio State University
1945: Doc Blanchard, FB, Army
1946: Glenn Davis, HB, Army
1947: John Lujack, QB, Notre Dame
1948: Doak Walker, RB, Southern Methodist University
1949: Leon Hart, E, Notre Dame
1950: Vic Janowicz, HB, Ohio State University
1951: Dick Kazmaier, RB, Princeton University
1952: Billy Vessels, RB, University of Oklahoma
1953: Johnny Lattner, HB, Notre Dame
1954: Alan Ameche, FB, University of Wisconsin
1955: Howard "Hopalong" Cassady, HB, Ohio State University
1956: Paul Hornung, QB, Notre Dame
1957: John David Crow, HB, Texas A&M University
1958: Pete Dawkins, HB, Army

A B C D E F G H I J K L M N O P Q R S T U V W X Y Z

Posers, continued from page 179

1959: Billy Cannon, HB, Louisiana State University
1960: Joe Bellino, HB, Navy
1961: Ernie Davis, RB, Syracuse University
1962: Terry Baker, QB, Oregon State University
1963: Roger Staubach, QB, Navy
1964: John Huarte, QB, Notre Dame
1965: Mike Garrett, RB, USC
1966: Steve Spurrier, QB, University of Florida
1967: Gary Beban, QB, UCLA
1968: O.J. Simpson, RB, USC
1969: Steve Owens, FB, University of Oklahoma
1970: Jim Plunkett, QB, Stanford University
1971: Pat Sullivan, QB, Auburn University
1972: Johnny Rodgers, RB, University of Nebraska
1973: John Cappelletti, RB, Penn State University
1974: Archie Griffin, RB, Ohio State University
1975: Archie Griffin, RB, Ohio State University
1976: Tony Dorsett, RB, University of Pittsburgh
1977: Earl Campbell, RB, University of Texas
1978: Billy Sims, RB, University of Oklahoma
1979: Charles White, RB, USC
1980: George Rogers, RB, University of South Carolina
1981: Marcus Allen, RB, USC
1982: Herschel Walker, RB, University of Georgia
1983: Mike Rozier, RB, University of Nebraska
1984: Doug Flutie, QB, Boston College
1985: Bo Jackson, RB, Auburn University
1986: Vinny Testaverde, QB, University of Miami
1987: Tim Brown, WR, Notre Dame
1988: Barry Sanders, RB, Oklahoma State University
1989: Andre Ware, QB, University of Houston
1990: Ty Detmer, QB, Brigham Young University
1991: Desmond Howard, WR, University of Michigan
1992: Gino Torretta, QB, University of Miami
1993: Charlie Ward, QB, Florida State University
1994: Rashaan Salaam, RB, University of Colorado
1995: Eddie George, RB, Ohio State University
1996: Danny Wuerffel, QB, University of Florida
1997: Charles Woodson, CB, University of Michigan
1998: Ricky Williams, RB, University of Texas
1999: Ron Dayne, RB, University of Wisconsin
2000: Chris Weinke, QB, Florida State University
2001: Eric Crouch, QB, University of Nebraska
2002: Carson Palmer, QB, USC
2003: Jason White, QB, University of Oklahoma
2004: Matt Leinart, QB, USC
2005: Reggie Bush, RB, USC
2006: Troy Smith, QB, Ohio State University
2007: Tim Tebow, QB, University of Florida

Pounds For Pounding

Boxing Weight Classes

According to the The Boxing Register, *the first boxing weight class was introduced in England in 1719. By the early 20th century, there were eight accepted classes. But as the sport and its governing bodies grew, so did the number of weight classes. Today, there are 17 for professional male boxers. Here they are, with the year they were first recognized, followed by the 11 recognized Olympic classes:*

PROFESSIONAL

Strawweight: up to 105 pounds (1988)
Junior flyweight: 108 pounds (1975)
Flyweight: 112 pounds (1913)
Junior bantamweight: 115 pounds (1980)
Bantamweight: 118 pounds (1887)
Junior featherweight: 122 pounds (1922)
Featherweight: 126 pounds (1890)
Junior lightweight: 130 pounds (1921)
Lightweight: 135 pounds (1896)
Junior welterweight: 140 pounds (1922)
Welterweight: 147 pounds (1888)
Junior middleweight: 154 pounds (1962)
Middleweight: 160 pounds (1853)
Super middleweight: 168 pounds (1984)
Light heavyweight: 175 pounds (1903)
Cruiserweight: 200 pounds (2003)
Heavyweight: over 200 pounds (1719)

OLYMPIC

Light flyweight: up to 106 pounds/48 kg
Flyweight: 112 pounds/51 kg
Bantamweight: 119 pounds/54 kg
Featherweight: 125 pounds/57 kg
Lightweight: 132 pounds/60 kg
Light welterweight: 141 pounds/64 kg
Welterweight: 152 pounds/69 kg
Middleweight: 165 pounds/75 kg
Light heavyweight: 178 pounds /81 kg
Heavyweight: 201 pounds/91 kg
Super heavyweight: Over 201 pounds/91 kg and over

Quantifiable

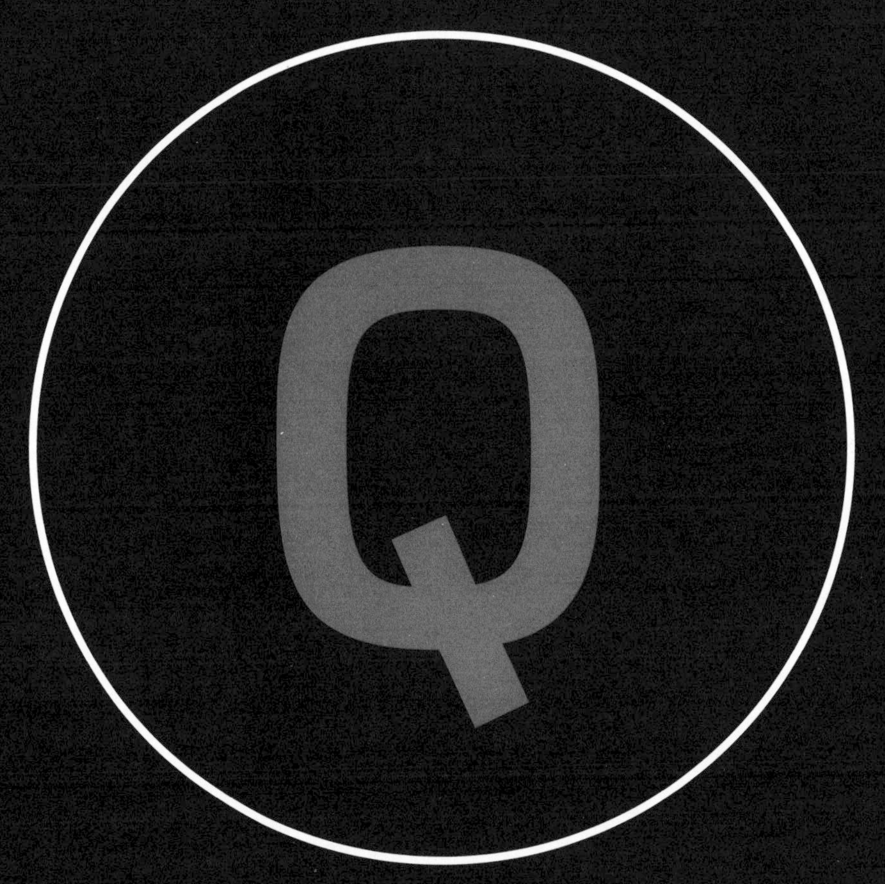

Quotable

Quantifiable Measures

Number Of Competitors In Various Team Sports

2: Badminton *(doubles)*, beach volleyball, paddleball *(doubles)*, racquetball *(doubles)*, rowing *(various)*, sailing *(various)*, table tennis *(doubles)*, tennis *(doubles)*, volleyball *(doubles)*

3: Arena polo, track cycling *(Olympic sprint)*, fencing *(team)*

4: Cycling *(team pursuit)*, Olympic curling, outdoor polo, rowing *(various)*, short track speed skating *(relays)*, swimming *(relays)*, track *(relays)*

5: Basketball, roller derby, in-line hockey

6: Dodgeball, ice hockey, indoor soccer, volleyball

7: Rugby sevens, team handball, water polo

8: Eight-man football, korfball, rowing

9: Baseball, softball

10: Lacrosse *(men's)*

11: Bandy, cricket, field hockey, football, soccer

12: Lacrosse *(women's)*

15: Rugby

18: Australian rules football

Questionable Math

The Formula For The NFL QB Rating

Developed by Don Smith of the Pro Football Hall of Fame and adopted in 1973, the formula for the NFL's quarterback rating is complicated. The calculation is based on four factors—percentage of completions per attempts, average yards gained per attempt, percentage of touchdown passes per attempt, and percentage of interceptions per attempts—and was designed so that a score of 85 is good, 100 is great, and (oddly) 158.3 is perfect.

1. Take the player's completion percentage, subtract 30, and multiply by .05. If the number falls between 0 and 2.375, the player gets that number. If the number is less than 0, the player gets nothing. If you get a number greater than 2.375, the player gets 2.375.

2. Take total yards passing, divide by attempts, and then subtract 3 from that number and multiply the result by .25. If you get 0 or less, give the player nothing. If you have 2.375 or higher, the player gets 2.375.

3. Take the number of TD passes, divide by attempts, and multiply by .20. The player gets that number. If the number is greater than 2.375, the player gets 2.375.

4. Divide the number of interceptions by passing attempts and multiply that number by .25, and then subtract the result from 2.375.

5. The four numbers are added, divided by 6, and multiplied by 100.

Quick Quencher

Original And Current Gatorade Recipes

To replenish dehydrated members of the University of Florida football team in 1965, school doctors whipped up a carbohydrate-electrolyte drink. The fortified Gators went 7-4 that year, 9-2 the next, and a legendary sports drink was born. In 1967, it was sold to food-and-beverage giant Stokely–Van Camp. Today, Gatorade (now owned by PepsiCo) is hydrating athletes around the world.

Original Recipe (Lemon–Lime)
Water, sodium, potassium,
glucose, lemon juice

Current Recipe (Lemon–Lime)
Water, sucrose syrup, glucose-fructose syrup, citric acid, natural lemon and lime flavors with other natural flavors, salt, sodium citrate,

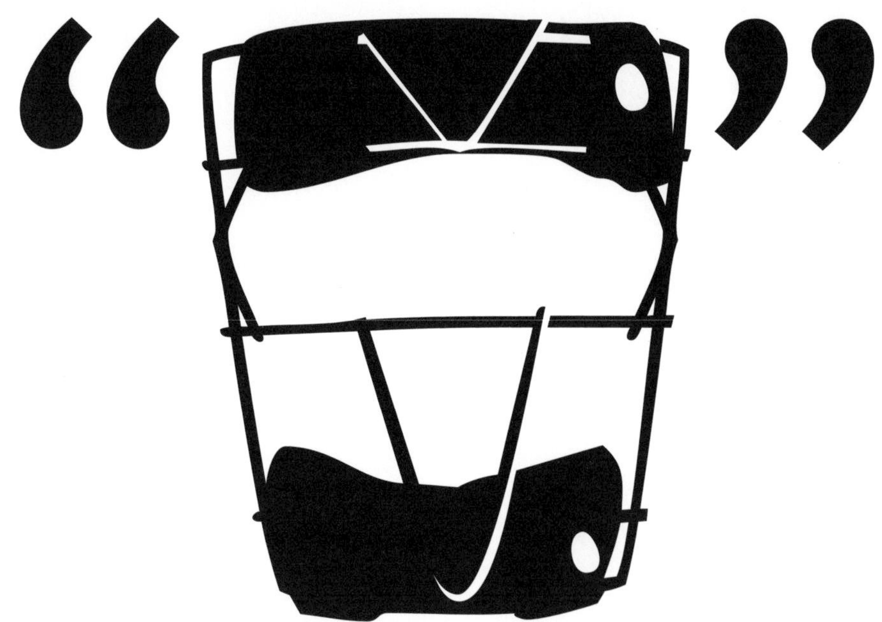

Quotable Yankee

What Yogi Berra Said

Hall of Fame New York Yankees catcher Yogi Berra, whose playing career spanned 1946–65, is known mostly for two things: the 10 World Series titles his teams won and his entertaining sound-bites. Here are some examples of the latter:

"It gets late early out there."

"All pitchers are liars or crybabies."

"How can you hit and think at the same time?"

"If people don't want to come out to the ballpark, nobody's going to stop them."

"I'm not going to buy my kids an encyclopedia. Let them walk to school like I did."

"In baseball, you don't know nothing."

"Baseball is 90% mental. The other half is physical."

"I always thought that record would stand until it was broken."

"I think Little League is wonderful. It keeps the kids out of the house."

"It's déjà vu all over again."

"Nobody goes there anymore because it's too crowded."

"He hits from both sides of the plate. He's amphibious."

"So I'm ugly. So what? I never saw anyone hit with his face."

"The future ain't what it used to be."

"In theory, there is no difference between theory and practice. In practice there is."

"It ain't over till it's over."

"The towels were so thick there I could hardly close my suitcase."

"You can observe a lot by watching."

"You should always go to other people's funerals. Otherwise, they won't come to yours."

"We made too many wrong mistakes."

"When you come to a fork in the road, take it."

"I never said most of the things I said."

Rapier

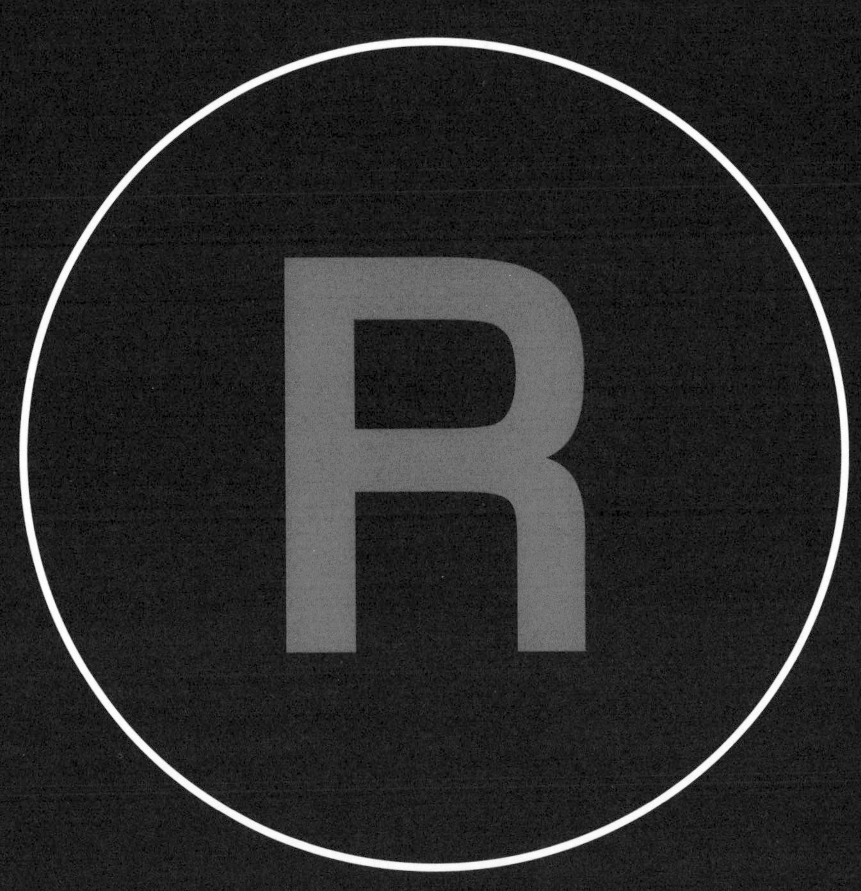

Ruthian

Rapier Bits

Basic Fencing Positions And Lines

Whether they wield foils, épées or sabres, fencers use one of eight principal parries, or blocks, to protect against attacks. Each calls for its own specific hand placement and wrist angle on the grip. They are:

PRIME: opponent's abdomen (low inside)
SECONDE: opponent's abdomen (low outside)
TIERCE: opponent's chest (high outside)
QUARTE: opponent's chest (high inside)
QUINTE: opponent's chest (high inside)
SIXTE: opponent's chest (high outside)
SEPTIME: opponent's abdomen (low inside)
OCTAVE: opponent's abdomen (low outside)

Raw Deals

A History Of Lopsided Trades

BASEBALL

1920: Boston Red Sox trade P/OF Babe Ruth (future Hall of Famer) to New York Yankees for $100,000 and a $350,000 loan.

1964: Chicago Cubs trade OF Lou Brock (future Hall of Famer), P Jack Spring, and P Paul Toth to St. Louis Cardinals for P Ernie Broglio, P Bobby Shantz, and OF Doug Clemens.

1965: Cincinnati Reds trade OF Frank Robinson (future Hall of Famer) to Baltimore Orioles for P Milt Pappas, P Jack Baldschun, and OF Dick Simpson.

1971: New York Mets trade P Nolan Ryan (future Hall of Famer), P Don Rose, OF Leroy Stanton, and C Francisco Estrada to California Angels for SS Jim Fregosi.

1977: New York Mets trade P Tom Seaver (future Hall of Famer) to Cincinnati Reds for 2B Doug Flynn, OF Steve Henderson, OF Dan Norman, and P Pat Zachry.

1982: Philadelphia Phillies trade 2B Ryne Sandberg (future Hall of Famer) and SS Larry Bowa to Chicago Cubs for SS Ivan DeJesus.

1992: Chicago White Sox trade OF Sammy Sosa and P Ken Patterson to Chicago Cubs for OF George Bell.

1993: Los Angeles Dodgers trade P Pedro Martinez to Montreal Expos for 2B Delino DeShields.

1997: Oakland A's trade 1B Mark McGwire to St. Louis Cardinals for P T.J. Mathews, P Blake Stein, and P Eric Ludwick.

FOOTBALL

1950: New York Bulldogs trade QB Bobby Layne (future Hall of Famer) to Detroit Lions for WR Bob Mann.

1983: Baltimore Colts trade rights to QB John Elway (future Hall of Famer) to Denver Broncos for QB Mark Herrmann, OT Chris Hinton, and a first-round pick in 1984 (G Ron Solt).

1987: Tampa Bay Buccaneers trade QB Steve Young (future Hall of Famer) to San Francisco 49ers for second- and fourth-round picks in 1987 (LB Winston Moss and WR Bruce Hill).

1989: Minnesota Vikings trade five players, six conditional picks over three years, and one first-round 1992 pick to Dallas Cowboys for RB Herschel Walker. Among players drafted by Dallas with Minnesota's picks were RB Emmitt Smith (all-time leading rusher), S Darren Woodson, and DT Russell Maryland.

1992: Atlanta Falcons trade QB Brett Favre to Green Bay Packers for a first-round pick in 1992, which the Packers trade to Cowboys for two draft picks (RB Tony Smith and CB Frankie Smith).

1996: St. Louis Rams trade RB Jerome Bettis to Pittsburgh Steelers for two draft picks (TE Ernie Conwell and T Ryan Tucker).

1999: Indianapolis Colts trade RB Marshall Faulk to St. Louis Rams for two draft picks (LB Mike Peterson and DE Brad Scioli).

BASKETBALL

1965: San Francisco Warriors trade C Wilt Chamberlain (future Hall of Famer) to Philadelphia 76ers for G Paul Neumann, F/C Connie Dierking, F Lee Shaffer, and $150,000.

1975: Milwaukee Bucks trade Kareem Abdul-Jabbar (future Hall of Famer) to Los Angeles Lakers for C Elmore Smith, G/F Junior Bridgeman, G/F Brian Winters, and F/C Dave Meyers.

1976: New York Nets trade F Julius Erving (future Hall of Famer) to Philadelphia 76ers for $3 million.

1980: Golden State Warriors trade C Robert Parish (future Hall of Famer) and No. 3 pick in 1980 draft (F Kevin McHale,

........➤

Raw Deals, continued from page 175

future Hall of Famer) to Boston Celtics for No. 1 (C Joe Barry Carroll) and No. 13 (F/C Rickey Brown) picks.

1987: Seattle SuperSonics trade rights to F Scottie Pippen to Chicago Bulls for rights to C Olden Polynice, a second-round pick in 1988 (F Sylvester Gray), and a future player (Brad Sellers).

1992: Philadelphia 76ers trade Charles Barkley (future Hall of Famer) to Phoenix Suns for C Andrew Lang, G Jeff Hornacek, and F Tim Perry.

1996: Los Angeles Lakers acquire draft rights of G Kobe Bryant from Charlotte Hornets for C Vlade Divac.

HOCKEY

1967: Chicago Black Hawks trade C Phil Esposito (future Hall of Famer), RW Ken Hodge, and LW Fred Stanfield to Boston Bruins for D Gilles Marotte, C Pit Martin, and G Jack Norris.

1975: Detroit Red Wings trade C Marcel Dionne (future Hall of Famer) and D Bart Crashley to Los Angeles Kings for D Terry Harper, LW Dan Maloney, and a second-round draft choice in 1976.

1986: Vancouver Canucks trade RW Cam Neely (future Hall of Famer) and a No. 1 pick (D Glen Wesley) to Boston Bruins for C Barry Pederson.

1988: Calgary Flames trade RW Brett Hull and F Steve Bozek to St. Louis Blues for D Rob Ramage and G Rick Wamsley.

1991: Hartford Whalers trade C Ron Francis, D Ulf Samuelsson, and D Grant Jennings to Pittsburgh Penguins for D Zarley Zalapski, C John Cullen, and F Jeff Parker.

1992: Chicago Blackhawks trade G Dominik Hasek to Buffalo Sabres for G Stéphane Beauregard and a fourth-round draft pick in 1993.

1992: Philadelphia Flyers trade C Peter Forsberg, LW Chris Simon, D Steve Duchesne, D Kerry Huffman, C Mike Ricci, G Ron Hextall, 1993 and 1994 first-round picks, and $15 million to Quebec Nordiques for rights to C Eric Lindros.

1995: Montreal Canadiens trade G Patrick Roy and RW Mike Keane to Colorado Avalanche for G Jocelyn Thibault, LW Martin Rucinsky, and RW Andrei Kovalenko.

Ring Leaders

International Olympic Committee Presidents

1. Demetrius Vikelas (1894-96)
2. Pierre de Coubertin (1896-1925)
3. Henri de Baillet-Latour (1925-42)
4. J. Sigfrid Edström (1946-52)
5. Avery Brundage (1952-72)
6. Lord Killanin (1972-80)
7. Juan Antonio Samaranch (1980-2001)
8. Jacques Rogge (2001-present)

Rink Requirements

The 1877 Rules Of Ice Hockey

The first organized ice hockey game was between McGill University students and a pickup team at Montreal's Victoria Skating Rink on March 3, 1875. On February 27, 1877, the first rules were published in The Gazette. *They are:*

1. The game shall be commenced and renewed by a Bully[1] in the centre of the ground. Goals shall be changed after each game.

2. When a player hits the ball, any one of the same side who at such moment of hitting is nearer to the opponents' goal line is out of play, and may not touch the ball himself, or in any way whatever prevent any other player from doing so, until the ball has been played. A player must always be on his own side of the ball.

3. The ball may be stopped, but not carried or knocked on by any part of the body. No player shall raise his stick above his shoulder. Charging from behind, tripping, collaring, kicking, or shinning shall not be allowed.

4. When the ball is hit behind the goal line by the attacking side, it shall be brought out straight 15 yards, and started again by a Bully; but, if hit behind by any one of the side whose goal line it is, a player of the opposite side shall hit it out from within one yard of the nearest corner, no player of the attacking side at that time shall be within 20 yards of the goal line, and the defenders, with the exception of the goal-keeper, must be behind their goal line.

5. When the ball goes off at the side, a player of the opposite side to that which hit it out shall roll it out from the point on the boundary line at which it went off at right angles with the boundary line, and it shall not be in play until it has touched the ice, and the player rolling it in shall not play it until it has been played by another player, every player being then behind the ball.

6. On the infringement of any of the above rules, the ball shall be brought back and a Bully shall take place.

7. All disputes shall be settled by the Umpires, or in the event of their disagreement, by the Referee

Note: "Bully" refers to a face-off. The word "game" generally refers to a "goal."

A
B
C
D
E
F
G
H
I
J
K
L
M
N
O
P
Q
R
S
T
U
V
W
X
Y
Z

Roster Ringers

Mr. Burns' 1992 Company Softball Team On *The Simpsons*

- Mike Scioscia, C
- Don Mattingly, 1B
- Steve Sax, 2B
- Ozzie Smith, SS
- Wade Boggs, 3B
- Jose Canseco, OF
- Ken Griffey Jr., OF
- Darryl Strawberry, OF
- Roger Clemens, P

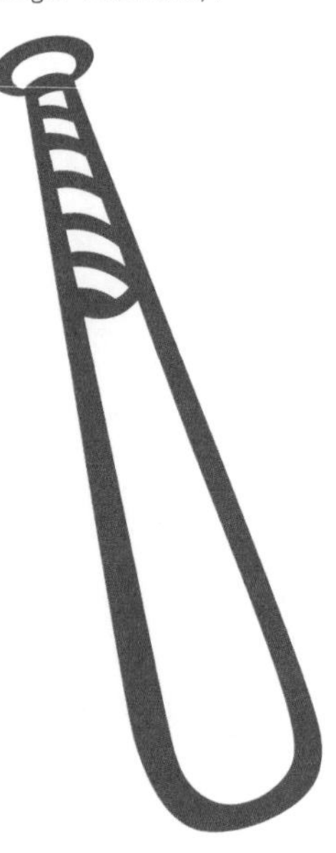

Round-Trippers

Home Run Euphemisms

- Babe Ruth
- Baker
- Ballantine blast
- Belt
- Big fly
- Big hit
- Big knock
- Big swat
- Blast
- Bomb
- Bye-bye ball
- Circuit belt
- Circuit blow
- Circuit clout
- Circuit drive
- Circuit smash
- Circuit tripper
- Circuit wallop
- Clout
- Dinger
- Dong
- Dome dong
- Downtowner
- Dr. Longball
- Five-dollar ride in a yellow cab
- Four-bagger
- Four-master
- Four-ply wallop
- Get-small-quick ball
- Gopher ball
- Home bagger
- Homer
- Homer ball
- Jack
- Jonrun
- Long ball
- Long potato
- Long tater
- Master fly
- Monster shot
- Moon shot
- Poke
- Poke off
- Potato
- Rainbow drop
- Rainmaker
- Rooftopper
- Round-tripper
- Seat-boomer
- Seeya
- Shot
- Space shot
- Tater
- Tonk
- Wallop
- Yardbird

Excerpted from *The New Dickson Baseball Dictionary* © 1999 by Paul Dickson. Reprinted with permission of Harcourt, Inc.

Rout Markers

Largest Margins Of Victory

COLLEGE FOOTBALL
222 points: Georgia Tech 222, Cumberland 0 (October 7, 1916)

COLLEGE BASKETBALL (DIVISION I WOMEN)
101 points: Louisiana Tech 126, Texas–Pan American 25 (February 18, 1989)

COLLEGE BASKETBALL (DIVISION I MEN)
91 points: Tulsa 141, Prairie View A&M 50 (December 7, 1995)

NFL
73 points: Chicago Bears 73, Washington Redskins 0 (December 8, 1940)

NBA
68 points: Cleveland Cavaliers 148, Miami Heat 80 (December 17, 1991)

WNBA
45 points: Houston Comets 110, Washington Mystics 65 (August 17, 1998)

MLB
25 runs: Boston Red Sox 29, St. Louis Browns 4 (June 8, 1950)

PGA
16 strokes: J. Douglas Edgar, Canadian Open, 1919; Joe Kirkwood, Sr., Corpus Christi Open, 1924; Bobby Locke, Chicago National Championship, 1948

NHL
15 goals: Detroit Red Wings 15, New York Rangers 0 (January 23, 1944)

LPGA
14 strokes: Louise Suggs, U.S. Open, 1949; Cindy Mackey, MasterCard International Pro-Am, 1986

NASCAR
14 laps: Ned Jarrett, Southern 500 (September 6, 1965)

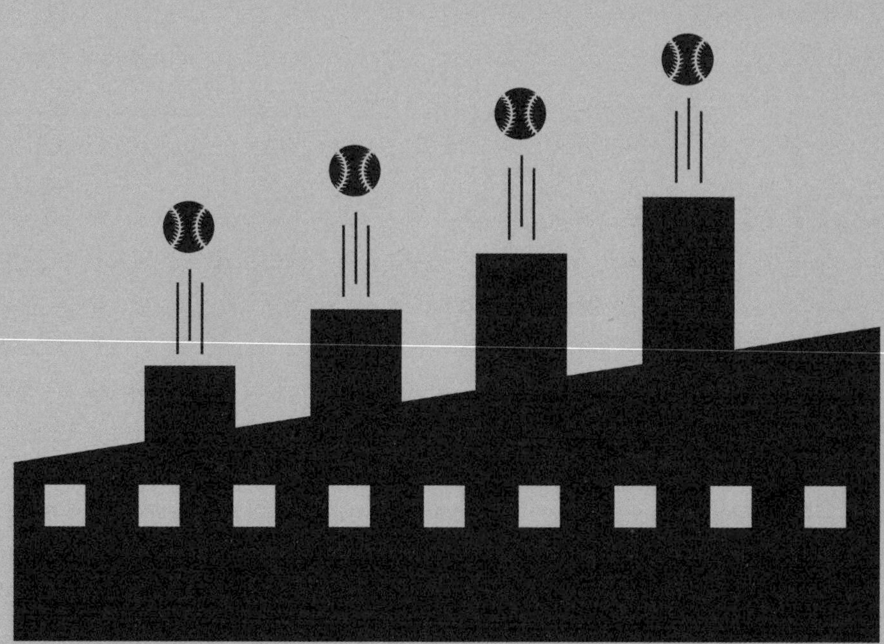

Run Factories

Baseball Teams That Scored In Every Inning Of A Game

In baseball's modern era, only nine MLB teams have scored at least one run in every inning of a game. Here they are:

NATIONAL LEAGUE

New York Giants 22, Philadelphia Phillies 8 (June 1, 1923)

St. Louis Cardinals 15, Chicago Cubs 2 (September 13, 1964)

Colorado Rockies 13, Chicago Cubs 6 (May 5, 1999)

AMERICAN LEAGUE

Boston Americans 14, Cleveland Naps 7 (September 16, 1903)

Cleveland Indians 27, Boston Red Sox 3 (July 7, 1923)

New York Yankees 14, St. Louis Browns 1 (July 26, 1939)

Chicago White Sox 12, Boston Red Sox 8 (May 11, 1949)

Kansas City Royals 16, Oakland A's 6 (September 14, 1998)

New York Yankees 17, Toronto Blue Jays 6 (April 29, 2006)

Ruthian References

Nicknames For The Babe

Seems like everyone who knew him—players, managers, friends, enemies, reporters—had a nickname for George Herman Ruth. Here are 34, many of them provided by Greg Schwalenberg, the curator of the Babe Ruth Museum in Baltimore.

- Babe (or, The Babe)
- Bambino
- The Barnstorming Babe
- Battering Bambino
- The Behemoth of Biff
- The Behemoth of Bust
- The Big Bam
- The Bulky Monarch
- The Caliph of Clout
- The Circuit Smasher
- The Colossus of Clout
- The Colossus of Club
- The Goliath of Grand Slam
- The Great Bambino
- Herman the Great
- His Eminence
- The High Priest of Swat
- Homeric Herman
- The Home Run King
- The Infant Swategy
- Jedge
- Jidge
- The King of Clout
- King of Diamonds
- King of Swing
- The Maharajah of Mash
- The Man
- The (Big) Monk
- The Prince of Pounders
- The Slambino
- The Sultan of Swat
- The Wally of Wallop
- The Wizard of Whack

Saturday

Suds

Saturday Night Specials

Sports Personalities Who Hosted *Saturday Night Live*

- **Fran Tarkenton:** January 29, 1977
- **O.J. Simpson:** February 25, 1978
- **Bill Russell:** November 3, 1979
- **John Madden:** January 30, 1982
- **Bob Uecker:** October 13, 1984
- **Alex Karras:** February 2, 1985
- **Hulk Hogan, Mr. T:** March 30, 1985
- **Howard Cosell:** April 13, 1985
- **Billy Martin:** May 24, 1986
- **Joe Montana, Walter Payton:** January 24, 1987
- **Wayne Gretzky:** May 13, 1989
- **Chris Evert:** November 11, 1989
- **George Steinbrenner:** October 20, 1990
- **Michael Jordan:** September 28, 1991
- **Charles Barkley:** September 25, 1993
- **Nancy Kerrigan:** March 12, 1994
- **George Foreman:** December 17, 1994
- **Deion Sanders:** February 18, 1995
- **The Rock:** March, 18, 2000; April 13, 2002
- **Derek Jeter:** December 1, 2001
- **Jonny Moseley:** March 2, 2002
- **Jeff Gordon:** January 11, 2003
- **Andy Roddick:** November 8, 2003
- **Tom Brady:** April 16, 2005
- **Lance Armstrong:** October 29, 2005
- **Peyton Manning:** March 24, 2007
- **LeBron James:** September 27, 2007
- **Michael Phelps:** September 13, 2008

Screen Gems

THE TOP-GROSSING SPORTS MOVIES OF ALL TIME

MOVIE	DOMESTIC REVENUE
1) *The Waterboy* (1998)	$161,491,646
2) *The Longest Yard* (2005)	$158,119,460
3) *Jerry Maguire* (1996)	$153,952,592
4) *Talladega Nights: The Ballad of Ricky Bobby* (2006)	$148,213,375
5) *Rocky IV* (1985)	$127,873,716
6) *Rocky III* (1982)	$125,049,125
7) *Seabiscuit* (2003)	$120,277,854
8) *Rocky* (1976)	$117,235,147
9) *Remember the Titans* (2000)	$115,654,751
10) *The Karate Kid, Part II* (1986)	$115,103,979
11) *Dodgeball: A True Underdog Story* (2004)	$114,326,736
12) *A League of Their Own* (1992)	$107,928,762
13) *Million Dollar Baby* (2004)	$100,492,203
14) *The Karate Kid* (1984)	$90,815,558
15) *Space Jam* (1996)	$90,418,342
16) *Rocky II* (1979)	$85,182,160
17) *Days of Thunder* (1990)	$82,670,733
18) *Nacho Libre* (2006)	$80,197,993
19) *White Men Can't Jump* (1992)	$76,253,806
20) *The Rookie* (2002)	$75,600,072

Slim Pickings

Inaugural Franchise Picks Inducted Into Canton

Only four NFL teams have selected a future Hall of Famer with the first pick in franchise history. These four:

YEAR	TEAM	PLAYER	INDUCTED
1936	Chicago Bears	Joe Stydahar	1967
1950	San Francisco 49ers	Leo Nomellini	1969
1961	Dallas Cowboys	Bob Lilly	1980
1976	Tampa Bay Buccaneers	Lee Roy Selmon	1995

Small World

The First Little League World Series Bracket

When the Little League World Series began in 1947, it was hardly a global competition. Of the 12 participating teams, 11 were from Pennsylvania—five from Williamsport itself—with the 12th from New Jersey. The Maynard League Midgets were the winners. Here are the original teams, in the original pairings:

GAME 1
Williamsport Little League (Williamsport, Pennsylvania) vs. Williamsport Sunday School League (Williamsport)

GAME 2
Lincoln League (Williamsport) vs. Montoursville (Montoursville, Pennsylvania)

GAME 3
Brandon League (Williamsport) vs. Montgomery (Montgomery, Pennsylvania)

GAME 4
Jersey Shore (Jersey Shore, Pennsylvania) vs. Maynard League (Williamsport)

GAME 5
Hammonton (Hammonton, New Jersey) vs. Milton Midget League (Milton, Pennsylvania)

GAME 6
Perry County Little League (Perry County, Pennsylvania) vs. Lock Haven (Lock Haven, Pennsylvania)

Smooth Talk

The Credo Of Curling

Yes, it has one. Here is the official "Spirit of Curling," from the people who should officially know: the World Curling Federation.

THE SPIRIT OF CURLING

Curling is a game of skill and of traditions. A shot well executed is a delight to see and so, too, it is a fine thing to observe the time-honoured traditions of curling being applied in the true spirit of the game. Curlers play to win but never to humble their opponents. A true curler would prefer to lose rather than win unfairly. A good curler never attempts to distract an opponent or otherwise prevent him from playing his best. No curler ever deliberately breaks a rule of the game or any of its traditions. But, if he should do so inadvertently and be aware of it, he is the first to divulge the breach. While the main object of the game of curling is to determine the relative skill of the players, the spirit of the game demands good sportsmanship, kindly feeling, and honourable conduct. This spirit should influence both the interpretation and application of the rules of the game and also the conduct of all.

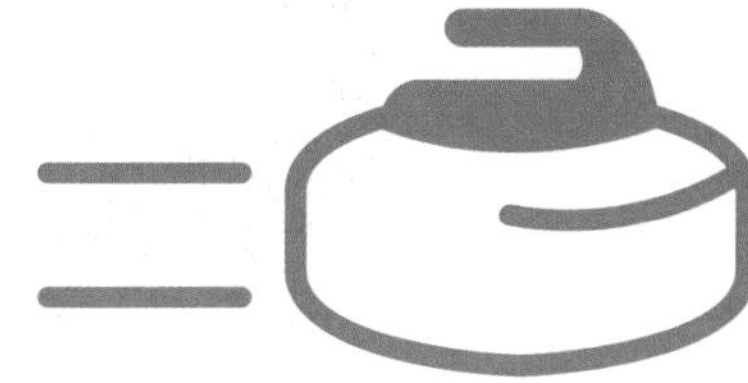

A
B
C
D
E
F
G
H
I
J
K
L
M
N
O
P
Q
R
S
T
U
V
W
X
Y
Z

Soccer Originals

The Founding Teams Of Major League Soccer

The United States hosted soccer's 1994 World Cup, but only after the sport's international governing body, FIFA, secured a promise from the U.S. Soccer Federation that the country would first create a competitive professional league. The league was formed in 1993, but the first season didn't begin until three years later. Here are the 10 original teams of MLS:

EASTERN DIVISION

Columbus Crew
D.C. United
New York/New Jersey MetroStars[1]
New England Revolution
Tampa Bay Mutiny

WESTERN DIVISION

Colorado Rapids
Dallas Burn[2]
Kansas City Wiz[3]
Los Angeles Galaxy
San Jose Clash[4]

Notes: [1]Now New York Red Bulls; [2]Now FC Dallas; [3]Now Wizards; [4]Now Houston Dynamo.

Spell Checks

Sports Curses Through The Years

CURSE OF THE BAMBINO

Boston Red Sox owner Harry Frazee sold Babe Ruth to the New York Yankees in 1920, and it plummeted the team into 84 years of bad luck. In 2004, the Red Sox finally won the World Series and the curse was lifted.

CURSE OF THE BILLY GOAT

In 1945, William Sianis showed up at Wrigley Field for Game 4 of the World Series. He had two tickets—for himself and for his pet goat, Sonovia. The pair was actually allowed in, but Chicago Cubs owner Phillip Wrigley had them kicked out, reportedly because of the odor (presumably the goat's). An irate Sianis placed a curse on the Cubs that they'd never play in a World Series again. And they haven't.

CURSE OF CHIEF NOC-A-HOMA

Back in the day, the Atlanta Braves had a Native American cheerleader who worked out of a tepee in the bleachers. On July 29, 1982, team owner Ted Turner replaced the tepee with more seats, and Atlanta won just two of its next 21 games. When the chief was reinstated later that summer, the team rallied to win the division. The chief was sent packing for good after the 1985 season, and although the Braves won 14 division titles, they've been World Series champs just once.

CURSE OF THE DISPLACED GYPSIES

The Middlesbrough (England) soccer squad has been playing since 1876 and has yet to win the English Premier League's prestigious FA cup. Blame the stadium. When Ayresome Park was built in 1903, some gypsies were evicted from the construction site. They responded, legend has it, by cursing the team. Middlesbrough relocated in 1995 to Riverside Stadium. They won the Carling Cup in 2004, but still no FA Cup.

CURSE OF LORD STANLEY'S ASHTRAY

In 1940, soon after the New York Rangers won the Stanley Cup for the third time, the team's owners paid off the mortgage on Madison Square Garden. In celebration, they burned the mortgage papers in the Cup itself. Apparently, Lord Stanley didn't appreciate the diss. The Rangers went 54 years before winning the Cup again in 1994.

CURSE OF ROCKY COLAVITO

Rocky Colavito was without question the most popular player on the 1959 Cleveland Indians. But at season's end, the team traded him to the Detroit Tigers for Harvey Kuenn, the American League batting champ. Kuenn couldn't make the Indians fans forget about Colavito, and although the Tribe reacquired him in 1965, they still spent much of the 1970s and 80s as uncompetitive also-rans and have only been to the World Series twice since.

CURSE OF WILLIAM PENN

In 1894, the founder of Pennsylvania was honored with a 37-foot statue atop Philadelphia's city hall. For the next 90 years, an informal agreement among city leaders kept all additions to the skyline below the statue. But in 1987, One Liberty Place was completed, reaching 397 feet above city hall. Since then, no local team has won a pro sports title.

KENTUCKY FRIED CURSE

After Hanshin's Tigers won the 1985 Japan Series, fans convinced player lookalikes to jump into a local river. For first baseman Randy Bass, a bearded white American, they dunked a statue of Colonel Sanders from a nearby KFC. The statue was lost. It's still MIA; so, too, the Tigers from the Japan Series' winner circle.

MADDEN COVER CURSE

In 2000, NFL players started to grace the cover of what has become the most popular video football game. Of the first seven players featured—Eddie George, Daunte Culpepper, Marshall Faulk, Michael Vick, Ray Lewis, Donovan McNabb, Shaun Alexander—six were either injured or had a noticeable decrease in productivity in the season that followed their cover billing. Only Lewis survived the curse's wrath.

SPORTS ILLUSTRATED COVER JINX

The story: If an athlete appears on the SI cover, bad things will happen. The truth: the two athletes who have appeared on the cover the most? Michael Jordan and Muhammad Ali.

A
B
C
D
E
F
G
H
I
J
K
L
M
N
O
P
Q
R
S
T
U
V
W
X
Y
Z

Springfield Standouts

Inaugural Inductees Into The Basketball Hall Of Fame

The Naismith Memorial Basketball Hall of Fame in Springfield, Massachusetts, inducted its first class in 1959. Here are the original inductees:

The first team (the 18 International YMCA Training School students in James Naismith's gym class who first played the game: Lyman W. Archibald, Franklin Everets Barnes, Wilbert Franklin Carey, William Richmond Chase, William Henry Davis, George Edward Day, Benjamin Snell French, Henry Gelan, Ernest Gotthold Hildner, Genzabaro Sadakni Ishikawa, Raymond Pimlott Kaighn, Eugene Samuel Libby, Finlay Grant MacDonald, Frank Mahan, Thomas Duncan Patton, Edwin Pakenham Ruggles, John George Thompson, George Radford Weller)

The Original Celtics (Dave Banks, Pete Barry, John Beckman, Bennie Borgmann, Eddie Burke, Dutch Dehnert, Swede Grimstead, George "Horse" Haggerty, Nat Holman, Joe Lapchick, Chris Leonard, Ernie Reich, Elmer Ripley, Mike Smolick, Joe Trippe, George Whitty)

Forrest Clare "Phog" Allen: coach; Baker University, Haskell Institute, Warrensburg Teachers College, University of Kansas (1908-09; 1920-56)

Henry Clifford Carlson: coach; University of Pittsburgh (1922-58)

Luther Gulick: builder; told James Naismith to create an indoor game; chairman of the Basketball Rules Organization

Edward J. Hickox: builder; laid groundwork for building Hall of Fame, executive secretary of Hall (1949-63)

Charles D. Hyatt: player; University of Pittsburgh (1926-30)

Matthew P. Kennedy: referee (1924-56)

Angelo Luisetti: player; Stanford University, popularized running one-handed shot (1934-38)

Walter E. Meanwell: coach; University of Wisconsin, University of Missouri (1911-34)

George L. Mikan: player; Chicago Gears, Minneapolis Lakers (1946-56)

Ralph Morgan: co-founder; College Basketball Rules Committee

James Naismith: builder; inventor of basketball

Harold G. Olsen: builder; led efforts to create NCAA postseason national playoffs

John J. Schommer: player; University of Chicago (1906-09)

Amos Alonzo Stagg: builder; inventor of five-man basketball

Oswald Tower: builder; editor of *Official Basketball Guide* (1915-59)

D'oH!

Springfield Walk-Ons

Sports Cameos On The Simpsons

"Homer Defined" (Aired October 17, 1991): Magic Johnson, Chick Hearn

"Homer at the Bat" (February 20, 1992): Wade Boggs, Jose Canseco, Roger Clemens, Ken Griffey Jr., Don Mattingly, Steve Sax, Mike Scioscia, Ozzie Smith, Darryl Strawberry

"Brother, Can You Spare Two Dimes" (August 27, 1992): Joe Frazier

"$pringfield (Or, How I Learned to Stop Worrying and Love Legalized Gambling)" (December 16, 1993): Gerry Cooney

"Homie the Clown" (February 12, 1995): Johnny Unitas

"Scenes From the Class Struggle in Springfield" (February 4, 1996): Tom Kite

"The Homer They Fall" (November 10, 1996): Michael Buffer

"Bart Star" (November, 9, 1997): Joe Namath, Roy Firestone

"Sunday, Cruddy Sunday" (January 31, 1999): Troy Aikman, Rosey Grier, John Madden, Dan Marino, Pat Summerall

"The Old Man and the 'C' Student" (April 25, 1999): Jack La Lanne

"Brother's Little Helper" (October 3, 1999): Mark McGwire

"Tennis the Menace" (February 11, 2001): Andre Agassi, Pete Sampras, Venus Williams, Serena Williams

"Helter Shelter" (December 1, 2002): Larry Holmes

"Pray Anything" (February 9, 2003): Lisa Leslie

"Barting Over" (February 16, 2003): Tony Hawk

"Treehouse of Horror XIV" (November 2, 2003): Oscar De La Hoya

"Homer and Ned's Hail Mary Pass" (February 6, 2005): Tom Brady, LeBronJames, Yao Ming, Warren Sapp, Michelle Kwan

"Treehouse of Horror XVI" (November 6, 2005): Terry Bradshaw, Dennis Rodman

"Regarding Margie" (May 7, 2006): Sal Bando, Gene Tenace

"Kill Gil (Volumes I and II)" (December 17, 2006): Elvis Stojko

Table

T

Two

Table Talk

Texas Hold 'Em Hole Card Nicknames

A–A: Pocket Rockets; Bullets; Sharp Tops
K–K: Cowboys; King Kong
Q–Q: Ladies; Siegfried & Roy
J–J: Fishhooks; Jaybirds; Dy-No-Mite!
10–10: Dimes; Tension
9–9: Barbara Feldon; Popeye's; Luftballoons
8–8: Snowmen; Piano Keys; Little Olds
7–7: Walking Sticks; Hockey Sticks
6–6: Route 66; Cherries
5–5: Speed Limit; Nickels
4–4: Magnum; Sailboats
3–3: Crabs; Treys
2–2: Ducks; Pocket Swans
A–K: Big Slick, Santa Barbara[1]; Anna Kournikova
A–Q: Big Chick; Little Slick
A–J: Ajax; Jackass; Apple Jacks
A–10: Bookends
A–9: Chris Ferguson[2]
A–8: Dead Man's Hand
A–5: High Five
A–4: Transvestite
A–3: Ash Tray; Baskin Robbins
A–2: Hunting Season
K–Q (s)[3]**:** Royal Couple
K–Q: Mixed Marriage
K–J (s): Kojak; King John
K–9: Canine; Fido
K–3: King Crab
Q–J: Oedipus; Maverick[4]
Q–10: Quint; Varkonyi[5]
Q–9: Quinine
Q–7: Computer Hand[6]
Q–4: Whores and Fours
Q–3: San Francisco Busboy
J–7: Jack Daniels
J–5: Jackson Five; Motown
J–4: Flat Tires[7]
10–9: Countdown
10–4: Convoy; Good Buddy; Roger That
10–2: Doyle Brunson, Texas Dolly[8]
9–8: Oldsmobile
6–9: Dinner for Two; Yin Yang
9–5: Dolly Parton; Hard-Working Man
9–2: Montana Banana[9]
8–4: Orwell
7–10: Split
7–8: RPM
7–6: Union Oil; Trombones
7–2: Beer Hand
5–10: Five & Dime; Woolworth's
5–7: Heinz; Chevy
4–K: Fork
4–9: Joe Montana Banana; San Francisco
4–7: AK-47; Machine Gun
4–5: Colt 45; Jesse James
3–9: Jack Benny
3–8: Raquel Welch
3–4: Waltz
2–9: Golf Bag
2–5: Quarter; Two Bits
2–4: Lumberman's Hand
2–3: Mississippi Slick[10]

Notes: [1]Reference to a long-ago oil slick off the coast of southern California; [2]Ferguson's winning hand in the 2000 World Series of Poker; [3](s) denotes suited cards; [4]Reference to TV's *Maverick,* the theme song of which included the line "Livin' on jacks and queens"; [5]Robert Varkonyi won the 2002 WSOP with this hand; [6]Thought to be the average starting hand or break even hand; [7]What's a jack for? [8]Brunson, a.k.a. Texas Dolly, won two WSOP titles with this hand; [9]Number of the proposition that legalized poker in Montana; [10]Opposite of Big Slick.

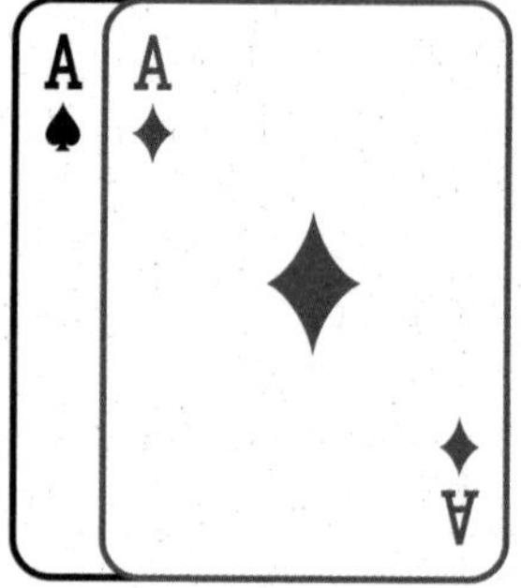

Talking Points

Some Rules Of Heckling

Pete Martin Adelis was a Philadelphia legend of sorts, the fanatic before the Phanatic. His presence at Philadelphia A's games and persistent badgering of opposing players eventually earned him the nickname The Iron Lung of Shibe Park and a feature in The Sporting News, *published on September 8, 1948. On the same page, the magazine published seven rules of heckling, which are as useful today as they were then.*

1. No profanity.
2. Nothing purely personal.
3. Keep pouring it on.
4. Know your players.
5. Don't be shouted down.
6. Take it as well as give it.
7. Give the old-timer a chance. He was a rookie once.

Tally Tallies

Points Needed To Win Various Games

Badminton: 15
Court Tennis (U.S.): 4*
Darts: 0 (counting down from 501)
Handball (U.S.): 21 (11 for tiebreakers)
Jai Alai (international): 10-40 (depending on country)
Jai Alai (U.S.): 7 or9
Paddle Ball (1-wall): 11, 15, 21, and 25* (in succession)
Paddle Ball (4-wall): 21 (11 for tiebreakers)
Racquetball: 15 (11 for tiebreakers)
Shuffleboard: 50, 75, or 100
Squash: 9 (9 or 10 for tiebreakers, at server's discretion)
Table Tennis: 11*
Volleyball: 25* (15 for tiebreakers)

Note: *Must win by 2.

A B C D E F G H I J K L M N O P Q R S T U V W X Y Z

Ten Pack

The Events Of The Olympic Decathlon

- 100-meter dash
- Long jump
- Shot put
- High jump
- 400-meter race
- 110-meter hurdles
- Discus throw
- Pole vault
- Javelin throw
- 1,500-meter race

Tendered Offers

The Largest Trades In Sports History

MLB

17 players, two teams

November 17–December 1, 1954

New York Yankees traded Gene Woodling, Harry Byrd, Jim McDonald, Hal Smith, Gus Triandos, Willie Miranda, Bill Miller, Kal Segrist, Don Leppert, and Ted Del Guercio to Baltimore Orioles for Don Larsen, Bob Turley, Billy Hunter, Mike Blyzka, Darrell Johnson, Jim Fridley, and Dick Kryhoski.

NFL

18 players, two teams

October 12, 1989

Dallas Cowboys traded Herschel Walker and four future draft picks to Minnesota Vikings for Jesse Solomon, Issiac Holt, Darrin Nelson, David Howard, Alex Stewart, and eight future draft picks.

NBA

15 players, five teams

August 2, 2005

Miami Heat traded Qyntel Woods, the draft rights to Albert Miralles and two second-round picks to Boston Celtics, Eddie Jones to Memphis Grizzlies, and Rasual Butler to New Orleans Hornets; Celtics traded Antoine Walker to Heat; Grizzlies traded Jason Williams, Andre Emmett, and James Posey to Heat, Greg Ostertag to Utah Jazz; Jazz trade Raul Lopez to Grizzlies, Kirk Snyder to Hornets, and Curtis Borchardt to Celtics; Hornets traded draft rights to Roberto Duenas to Heat.

NHL

10 players, two teams

January 2, 1992

Calgary Flames traded Doug Gilmour, Jamie Macoun, Ric Nattress, Rick Wamsley, and Kent Manderville to Toronto Maple Leafs for Gary Leeman, Michel Petit, Jeff Reese, Craig Berube, and Alexander Godynyuk.

Terrible Tribe

The Roster Of *Major League*'s Cleveland Indians

Released in 1989, the movie Major League *tells the story of the downtrodden Indians' attempt to reclaim baseball legitimacy. The batting order of the fictional team wasn't constant, and, in fact, some roles were so small players weren't even given full names. Still, determining manager Lou Brown's assignments is possible, although even the movie's writers clearly struggled: At one point, the Tribe's shortstop is called Molina by announcer Harry Doyle (Bob Uecker), although his uniform reads Reyna.*

- Willie Hayes, CF
- Jake Taylor, C
- Roger Dorn, 3B
- Pedro Cerrano, RF
- Metcalf, 1B
- Larson, 2B
- Reyna, SS
- Tomlinson, LF
- Eddie Harris, SP
- Rick Vaughn, RP

Today's Lineup

The Roster In Abbott & Costello's "Who's On First?" Routine

Comedians Bud Abbott and Lou Costello are the only people represented in the Baseball Hall of Fame who never played, managed, umped, or were involved with a team in any way. They got there on the merits of their classic "Who's on First?" routine, which was originally performed in 1938 on radio and described the roster of a fictional team. The one missing position? Right field.

- C Today
- 1B Who
- 2B What
- 3B I Don't Know
- SS I Don't Give a Darn
- LF Why
- CF Because
- P Tomorrow

A B C D E F G H I J K L M N O P Q R S T U V W X Y Z

A B C D E F G H I J K L M N O P Q R S T U V W X Y Z

Tools Of The Trade

Sporting Implements

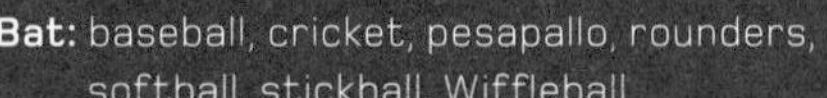

Bat: baseball, cricket, pesapallo, rounders, softball, stickball, Wiffleball
Bow: archery
Broom: broomball, curling
Caman: shinty
Cesta: jai alai
Club: golf
Crosse: lacrosse
Cue: billiards, bumper pool, shuffleboard, snooker
Épée: fencing
Foil: fencing
Hurley: camogie, hurling
Lance: jousting
Mallet: bicycle polo, croquet, polo
Paddle: kadima, pickleball, platform paddle tennis, table tennis
Paleta: Basque pelota
Pole: pole vault, skiing
Racket: tennis
Racquet: racquetball, squash
Rod: fishing
Sabre: fencing
Stick: bandy, field hockey, floorball, ice hockey, in-line hockey, ringette, street hockey

Totemic Tournaments

Major Championships In Golf And Tennis

Through the years, the major tournaments that comprise the quartet of most-coveted titles in golf have changed. Originally, the majors were the U.S. and British amateur and Open championships, at a time when the best golfers in the world weren't professionals and could compete in all four. These days, all the majors in both golf and tennis are pro events. Here they are:

PROFESSIONAL GOLF (MEN)

The Masters
British Open
U.S. Open
PGA Championship

PROFESSIONAL GOLF (WOMEN)

U.S. Women's Open
Kraft Nabisco Championship
Women's British Open
LPGA Championship

TENNIS

Australian Open
French Open
Wimbledon
U.S. Open

Note: Previous women's majors include the Western Open, Titleholders Championship, and du Maurier Classic.

Tournament Topplers

March Madness 12-seeds That Upset 5-seeds

It's almost an office pool lock: since the NCAA men's basketball tourney expanded to 64 teams in 1985 (and to 65 in 2001), 29 teams seeded 12th have defeated their first-round 5th-seed rivals.

1985 University of Kentucky over University of Washington

1986 DePaul University over University of Virginia

1987 University of Wyoming over University of Virginia

1989 DePaul University over University of Memphis

1990 Ball State University over Oregon State University; University of Dayton over University of Illinois

1991 Eastern Michigan University over Mississippi State University

1992 New Mexico State University over DePaul University

1993 George Washington University over University of New Mexico

1994 University of Wisconsin-Green Bay over University of California; University of Tulsa over UCLA

1995 Miami University (Ohio) over University of Arizona

1996 Drexel University over University of Memphis; University of Arkansas over Penn State University

1997 College of Charleston over University of Maryland

1998 Florida State University over Texas Christian University

1999 Southwest Missouri State University[1] over University of Wisconsin; University of Detroit over UCLA

2001 Gonzaga University over University of Virginia; Utah State University over Ohio State University

2002 University of Missouri over University of Miami; University of Tulsa over Marquette University; Creighton University over University of Florida

2003 Butler University over Mississippi State University

2004 Pacific University over Providence College; Manhattan College over University of Florida

2005 University of Wisconsin-Milwaukee over University of Alabama

2006 Texas A&M University over Syracuse University; University of Montana over University of Nevada

2008 Western Kentucky over Drake University; Villanova University over University of Clemson

Note: [1]Now Missouri State University.

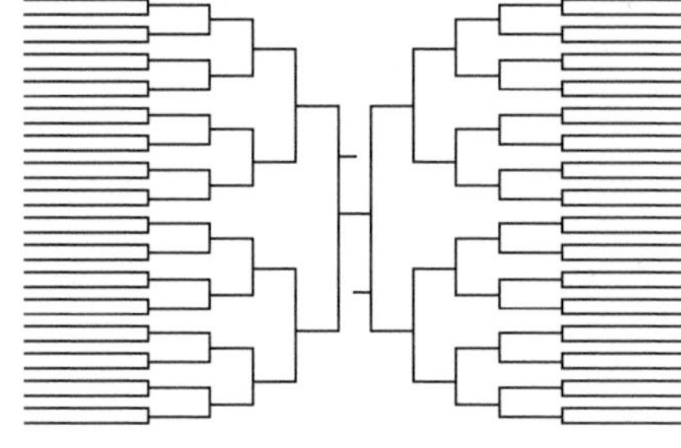

A
B
C
D
E
F
G
H
I
J
K
L
M
N
O
P
Q
R
S
T
U
V
W
X
Y
Z

Traveling Batsmen

International Firsts In Professional Baseball

Baseball may be America's national pastime, but an awful lot of people have come from other lands to play it professionally. Here are the first players to make it to the bigs from their country:

Afghanistan: Jeff Bronkey (2003; Texas Rangers)

American Samoa: Tony Solaita (1968; New York Yankees)

Aruba: Gene Kingsale (1996; Baltimore Orioles)

Australia: Joe Quinn (1884; St. Louis Maroons)

Austria: Kurt Krieger (1949; St. Louis Cardinals)

Austria-Hungary: Frank Rooney (1914; Indianapolis Hoosiers)

Bahamas: Andre Rodgers (1957; New York Giants)

Belgium: Brian Lesher (1996; Oakland Athletics)

Belize: Chito Martinez (1991; Baltimore Orioles)

Canada: Bill Phillips (1879; Cleveland Blues)

Canal Zone: Pat Scantlebury (1956; Cincinnati Reds)

China: Harry Kingman (1914; New York Yankees)

Colombia: Luis Castro (1902; Philadelphia Athletics)

Cuba: Rafael Almeida, Armando Marsans (1911; Cincinnati Reds)

Curaçao: Hensley Meulens (1989; New York Yankees)

Czechoslovakia: Amos Cross (1885; Louisville Colonels)

Denmark: Olaf Henriksen (1911; Boston Red Sox)

Dominican Republic: Ozzie Virgil (1956; New York Giants)

Finland: John Michaelson (1921; Chicago White Sox)

France: Joe Woerlin (1895; Washington Senators)

Germany: Charlie Getzein (1884; Detroit Wolverines)

Greece: Al Campanis (1943; Brooklyn Dodgers)

Guam: John Hattig (2006; Toronto Blue Jays)

Honduras: Gerald Young (1987; Houston Astros)

Indonesia: Tom Mastny (2006; Cleveland Indians)

Italy: Julio Bonetti (1937; St. Louis Browns)

Jamaica: Chili Davis (1981; San Francisco Giants)

Japan: Masanori Murakami (1964; San Francisco Giants)

Mexico: Mel Almada (1933; Boston Red Sox)

Netherlands: John Houseman (1894; Chicago Colts)

Nicaragua: Dennis Martinez (1976; Baltimore Orioles)

Norway: John Anderson (1894; Brooklyn Bridegrooms)

Panama: Humberto Robinson (1955; Milwaukee Braves)

Philippines: Bobby Chouinard (1996; Oakland Athletics)

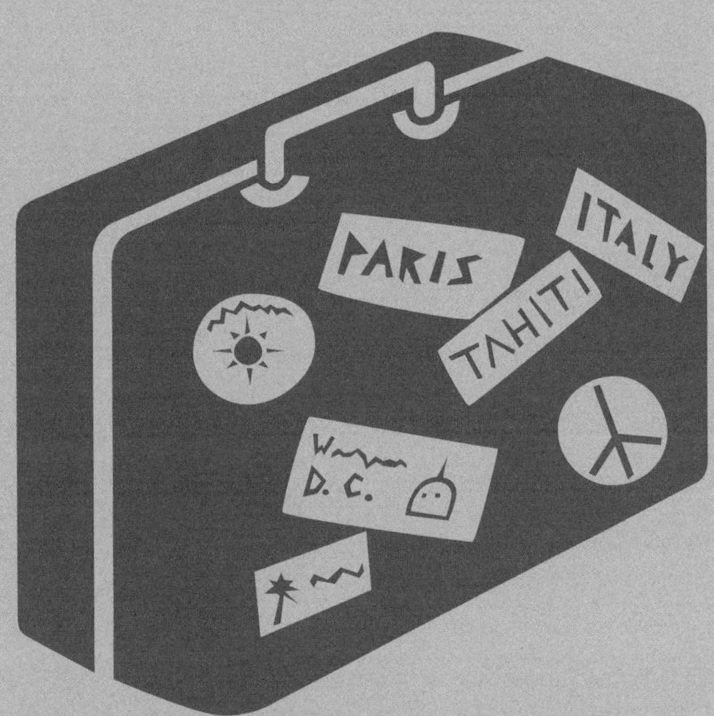

Poland: Henry Peploski (1929; Boston Braves)

Puerto Rico: Hiram Bithorn (1942; Chicago Cubs)

Russia: Jake Gettman (1897; Washington Senators)

Scotland: Jim McCormick (1878; Indianapolis Browns)

Singapore: Robin Jennings (1996; Chicago Cubs)

South Korea: Chan Ho Park (1994; Los Angeles Dodgers)

South Vietnam: Danny Graves (1996; Cleveland Indians)

Spain: Al Cabrera (1913; St. Louis Cardinals)

Sweden: Charlie Hallstrom (1885; Providence Grays)

Switzerland: Otto Hess (1902; Cleveland Indians)

Taiwan: Chin-Feng Chen (2002; Los Angeles Dodgers)

USSR: Victor Cole (1992; Pittsburgh Pirates)

Venezuela: Alex Carrasquel (1939; Washington Senators)

Virgin Islands: Joe Christopher (1959; Pittsburgh Pirates)

Wales: Ted Lewis (1896; Boston Beaneaters)

West Germany: Rob Belloir (1975; Atlanta Braves)

A B C D E F G H I J K L M N O P Q R S T U V W X Y Z

A B C D E F G H I J K L M N O P Q R S T U V W X Y Z

Two-fers

CURRENT TEAM NAMES USED MORE THAN ONCE IN PRO U.S. SPORTS

TEAM NAME	FRANCHISES
Cardinals	Arizona (NFL), St. Louis (MLB)
Giants	New York (NFL), San Francisco (MLB)
Kings	Los Angeles (NHL), Sacramento (NBA)
Panthers	Carolina (NFL), Florida (NHL)
Predators	Nashville (NHL), Orlando (AFL)
Rangers	New York (NHL), Texas (MLB)
Sun(s)	Connecticut (WNBA), Phoenix (NBA)
Wizards	Kansas City (MLS), Washington (NBA)

Two-Point Conversions

DARRYL DAWKINS' DUNK NAMES

Drafted by the Philadelphia 76ers in 1975 out of Maynard Evans High School in Orlando, Florida, Darryl Dawkins was more than just a trailblazer in the prep-to-pro jump. Nicknamed Chocolate Thunder, Dawkins had a 14-year NBA career that was filled with flamboyant and aggressive play (his 386 personal fouls in 1983-84 are still a record). The self-proclaimed "alien from Lovetron" was most famous for naming his thunderous dunks, often borrowing Parliament Funkadelic lingo. Here are some of his more memorable dunk names:

Heart Stopper

Get Out the Wayin', Back-door Swayin', Game-Delayin', If You Ain't Groovin' You Best Get Movin' Dunk

Yo' Mama

In Your Face Disgrace

Cover Yo' Damn Head

The Turbo Sexphonic Delight

Go-rilla Dunk

Left-Handed Spine Chiller Supreme

Hammer of Thor

Candy Slam

Earthquaker Shaker

Dunk You Very Much

Look Out Below

Rim Wrecker

Greyhound Bus

Chocolate Thunder-Flying, Robinzine-Crying, Teeth-Shaking, Glass-Breaking, Rump-Roasting, Bun-Toasting, Wham, Bam, Glass Breaker I Am Jam

Two Timers, Part One

PLAYERS WHO APPEARED IN THE LITTLE LEAGUE AND MLB WORLD SERIES

Boog Powell: Lakeland, Florida, 1954; Baltimore Orioles, 1966
Jim Barbieri: Schenectady, New York, 1955; Los Angeles Dodgers, 1966
Rick Wise: Portland, Oregon, 1958; Boston Red Sox, 1975
Carney Lansford: Santa Clara, California, 1969; Oakland A's, 1988 and 1990
Ed Vosberg: Tucson, Arizona, 1973; Florida Marlins, 1997
Charlie Hayes: Hattiesburg, Mississippi, 1977; New York Yankees, 1996
Derek Bell: Tampa, Florida, 1980 and 1981; Toronto Blue Jays, 1992
Gary Sheffield: Tampa, Florida, 1980; Florida Marlins, 1997
Jason Varitek: Altamonte Springs, Florida, 1984; Boston Red Sox, 2004
Jason Marquis: Staten Island, New York, 1991; St. Louis Cardinals, 2004

Two Timers, Part Two

SUMMER AND WINTER OLYMPIC MEDALISTS

Only four athletes have won medals in both the Winter and Summer Games:

Eddie Eagan (U.S.): light heavyweight boxing, gold (1920); four-man bobsled, gold (1932)
Jacob Tullin Thams (Norway): ski jumping, gold (1924); eight-meter yachting, silver (1936)
Christa Luding-Rothenburger (East Germany): 500-meter speed skating, gold (1984) and 1,000-meter, gold (1988), 500-meter, silver (1988) and 500-meter, bronze (1992); match sprint cycling, silver (1988)[1]
Clara Hughes (Canada): individual road race cycling bronze and individual time trial cycling, bronze (1996); 5,000m speed skating, bronze (2002)

Note: [1]Only athlete to win medals in both Games in same year.

Unforgettable

U

Unrealized

A B C D E F G H I J K L M N O P Q R S T U V W X Y Z

Unforgettable Lines

The Best Sports Movie Quotes

In 2005, ESPN.com named the 100 best sports movie quotes. Here are the top 20:

20. "What about Brett Fav-ruh?" —*There's Something About Mary*

19. "I'm gonna make Gretzky's head bleed for SuperFan99 over here."—*Swingers*

18. "Jocks only think about sports. Nerds only think about sex." —*Revenge of the Nerds*

17. "Mike Eruzione! Winthrop, Massachusetts! I play for the United States of America!"—*Miracle*

16. "Well, Nuke's scared because his eyelids are jammed and his old man's here. We need a live ... is it a live rooster? We need a live rooster to take the curse off Jose's glove, and nobody seems to know what to get Millie or Jimmy for their wedding present."—*Bull Durham*

15. "Fat man, you shoot a great game of pool."—*The Hustler*

14. "There's one thing I want you to do for me. Win. Win!"—*Rocky II*

13. "Pick me out a winner, Bobby." —*The Natural*

12. "Noonan!"—*Caddyshack*

11. "If you build it, he will come." —*Field of Dreams*

10. "You're gonna eat lightning, and you're gonna crap thunder!"—*Rocky*

9. "Oh, there they go. There they go. Every time I start talkin' 'bout boxing, a white man got to pull Rocky Marciano out their ass. That's their one, that's their one. Rocky Marciano! Rocky Marciano!" —*Coming to America*

8. "You guys. You lollygag the ball around the infield. You lollygag your way down to first. You lollygag in and out of the dugout. You know what that makes you?" —*Bull Durham*

7. "There's no crying in baseball!" —*A League of Their Own*

6. "Sweep the leg."—*The Karate Kid*

5. "I'm out there busting my buns every night. Tell your old man to drag Walton and Lanier up and down the court for 48 minutes."—*Airplane!*

4. "Juuuust a bit outside!"—*Major League*

3. "Show me the money!"—*Jerry Maguire*

2. "You don't understand. I coulda had class. I coulda been a contender. I coulda been somebody, instead of a bum, which is what I am. Let's face it. It was you, Charley."—*On The Waterfront*

1. "Yo, Adrian!"—*Rocky*

United Skates

International Firsts In The NHL

Harry Mummery of the Toronto Arenas was the first American to play in the National Hockey League, starting in 1917. Here are the first NHLers from other countries:

Austria Reinhard Divis (debut season 2001-02; St. Louis Blues)

Belarus Ruslan Salei (1996-97; Anaheim Mighty Ducks)

Belgium Jan Benda (1997-98; Washington Capitals)

Brazil Mike Greenlay (1989-90; Edmonton Oilers)

Czechoslovakia Stan Mikita (1958-59; Chicago Blackhawks)

Denmark Poul Popiel (1965-66; Boston Bruins)

Finland Matti Hagman (1976-77; Boston Bruins)

France Andre Peloffy (1974-75; Washington Capitals)

Germany Uwe Krupp (1986-87; Buffalo Sabres)

Haiti Claude Vilgrain (1987-88; Vancouver Canucks)

Ireland Jack Riley (1932-33; Detroit Red Wings)

Italy Nelson Debenedet (1973-74; Detroit Red Wings)

Jamaica Graeme Townshend (1989-90; Boston Bruins)

Kazakhstan Evgeni Nabokov (1999-2000; San Jose Sharks)

Korea Jim Paek (1990-91; Pittsburgh Penguins)

Latvia Helmut Balderis (1989-90; Minnesota North Stars)

Lebanon Ed Hatoum (1968-69; Detroit Red Wings)

Nigeria Rumun Ndur (1996-97; Buffalo Sabres)

Norway Bjorn Skaare (1978-79; Detroit Red Wings)

Paraguay Willi Plett (1975-76; Atlanta Flames)

Poland John Miszuk (1963-64; Detroit Red Wings)

Russia Johnny Gottselig (1928-29; Chicago Blackhawks)

South Africa Olaf Kolzig (1989-90; Washington Capitals)

Sweden Ulf Sterner (1964-65; New York Rangers)

Switzerland Mark Hardy (1979-80; Los Angeles Kings)

Tanzania Chris Nielsen (2000-01; Columbus Blue Jackets)

Venezuela Rick Chartraw (1974-75; Montreal Canadiens)

Yugoslavia Stan Smrke (1956-57; Montreal Canadiens)

Universe Expanders

Other "World Series"

- Adventure Racing World Series
- Air Race World Series
- Caribbean World Series
- Champ Car World Series
- Junior College World Series
- Little League World Series
- Little League Softball World Series
- NAIA Baseball World Series
- NCAA College World Series
- Wakeboarding World Series
- Women's College World Series
- Women's World Series
- World Series of Barbecue
- World Series of Birding
- World Series of Blackjack
- World Series of Golf
- World Series of Martial Arts
- World Series of Poker

Unknown Aliases

Given Names of Sports Figures

Kareem Abdul-Jabbar: Ferdinand Lewis Alcindor Jr.
Karim Abdul Jabbar: Sharmon Shah
Muhammad Ali: Cassius Marcellus Clay Jr.
Red Auerbach: Arnold Auerbach
Dusty Baker: Johnnie B. Baker Jr.
Cool Papa Bell: James Thomas Bell
Yogi Berra: Lawrence Peter Berra
Rocky Bleier: Robert Bleier
Muggsy Bogues: Tyrone Curtis Bogues
Swin Cash: Swintayla Marie Cash
Speedy Claxton: Craig Claxton
Coco Crisp: Covelli Loyce Crisp
Daffy Dean: Paul Dee Dean
Dizzy Dean: Jay Hanna Dean
Bucky Dent: Russell Earl O'Dey
Babe Didrikson: Mildred Ella Didrikson
Boomer Esiason: Norman Julius Esiason
Cotton Fitzsimmons: Lowell Fitzsimmons
Sleepy Floyd: Eric Augustus Floyd
World B. Free: Lloyd B. Free
Lefty Gomez: Vernon Louis Gomez
Goose Gossage: Richard Michael Gossage
He Hate Me: Rod Smart
Bo Jackson: Vincent Edward Jackson
Magic Johnson: Earvin Johnson
Chipper Jones: Larry Wayne Jones
Pacman Jones: Adam Bernard Jones
Pepper Martin: Johnny Leonard Roosevelt Martin
Bake McBride: Arnold Ray McBride
Tug McGraw: Frank Edwin McGraw Jr.
Mercury Morris: Eugene Morris
Bronko Nagurski: Bronsilau Nagurski
Jesse Owens: James Cleveland Owens
Satchel Paige: Leroy Robert Paige
Smush Parker: William Henry Parker
Pelé: Edson Arantes Do Nascimento
Scoonie Penn: James Penn
Bum Phillips: Oail Andrew Phillips
Boog Powell: John Wesley Powell
Ahmad Rashad: Bobby Moore
Pee Wee Reese: Harold Henry Reese
Pokey Reese: Calvin Reese
Pooh Richardson: Jerome Richardson Jr.
Chi Chi Rodriguez: Juan Rodriguez
Preacher Roe: Elwin Charles Roe
Ronaldinho: Ronaldo De Assis Moreira
Spider Sabich: Vladimir Peter Sabich Jr.
Flip Saunders: Philip Saunders
Bo Schembechler: Glen Edward Schembechler
Red Schoendienst: Albert Fred Schoendienst
O.J. Simpson: Orenthal James Simpson
Bubba Smith: Charles Aaron Smith
Duke Snider: Edwin Donald Snyder
Rusty Staub: Daniel Joseph Staub
Casey Stengel: Charles Dillon Stengel
Bubba Watson: Gerry Watson
Spud Webb: Anthony Jerome Webb
Bonzi Wells: Gawen Deangelo Wells
Jamaal Wilkes: Jackson Keith Wilkes
Mookie Wilson: William Hayward Wilson
Ickey Woods: Elbert L. Woods
Tiger Woods: Eldrick T. Woods

A B C D E F G H I J K L M N O P Q R S T U V W X Y Z

Unparalleled Leadership

The Follies Of Charley Finley

Charles O. Finley, who bought the Kansas City A's in 1960 and later moved them to Oakland, was one of baseball's most innovative—and reviled—owners. A penny-pinching egomaniac who often fought with his players, MLB officials, and politicians, Finley was also the man whose team won three straight World Series in the 1970s, and was the guiding force behind many of baseball's best ideas. A couple of the worst ones, too. Here's a sample:

- Designated hitter
- Outfield sheep[1]
- Mechanical ball rabbits[2]
- Flamboyant uniforms[3]
- Orange baseballs[4]
- Postseason night games
- Interleague play
- Ball girls
- 20-second pitch clock
- Fan-friendly schedule changes[5]
- In-stadium fan attractions[6]
- Three-ball walks[7]

Notes: [1]Grazed beyond outfield fence in K.C. and lowered mowing costs; [2]In K.C., popped up to deliver new balls to umpires; [3]First MLB owner to change team's primary uniform to color other than white or gray (green and gold with white shoes); [4]Were used in one exhibition game but players couldn't see them; [5]7 p.m. games on weekdays (after working people clocked out); 2 p.m. on Sundays (after lunch and church) and weekend Opening Days (so whole family could come); [6]For example, exploding scoreboard in right field; [7]Tried in one exhibition game—19 walks were issued.

Unrealized Potential

A Partial List Of Olympic Demonstration Sports

Demonstration sports—the non-medal competitions of each Olympic Games—generally reflect the particular sporting or cultural influence of the host nation. Some, such as curling and moguls skiing, have become official Olympic sports. Not these:

WINTER GAMES

Military ski patrol (precursor to biathlon): 1928 (St. Moritz), 1936 (Garmisch-Partenkirchen), 1948 (St. Moritz)

Skijoring (skiing behind horses): 1928 (St. Moritz)

Dogsled racing: 1932 (Lake Placid)

Winter pentathlon (cross-country skiing, shooting, downhill skiing, fencing, horse riding): 1948 (St. Moritz)

Bandy (players use a stick to hit ball into goal on ice): 1952 (Oslo)

Speed skiing: 1992 (Albertville)

SUMMER GAMES

Bicycle polo: 1908 (London)

Korfball (Dutch basketball): 1920 (Antwerp), 1928 (Amsterdam)

French boxing (fighting with both fists and feet): 1924 (Paris)

Kaatsen (relative of American handball): 1928 (Amsterdam)

American football: 1932 (Los Angeles)

Gliding: 1936 (Berlin)

Pesapallo (Finnish baseball): 1952 (Helsinki)

Australian Rules football: 1956 (Melbourne)

Bowling: 1988 (Seoul)

Roller hockey: 1992 (Barcelona)

Water skiing: 1972 (Munich)

Basque pelota (relative of jai alai or handball): 1924 (Paris), 1968 (Mexico City), 1992 (Barcelona)

A B C D E F G H I J K L M N O P Q R S T U V W X Y Z

Valuable

V

Vote

Valuable Skaters

Inaugural Inductees Into The Hockey Hall Of Fame

The Hockey Hall of Fame in Toronto was founded in 1943. Here is the original class, inducted in 1945:

Sir Montagu Allan: NHL builder

Donald H. (Dan) Bain: C, Winnipeg Victorias (1894-1902)

Hobart Amery Hare (Hobey) Baker: Rover[1], Princeton Tigers (1910-14)

Russell (Dubbie) Bowie: C, Montreal St. John's, Montreal Tuckers, Montreal Comets, Montreal Victorias (1892-1910)

Charles Robert (Chuck) Gardiner: G, Winnipeg Tigers, Selkirk Fishermen, Winnipeg Marrons, Chicago Blackhawks (1921-34)

Edward George (Eddie) Gerard: D, Ottawa Seconds, Ottawa New Edinburghs, Toronto St. Pats, Ottawa Senators (1907-23)

Francis (Frank) McGee: F, Ottawa Seconds, Ottawa Aberdeens, Ottawa Silver Seven, Ottawa Senators (1899-1906)

Howard William (Howie) Morenz: F, Stratford Midgets, Stratford Indians, Montreal Canadiens, Chicago Blackhawks, New York Rangers (1920-36)

Thomas N. (Tommy) Phillips: F, Montreal Shamrocks, Montreal AAA, Toronto Marlboros, Rat Portage/Kenora Thistles, Ottawa Senators (1901-08)

Harvey Pulford: D, Ottawa Hockey Club, Ottawa Silver Seven, Ottawa Senators (1893-1908)

Arthur Howie (Art) Ross: D, Montreal Westmount, Montreal Merchants, Brandon Elks, Kenora Thistles, Pembroke Lumber Kings, Cobalt Silver Kings, Montreal Wanderers, Ottawa Senators (1902-16)

Lord (of Preston) Stanley: NHL builder, donor of Stanley Cup

William H. (Hod) Stuart: D, Rat Portage Thistles, Ottawa Silver Seven, Quebec Bulldogs, Pittsburgh Bankers, Portage Lakes, Calumet Miners, Pittsburgh Pros, Montreal Wanderers (1895-1907)

Georges Vezina: G, Chicoutimi Sagueneens, Montreal Canadiens (1909-26)

Note: [1]Obsolete position from pre-1920s hockey.

Vanished Bowls

Defunct NCAA Postseason Football Games

What is now the Champs Sports Bowl was once the Blockbuster Bowl, the Carquest Bowl, the Micron PC Bowl, the MicronPC.com Bowl, the Visit Florida Tangerine Bowl, and the Mazda Tangerine Bowl. And yet it still thrives. Here are some that weren't so lucky:

Alamo Bowl (San Antonio): 1947
All-American/Hall of Fame Classic (Birmingham, Alabama): 1977-90
Aloha Bowl (Honolulu): 1982-2000
Aviation Bowl (Dayton, Ohio): 1961
Bacardi Bowl (Havana): 1937
Bean Bowl[1] (Scottsbluff, Nebraska): 1949-50
Beaver Bowl[1] (Corry, Pennsylvania): 1958
Bluebonnet Bowl/Astro-Bluebonnet Bowl (Houston): 1959-87
Bluegrass Bowl (Louisville): 1958
California Bowl (Fresno, California): 1981-91
Camellia Bowl (Lafayette, Louisiana): 1948
Cattle Bowl[1] (Fort Worth, Texas): 1947-48
Cement Bowl[1] (Allentown, Pennsylvania): 1962
Cherry Bowl (Pontiac, Michigan): 1984-85
Delta Bowl (Memphis, Tennessee): 1948-49
Dixie Bowl (Birmingham, Alabama): 1948-1949
Dixie Classic (Dallas): 1922, 1925, 1934
Fish Bowl[1] (Corpus Christi,Texas): 1948
Fish Bowl[1] (Norfolk, Virginia): 1948
Fort Worth Classic (Forth Worth, Texas): 1921
Freedom Bowl (Anaheim, California): 1984-94
Garden State Bowl (East Rutherford, New Jersey): 1978-81
Glass Bowl[1] (Toledo, Ohio): 1946-49
Gotham Bowl (New York): 1961-62
Great Lakes Bowl (Cleveland): 1947
Harbor Bowl (San Diego): 1947-49
Iodine Bowl[1] (Charleston, South Carolina): 1949-53
Los Angeles Christmas Festival (Los Angeles): 1924
Mercy Bowl (Los Angeles): 1961
Oil Bowl (Houston): 1946-47
Optimist Bowl[1] (Houston): 1946
Pasadena Bowl/Junior Rose Bowl (Pasadena, California): 1967-71
Peanut Bowl[1] (Dothan, Alabama): 1968
Poultry Bowl[1] (Gainesville, Georgia): 1973-74
Presidential Cup (College Park, Maryland): 1950
Pretzel Bowl[1] (Reading, Pennsylvania): 1951
Raisin Bowl (Fresno, California): 1946-49
Refrigerator Bowl[1] (Evansville, Indiana): 1948-56
Salad Bowl (Phoenix): 1948-52
San Diego East-West Christmas Classic (San Diego): 1921-22
Jeep Oahu Classic/Seattle Bowl (Honolulu, Seattle): 1998-2002
Shrine Bowl (Little Rock): 1948
Silicon Valley Football Classic/Silicon Valley Classic (San Jose): 2000-04
Vulcan Bowl[1] (Birmingham, Alabama): 1942-49
Will Rogers Bowl[1] (Oklahoma City): 1947
Yam Bowl[1] (Dallas): 1946-47

Note: [1]Not sanctioned by NCAA.

A B C D E F G H I J K L M N O P Q R S T U V W X Y Z

Visionary Moments

Sports Television Firsts

The first sporting event ever televised in the United States was a baseball game between Columbia University and Princeton University on May 17, 1939. Here are some other firsts in televised sports:

BOXING
Max Baer vs. Lou Nova; Yankee Stadium, June 1, 1939

TENNIS
Eastern Grass Court championship matches; Westchester (New York) Country Club, August 9, 1939

FOOTBALL
Fordham University vs. Waynesburg College; New York City, September 30, 1939

HOCKEY
New York Rangers vs. Montreal Canadiens; Madison Square Garden, February 25, 1940

BASKETBALL
Fordham University vs. University of Pittsburgh; Madison Square Garden, February 28, 1940

TRACK & FIELD
AAAA Track and Field Championships; Madison Square Garden, March 2, 1940

OLYMPICS
Winter Games; Squaw Valley (California), February 18, 1960

Vocal Heroes

Athletes With Albums

Bronson Arroyo (MLB) Debut album "Covering the Bases" (2005; rock)

Ron Artest (NBA) "My World" (2006; hip-hop/R&B)

Terry Bradshaw (NFL) "I'm So Lonesome I Could Cry" (1976; country)

Ben Broussard (MLB) "Ben Broussard" (2005; folk rock)

Kobe Bryant (NBA) "K.O.B.E." (2000; hip hop)

Cassius Clay (boxing) "I Am the Greatest" (1963; poetry)

Tony Conigliaro (MLB) "Playing the Field" (1965; pop)

John Daly (golf) "My Life" (2002; country)

Oscar De La Hoya (boxing) "Oscar De La Hoya" (2000; Latin pop)

Buddy Dial (NFL) "Buddy Dial Sings" (1961; gospel)

Doug Flutie w/Flutie Gang (NFL/CFL) "Ramblin' Scramblin' Man" (1999; rock)

Raghib Ismail (NFL) "The Reign Cometh" (2002; gospel rap)

Allen Iverson (NBA) "Misunderstood" (2001, unreleased; hip-hop)

Peter Jacobson w/Jake Trout & the Flounders (golf) "I Love to Play" (1998; comedy rock)

Jack Johnson (surfing) "In Between Dreams" (2005; folk pop)

Roy Jones Jr. (boxing) "Round One: The Album" (2002; hip-hop)

Alexei Lalas (soccer) "Ginger" (1998; pop rock)

Carl Lewis (track) "Break It Up" (1987; pop)

Arthur Lee Maye w/Arthur Lee Maye and the Crowns (MLB) "Set My Heart Free" (1955; R&B)

Darren McCarty w/Grinder (NHL) "Out of Our Heads" (2005; rock)

Walter McCarty (NBA) "Moment for Love" (2003; R&B)

Jack McDowell w/View (MLB) "Extendagenda" (1991; pop rock)

John McEnroe w/McEnroe and Cash (tennis) "Rock and Roll" (1991; rock)

Yannick Noah (tennis) "Urban Tribu" (1993; world music)

Shaquille O'Neal (NBA) "Shaq Diesel" (1993; hip-hop)

Scott Radinsky w/Ten Foot Pole (MLB) "Rev" (1994; punk)

Mike Reid (NFL) "Turning for Home" (1991; country)

Deion Sanders (NFL) "Prime Time" (1995; hip-hop)

Kelly Slater w/The Surfers (surfing) "Songs from the Pipe" (1998; surf rock)

Wayman Tisdale (NBA) "Power Forward" (1995; jazz)

Chris Webber (NBA) "2 Much Drama" (1999; hip-hop)

Bernie Williams (MLB) "The Journey Within" (2003; smooth jazz)

Walt Williams (NBA) "Insight of a Wizzard" (2002; hip-hop)

A B C D E F G H I J K L M N O P Q R S T U V W X Y Z

Voice Squads

Famous Home Run Calls

"Going, going, gone!"
"How about that!"
Mel Allen (New York Yankees, New York Giants)

"Back, back, back, back, back … Gone!"
Chris Berman (ESPN)

"Hey, hey!"
"Whoo, boy! Next time around, bring me back my stomach!"
Jack Brickhouse (Chicago Cubs, Chicago White Sox)

"Bonsoir, elle est partie!" (French for "Good night, she's gone!")
Rodger Brulotte (Montreal Expos)

"Swing and a long one … it may go!"
Jack Buck (St. Louis Cardinals)

"It could be, it might be … it is! A home run!"
Harry Caray (Chicago Cubs, Chicago White Sox, Oakland A's, St. Louis Cardinals)

"They usually show movies on a flight like that."
Ken Coleman (Cleveland Indians, Cincinnati Reds, Boston Red Sox)

"Whattaya think about that?"
Rob Faulds (Toronto Blue Jays)

"Adios!"
Wayne Hagin (St. Louis Cardinals, Colorado Rockies, Chicago White Sox, San Francisco Giants, Oakland A's)

"You can put it on the board. Yesssssss!"
Ken "Hawk" Harrelson (Chicago White Sox, New York Yankees, Boston Red Sox)

"It's going, going ... gone!"
Harry Hartman (Cincinnati Reds)

"Long gone!"
Ernie Harwell (Detroit Tigers, Baltimore Orioles, New York Giants, Brooklyn Dodgers)

"Tell it bye bye, baby!"
Russ Hodges (New York/San Francisco Giants, New York Yankees, Washington Senators, Chicago Cubs, Cincinnati Reds)

"Watch that baby ... Outta here!"
Harry Kalas (Philadelphia Phillies, Houston Astros)

"Going back, [outfielder's name], at the track, at the wall ... seeeeya!"
Michael Kay (New York Yankees)

"That ball is going and it ain't coming back!"
Jeff Kingery (Colorado Rockies)

"That ball is history!"
Eric Nadel (Texas Rangers)

"Get out the rye bread and mustard, grandma, cause it's grand salami time!"
Dave Niehaus (Seattle Mariners, California Angels, New York Yankees, Los Angeles Dodgers)

"Kiss it good bye!"
Bob Prince (Houston Astros, Pittsburgh Pirates)

"Track ... wall ... see ... you ... later!"
Michael Reghi (Baltimore Orioles)

"Good bye baseball!"
Dick Risenhoover (Texas Rangers)

"Holy cow!"
Phil Rizzuto (New York Yankees)

"Get upstairs, Aunt Minnie, and raise the window, here she comes!"
Rosey Rowswell (Pittsburgh Pirates)

"Warning track, wall, you can touch 'em all."
Greg Schulte (Arizona Diamondbacks)

"Forget it!"
Vin Scully (Brooklyn/Los Angeles Dodgers)

"Tell it good bye!"
Lon Simmons (Oakland A's, San Francisco Giants)

"That ball is high! It is far! It is ... gone!"
John Sterling (New York Yankees, Atlanta Braves)

"Swing and there it goes! WAY BACK! WAAAY BACK! HOME RUN!"
Jerry Trupiano (Boston Red Sox, Montreal Expos, Houston Astros)

"Get up, get up, get outta here, gone!"
Bob Uecker (Milwaukee Brewers)

Voracious Appetites

Professional Eating Contest Records

Takeru Kobayashi might be the most famous eater in the world today, having inhaled a record 53¾ Nathan's Famous hot dogs and buns in 12 minutes. Here are some other (nauseating) records:

Baked Beans
Don Lerman
6 pounds; 1:48

Birthday Cake
Richard LeFevre
5 pounds; 11:26

Butter
Don Lerman
7 quarter-pound sticks (salted); 5:00

Cow Brains
Takeru Kobayashi
17.7 pounds; 15:00

Doughnuts
Eric Booker
49 (glazed); 8:00

Hard-boiled Eggs
Sonya Thomas
65; 6:40

Mayonnaise
Oleg Zhornitskiy
Four 32-ounce bowls; 8:00

Meat Pies
Boyd Bulot
16 six-ounce pies; 10:00

Pasta
Cookie Jarvis
6⅔ pounds (linguine); 10:00

SPAM
Richard LeFevre
6 pounds; 12:00

Sweet Corn
Joe LaRue
34 ears; 12:00

Watermelon
Jim Reeves
13.22 pounds; 15:00

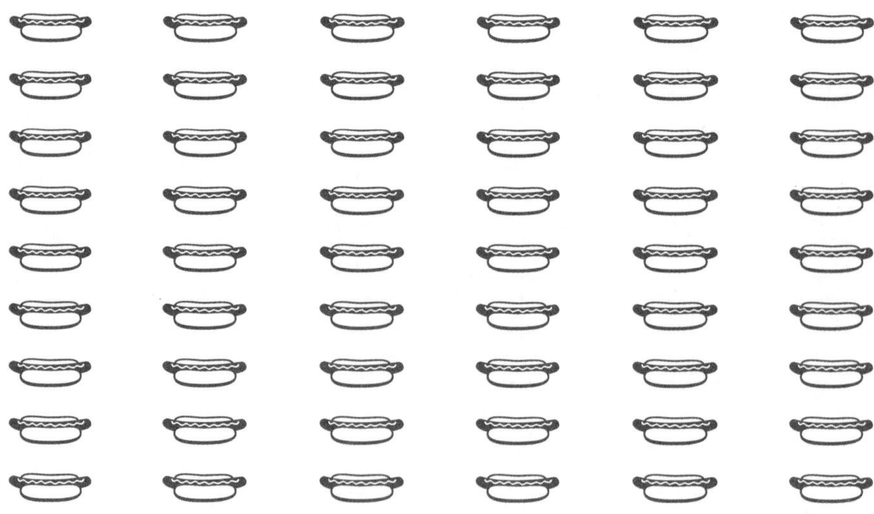

Vote Getters

Star Athletes Who Became Politicians

Bill Bradley: NBA forward/U.S. Senator (D-New Jersey)

Jim Bunning: MLB pitcher/U.S. Senator (R-Kentucky)

George H.W. Bush: College baseball player/ U.S. President (R-Connecticut)

Ben (Nighthorse) Campbell: Olympic judo/ U.S. Senator (D/R-Colorado)

Sebastien Coe: Olympic runner/British Member of Parliament

Ken Dryden: NHL goaltender/Canadian Member of Parliament

Dennis Hastert: college wrestler/U.S. Congressman (R-Illinois)

Baron Hill: college basketball player/ U.S. Congressman (D-Indiana)

Gerald Ford: college football player/U.S. President (R-Michigan)

Jack Kemp: NFL quarterback/ U.S. Congressman (R-New York)

Steve Largent: NFL wide receiver/ U.S. Congressman (R-Oklahoma)

Frank Mahovlich: NHL forward/ Canadian Senator

Judy Martz: Olympic speedskater/ Governor (R-Montana)

Bob Mathias: Olympic decathlete/ U.S. Congressman (R-California)

Tom McMillen: NBA forward/ U.S. Congressman (D-Maryland)

Howie Meeker: NHL forward/Canadian Member of Parliament

Tom Osborne: college football quarterback/U.S. Congressman (R-Nebraska)

Alan Page: NFL lineman/Minnesota Supreme Court justice

Rick Renzi: college football player/ U.S. Congressman (R-Arizona)

Jim Ryun: Olympic runner/U.S. Congressman (R-Kansas)

Heath Shuler: NFL quarterback/U.S. Congressman (D-North Carolina)

Arnold Schwarzenegger: bodybuilder/ Governor (R-California)

Jesse Ventura: professional wrestler/ Governor (Ind.-Minnesota)

J.C. Watts: college quarterback/ U.S. Congressman (R-Oklahoma)

Waist

W

Words

Waist Materials

Martial Arts Belt Colors

Color	KARATE	JUJITSU	JUDO	TAE KWON DO
White	10th kyu	8th kyu	6th kyu	10th keup
White (yellow stripes)				9th keup
Gold	9th kyu			
Yellow	8th kyu	7th kyu	5th kyu	8th keup
Yellow (green stripes)				7th keup
Orange	7th kyu		4th kyu	
Green	5th kyu	6th to 5th kyu	3rd kyu	6th keup
Green (blue stripes)				5th keup
Blue	6th kyu	2nd kyu	2nd kyu	4th keup
Blue (red stripes)				3rd keup
Purple	4th kyu	4th kyu		
Brown	3rd to 1st kyu		1st kyu	
Brown (red stripes)		3rd to 1st kyu		
Black	1st to 10th dan	1st to 5th dan	1st to 5th dan	
Red and white		6th to 7th dan	6th to 8th dan	
Red		8th to 10th dan	9th to 10th dan	2nd keup
Red (black stripes)				1st keup
Black (gold stripes)				1st to 10th dan

Note: Levels listed from lowest to highest.

Water Works

Famous Spitting Incidents

1939 New York Giants infielder Billy Jurges is suspended 10 days for spitting on umpire George Magerkurth, who is suspended 10 days himself—for his one-punch decking of Jurges in retaliation.

1956 Boston Red Sox great Ted Williams spits at the Fenway Park crowd. Afterwards he says, "I'm not a bit sorry for what I did. I was right and I'd spit again at the same fans who booed me today. Some of them are the worst in the world. Nobody's going to stop me from spitting."

1964 California Angels first baseman Vic Power is fined and suspended 10 days for spitting at umpire Jim Honochick.

1991 Philadelphia 76ers forward Charles Barkley, playing on the road in New Jersey, spits at a heckling fan but accidentally hits a little girl. He later apologizes.

1996 Baltimore Orioles infielder Roberto Alomar spits in the face of umpire John Hirschbeck and is given a five-game suspension.

1997 Tampa Bay Buccaneers linebacker Hardy Nickerson spits on San Francisco 49ers fullback William Floyd. The next year, Nickerson faces Floyd, now with the Carolina Panthers—and spits on him again.

1997 Portland Trail Blazers guard Isaiah Rider spits on a fan during halftime warm-ups and is suspended for three games.

1997 Denver Broncos linebacker Bill Romanowski spits on San Francisco 49ers wideout J.J. Stokes and is fined $7,500.

2000 Oakland Raiders defensive end Regan Upshaw spits at Pittsburgh Steelers punter Josh Miller and is fined $29,411.

2004 St. Louis Cardinals outfielder Roger Cedeno spits on umpire Rick Reed and is suspended for four games.

2004 Numerous Tour de France fans spit at U.S. cyclist Lance Armstrong during a time trial.

2004 Boston Celtics forward Paul Pierce spits in the direction of the Cleveland Cavaliers bench during a preseason game and is fined $15,000.

2004 Pittsburgh Steelers linebacker Joey Porter and Cleveland Browns running back William Green are ejected for fighting before a game. Both accuse the other of spitting, but neither owns up to it. Each player is fined $10,000.

2006 Washington Redskins Sean Taylor is fined $17,000 for spitting at Tampa Bay Buccaneers running back Michael Pittman in a playoff game.

2006 Dallas Cowboys wide receiver Terrell Owens spits in the face of Atlanta Falcons cornerback DeAngelo Hall during a game. He is fined $35,000.

A B C D E F G H I J K L M N O P Q R S T U V W X Y Z

Wave Makers

Members Of The Surfers' Hall Of Fame

Grauman's Chinese Theatre in Hollywood was the inspiration for the Surfers' Hall of Fame in Huntington Beach, California, right down to the hand- and footprints display.

Lisa Andersen (inducted in 2002): Won four straight world titles.

Robert August (2002): Starred in classic surf movie *The Endless Summer.*

Layne Beachley (2006): Seven-time world champ.

Corky Carroll (2002): Surfing's first real pro, five-time U.S. champ.

Tom Carroll (2005): Dominated surfing in 1980's, winning two world titles.

Tom Curren (2003): Two-time West Coast, U.S., and world amateur champion; three-time pro world title-holder.

Mike Doyle (2003): Voted best surfer in 1964 and 1965 *Surfer Magazine* poll; won 1969 Duke Kahanamoku Classic and 1970 World Championships.

Jack Haley (2004): Won 1959 West Coast Surfing Championships (first U.S. Open of Surfing event); opened venerable surfer hangout Captain Jack's.

Laird Hamilton (2002): Eschewed competition to concentrate exclusively on surfing the biggest, most dangerous swells; in 2000, rode what's considered the heaviest wave ever conquered, in Tahitian surf-mecca, Teahupoo.

Carl Hayward (2005): Surfboard shaper, created popular Rocket Fish model.

Bob Hurley (2006): Created Billabong USA; founded Hurley International, surf-inspired apparel company.

Andy Irons (2003): Won 1996 HIC Pipeline Pro while still in high school; won 1997 six-star G-Shock U.S. Open and Op Pro; three-time world champion.

Bruce Irons (2007): Talented regular foot surfer from Hanalei, Kauai and younger brother of three-time world champion Andy Irons. Won Pipeline Masters event (2001) and "Quiksilver In Memory of Eddie Aikau" event (2004) at Oahu's Waimea Bay.

Bud Llamas (2003): First U.S. amateur champion (1978).

Gerry Lopez (2004): Two-time Pipe Masters champ.

Rob Machado (2006): Twelve WCT event titles, including a Pipe Masters win.

Robert McKnight (2005): Founder and CEO of Quiksilver, major surf apparel company.

Al Merrick (2007): Elite surfboard shaper for Shaun Tomson, Tom Curren, and Kelly Slater. As surfers' status reached epic proportions, so did Merrick's surfboard label, Channel Islands.

Sofia Mulanovich (2007): First Peruvian to win the WCT event and first South American to win the world title. Also won the Vans Triple Crown of Surfing, U.S. Open of Surfing, and the Surfer Poll.

Greg Noll (2006): "Da Bull," pioneer of big wave surfing; in first group to surf Waimea Bay in Hawaii.

David Nuuhiwa Sr. (2004): Hawaiian community patriarch, father of surfing legend David Jr.

Mark Occhilupo (2004): Sensation at 17 with performances at World Championship Tour; played himself in surf movie *North Shore*; after dropping out of competition for years, came back to win first title at age 33.

Martin Potterthe (2007): Nicknamed "Pottz" and "Eggy Potter," a British born surfer considered the best "free-surfer" of his generation. Won the world title in 1989.

Jack O'Neill (2003): Invented wet suit; opened one of California's first surf shops in 1952.

Jericho Poppler (2004): One of first great female surfers (1970s); co-founded Women's International Surfing Association.

Mark Richards (2005): Won four straight world titles.

Kelly Slater (2002): Amateur titleholder in his teens; won world title at 21 to become youngest champion ever; won six more titles, including 2005, making him oldest champ ever.

Paul Strauch (2003): Influential surfer in 1960s best known for signature "Paul Strauch Five"or "Cheater 5" move; one of four riders on Duke Kahanamoku Surf Team.

Shaun Tomson (2003): Won world title in 1977; regular foot rider who redefined art of tuberiding (surfing inside a breaking wave).

Peter Townend (2004): World champion surfer in late 1970s; won first World Championship in 1976.

Joel Tudor (2002): Known for longboard prowess; became famous at 14 for breaking onto pro circuit and appearing in longboard video *On Safari to Stay*.

Robert "Wingnut" Weaver (2002): Appeared in *The Endless Summer II* and kept alive longboard surfing during downturn in popularity.

Wave Riders

WINNING AMERICA'S CUP CAPTAINS

The America's Cup is the most prestigious trophy in yachting—and the oldest active trophy in international sports—and winning captains often become more famous than their boats. Here are all the winners, and the yachts they skippered:

Richard Brown: 1851, *America*
Andrew Comstock: 1870, *Magic*
Andrew and Nelson Comstock: 1871, *Columbia*
Josephus Williams: 1876, *Madeleine*
Nathanael Clock: 1881, *Mischief*
Aubrey Crocker: 1885, *Puritan*
Martin Stone: 1886, *Mayflower*
Henry Haff: 1887, *Volunteer*
William Hansen: 1893, *Vigilant*
Henry Haff: 1895, *Defender*
Charles Barr: 1899, *Columbia*
Charles Barr: 1901, *Columbia*
Charles Barr: 1903, *Reliance*
Charles F. Adams: 1920, *Resolute*
Harold Vanderbilt: 1930, *Enterprise*
Harold Vanderbilt: 1934, *Rainbow*
Harold Vanderbilt: 1937, *Ranger*
Briggs Cunningham: 1958, *Columbia*
Bus Mosbacher: 1962, *Weatherly*
Bob Bavier and Eric Ridder: 1964, *Constellation*
Bus Mosbacher: 1967, *Intrepid*
Bill Ficker: 1970, *Intrepid*
Ted Hood: 1974 *Courageous*
Ted Turner: 1977, *Courageous*
Dennis Conner: 1980, *Freedom*
John Bertrand (Australia): 1983, *Australia II*
Dennis Conner: 1987, *Stars & Stripes*
Dennis Conner: 1988, *Stars & Stripes*
Bill Koch and Buddy Melges: 1992, *America3*
Russell Coutts (New Zealand): 1995, *Black Magic*
Russell Coutts & Dean Barker (New Zealand): 2000, *NZL60*
Russell Coutts (Switzerland): 2003, *Alinghi*
Brad Butterworth (Switzerland): 2007, *Alinghi*

Williamsport Winners

Little League World Series Champions

1947 Williamsport, Pennsylvania
1948 Lock Haven, Pennsylvania
1949 Hammonton, New Jersey
1950 Houston, Texas
1951 Stamford, Connecticut
1952 Norwalk, Connecticut
1953 Birmingham, Alabama
1954 Schenectady, New York
1955 Morrisville, Pennsylvania
1956 Roswell, New Mexico
1957 Monterrey, Mexico
1958 Monterrey, Mexico
1959 Hamtramck, Michigan
1960 Levittown, Pennsylvania
1961 El Cajon/La Mesa, California
1962 San Jose, California
1963 Granada Hills, California
1964 Staten Island, New York
1965 Windsor Locks, Connecticut
1966 Houston, Texas
1967 Tokyo, Japan
1968 Osaka, Japan
1969 Taipei, Taiwan
1970 Wayne, New Jersey
1971 Tainan, Taiwan
1972 Taipei, Taiwan
1973 Tainan City, Taiwan
1974 Kao Hsiung, Taiwan
1975 Lakewood, New Jersey
1976 Tokyo, Japan
1977 Li-Teh, Taiwan
1978 Pin-Tung, Taiwan
1979 Pu-Tzu Town, Taiwan
1980 Hua Lian, Taiwan
1981 Tai-Chung, Taiwan
1982 Kirkland, Washington
1983 Marietta, Georgia
1984 Seoul, South Korea
1985 Seoul, South Korea
1986 Tainan Park, Taiwan
1987 Hua Lian, Taiwan
1988 Tai-Chung, Taiwan
1989 Trumbull, Connecticut
1990 Tainan County, Taiwan
1991 Tai-Chung, Taiwan
1992 Long Beach, California*
1993 Long Beach, California
1994 Maracaibo, Venezuela
1995 Tainan, Taiwan
1996 Kao-Hsuing City, Taiwan
1997 Guadalupe, Mexico
1998 Toms River, New Jersey
1999 Osaka, Japan
2000 Maracaibo, Venezuela
2001 Tokyo, Japan
2002 Louisville, Kentucky
2003 Tokyo, Japan
2004 Willemstad, Curacao
2005 Ewa Beach, Hawaii
2006 Columbus, Georgia
2007 Warner Robins, Georgia
2008 Waipi`o, Hawaii

Note: *Long Beach declared 6-0 winner when Zamboanga City, Philippines, was found to have used players from outside city limits.

Winter War

Types Of Snomobile Races

SNOCROSS: A 12- to 24-lap circuit race on a 300-meter to one-kilometer course. Nine qualifying heats and a Last Chance Qualifier bring 15 finalists to race through a series of technical whoopses (small jumps), banked turns, and large jumps.

HILLCLIMB: Snowmobilers are timed racing one at a time up steep pitches (up to 45 degrees) or mountains.

HILLCROSS: A combination of Hillclimb and Snocross in which multiple racers start at the bottom of a hill (usually a ski slope) and head up, over jumps, straight to the finish at the top.

WATERCROSS: Racers round buoys on a water circuit during the summer.

EXTREME ICE: Racing typically done on frozen lakes, either as ice drag (one-on-one in a straight line) or as an oval circuit with multiple racers.

FREESTYLE SNOCROSS: Similar to Freestyle Motocross, FSX'ers perform tricks over a series of large jumps during one- to two-minute runs. They are judged on difficulty, style, continuity, amplitude, and originality.

Winter Wear

Figure Skating Dress Code

Rule 304.2 of the International Skating Union regulations states exactly what attire is—and isn't—allowed on the ice.

At ISU Championships, the Olympic Winter Games and International Competitions, the clothing of the competitors must be modest, dignified, and appropriate for athletic competition—not garish or theatrical in design. Clothing may, however, reflect the character of the music chosen.

a) The clothing must not give the effect of excessive nudity for athletic sport. Men must wear trousers; no tights are permitted. Accessories and props are not permitted.

b) Clothing not meeting the foregoing requirements must be penalized by a deduction of 1.0 point.

Words To Leave By

Lou Gehrig's Farewell Speech

Two years before his death from ALS in 1941, the legendary New York Yankees first baseman delivered these remarks at Yankee Stadium at a ceremony in his honor:

"Fans, for the past two weeks you have been reading about the bad break I got. Yet today **I consider myself the luckiest man on the face of the earth.** I have been in ballparks for seventeen years and have never received anything but kindness and encouragement from you fans. Look at these grand men. Which of you wouldn't consider it the highlight of his career just to associate with them for even one day? Sure, I'm lucky. Who wouldn't consider it an honor to have known Jacob Ruppert? Also, the builder of baseball's greatest empire, Ed Barrow? To have spent six years with that wonderful little fellow, Miller Huggins? Then to have spent the next nine years with that outstanding leader, that smart student of psychology, the best manager in baseball today, Joe McCarthy? Sure, I'm lucky. When the New York Giants, a team you would give your right arm to beat, and vice versa, sends you a gift—that's something. When everybody down to the groundskeepers and those boys in white coats remember you with trophies—that's something. When you have a wonderful mother-in-law who takes sides with you in squabbles with her own daughter—that's something. When you have a father and a mother who work all their lives so you can have an education and build your body—it's a blessing. When you have a wife who has been a tower of strength and shown more courage than you dreamed existed—that's the finest I know. So I close in saying that I might have been given a bad break, but I've got an awful lot to live for. Thank you."

A B C D E F G H I J K L M N O P Q R S T U V W X Y Z

X-ed
X
X-Men

X-ed Out
Discontinued X Games Events

SUMMER X

Aggressive In-line: High Air (discontinued in 1995), Best Trick (1996), Downhill In-line (1998), Street (1999), Vert Triples (1999), Park (2003), Vert (2004)

Barefoot Jumping (1998)

BMX Freestyle: Vert Doubles (1998), Street (1999), Flatland (2003), Downhill BMX (2003)

Bungy (1996)

Climbing: Bouldering/Difficulty (1999), Speed (2002)

Mountain Biking: Dual Slalom (1995), Dual Downhill (1995)

Skateboard: High Air (1995), Street Best Trick (2003), Park (2003), Vert Doubles (2003)

Skysurfing: (2000)

Street Luge: Mass (1998), Dual (2000), Super Mass (2001), King of the Hill (2001)

Wakeboard (2006)

Windsurfing (1995)

Xventure Race (1997)

WINTER X

Crossover (1997)

Ice Climbing: Speed (1998), Difficulty (1999)

Kiteskiing (1995)

Skiboarding: Triple Air (1999), Slopestyle (2000)

Skiing: Big Air (2001)

SnoCross: HillCross (2004)

Snowboard: Half Pipe (1999), Big Air (2001)

Snow Mountain Bike: Speed (1998), Downhill (1998), Biker X (2000)

Super-Modified Shovel Racing (1997)

UltraCross (2005)

X-Men

Multi-sport Pro Athletes

Danny Ainge: MLB (Toronto Blue Jays, 1979-81); NBA (Boston Celtics, Sacramento Kings, Portland Trail Blazers, Phoenix Suns, 1982-95)

Morris (Red) Badgro: MLB (St. Louis Browns, 1929-30); NFL (New York Yankees, New York Giants, Brooklyn Dodgers, 1927-36)

Josh Booty: MLB (Florida Marlins, 1996-98); NFL (Cleveland Browns 2001-03)

John Brodie: NFL (San Francisco 49ers; 1957-73); Senior PGA Tour (1985-98)

Tom Brown: MLB (Washington Senators, 1963); NFL (Green Bay Packers, Washington Redskins, 1964-69)

Lionel Conacher: NHL (Pittsburgh Pirates, New York Americans, Montreal Maroons, Chicago Blackhawks, 1925-37); CFL (Toronto Argonauts, 1921-22); wrestling (Canadian and U.S. pro, 1932-33); International Indoor Professional Lacrosse League (Montreal Maroons, 1931); International Professional Baseball League (Toronto Maple Leafs, 1926)

Gene Conley: MLB (Boston/Milwaukee Braves, Philadelphia Phillies, Boston Red Sox, 1952-63); NBA (Boston Celtics, New York Knicks, 1953, 1959-64)

Chuck Connors: MLB (Brooklyn Dodgers, Chicago Cubs, 1949, 1951); NBA (Boston Celtics, 1947-48)

Dave DeBusschere: NBA (Detroit Pistons, New York Knicks, 1963-74); MLB (Chicago White Sox, 1962-63)

John (Paddy) Driscoll: MLB (Chicago Cubs, 1917); pro football (Hammond Pros, Decatur Staleys, Chicago Cardinals, Chicago Bears, 1919-29)

Dick Groat: MLB (Pittsburgh Pirates, St. Louis Cardinals, Philadelphia Phillies, New York/San Francisco Giants,

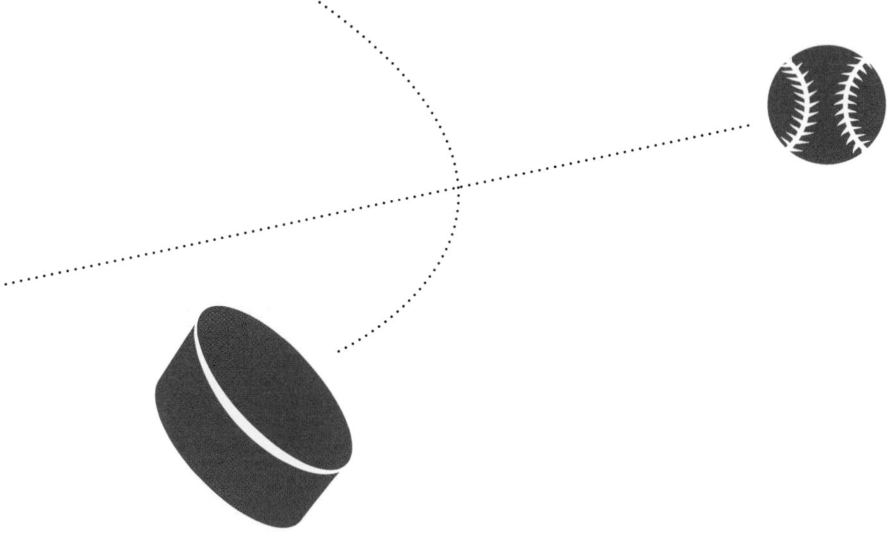

1952-67); NBA (Fort Wayne Pistons, 1952-53)

George Halas: MLB (New York Yankees, 1919); NFL (Chicago Bears, 1920-28)

Mark Hendrickson: NBA (Philadelphia 76ers, Sacramento Kings, New Jersey Nets, Cleveland Cavaliers, 1996-2000); MLB (Toronto Blue Jays, Tampa Bay Devil Rays, Los Angeles Dodgers, 2002-present)

Bo Jackson: MLB (Kansas City Royals, Chicago White Sox, California Angels, 1986-94); NFL (Los Angeles Raiders, 1987-90)

Brian Jordan: MLB (St. Louis Cardinals, Atlanta Braves, Los Angeles Dodgers, Texas Rangers, Atlanta Braves, 1992-present); NFL (1989-91; Atlanta Falcons)

Ernie Nevers: MLB (St. Louis Browns, 1926-28); NFL (Duluth Eskimos, Chicago Cardinals, 1926-31)

Clarence (Ace) Parker: MLB (Philadelphia Athletics, 1937-38); pro football (Brooklyn Dodgers, Boston Yanks, New York Yankees, 1937-46)

Ron Reed: NBA (Detroit Pistons, 1965-67); MLB (Atlanta Braves, St. Louis Cardinals, Philadelphia Phillies, Chicago White Sox, 1966-84)

Deion Sanders: MLB (New York Yankees, Atlanta Braves, Cincinnati Reds, San Francisco Giants, Cincinnati Reds, 1989-97, 2001); NFL (Atlanta Falcons, San Francisco 49ers, Dallas Cowboys, Washington Redskins, Baltimore Ravens, 1989-2000, 2004-05)

Jim Thorpe: MLB (New York Giants, Cincinnati Reds, Boston Braves, 1913-19); pro football (Canton Bulldogs, Cleveland Indians, Oorang Indians, Rock Island Independents, New York Giants, Chicago Cardinals, 1915-28)

Yanks
Y
Youthful

Yanks For The Memories

The Lineup In Monument Park

There are numerous plaques[1] and retired numbers[2] in Yankee Stadium's famed Monument Park, but only six actual monuments. Here is what they say:

MILLER JAMES HUGGINS
MANAGER OF THE NEW YORK YANKEES,
1918-1929
PENNANT WINNERS
1921-22-23, 1926-27-28
WORLD CHAMPIONS 1923, 1927 AND 1928
AS A TRIBUTE TO A SPLENDID
CHARACTER WHO MADE PRICELESS
CONTRIBUTION TO BASEBALL AND ON
THIS FIELD BROUGHT GLORY TO THE NEW
YORK CLUB OF THE AMERICAN LEAGUE
THIS MEMORIAL ERECTED BY COL. JACOB
RUPPERT AND BASEBALL WRITERS OF
NEW YORK MAY 30, 1932

GEORGE HERMAN "BABE" RUTH
1895-1948
A GREAT BALL PLAYER, A GREAT
MAN, A GREAT AMERICAN
ERECTED BY THE YANKEES AND
THE NEW YORK BASEBALL WRITERS
APRIL 19, 1949

HENRY LOUIS GEHRIG
JUNE 19th, 1903 – JUNE 2nd, 1941
A MAN, A GENTLEMAN AND A GREAT
BALL PLAYER WHOSE AMAZING RECORD
OF 2,130 CONSECUTIVE GAMES SHOULD
STAND FOR ALL TIME.
THIS MEMORIAL IS A TRIBUTE
FROM THE YANKEES PLAYERS
TO THEIR BELOVED CAPTAIN
AND TEAMMATE.
JULY THE FOURTH, 1941

MICKEY MANTLE
"A GREAT TEAMMATE"
1931-1996
536 HOME RUNS
WINNER OF THE TRIPLE CROWN 1956
MOST WORLD SERIES HOMERS 18
SELECTED TO ALLSTAR GAME 20 TIMES
WON MVP AWARD 1956, 1957 & 1962
ELECTED TO HALL OF FAME 1974
A MAGNIFICENT YANKEE WHO LEFT A
LEGACY OF UNEQUALLED COURAGE
DEDICATED BY THE NEW YORK YANKEES
AUGUST 25, 1996

A B C D E F G H I J K L M N O P Q R S T U V W X Y Z

JOSEPH PAUL DIMAGGIO
"THE YANKEE CLIPPER"
1914 - 1999
RECOGNIZED AS BASEBALL'S
"GREATEST LIVING PLAYER"
LIFETIME BATTING AVERAGE .325
WON MVP AWARD 1939, 1941, 1947
SELECTED TO THE
ALL-STAR GAME 13 TIMES
AMERICAN LEAGUE
BATTING TITLE 1939, 1940
ELECTED TO HALL OF FAME 1955
SET ONE OF BASEBALL'S
MOST ENDURING RECORDS,
56-GAME HITTING STREAK,
MAY 15 TO JULY 16, 1941
LED THE YANKEES TO AN INCREDIBLE
NINE WORLD CHAMPIONSHIPS
IN HIS 13-YEAR CAREER
A BASEBALL LEGEND
AND AN AMERICAN ICON
"HE HAS PASSED, BUT
HE WILL NEVER LEAVE US."
DEDICATED BY THE NEW YORK YANKEES
APRIL 25, 1999

SEPTEMBER 11, 2001 TRIBUTE
WE REMEMBER ...
ON SEPTEMBER 11, 2001, DESPICABLE ACTS OF TERRORISM WERE PERPETRATED ON OUR COUNTRY. IN TRIBUTE TO THE ETERNAL SPIRIT OF THE INNOCENT VICTIMS OF THESE CRIMES AND TO THE SELFLESS COURAGE SHOWN BY BOTH PUBLIC SERVANTS AND PRIVATE CITIZENS. WE DEDICATE THIS PLAQUE. THESE VALIANT SOULS, WITH UNFETTERED RESOLVE, EXEMPLIFY THE TRUE CHARACTER OF THIS GREAT NATION. THEIR UNITY AND RESILIENCE DURING THIS TIME OF DISTRESS DEFINED AMERICAN HEROISM FOR FUTURE GENERATIONS. DEDICATED BY THE NEW YORK YANKEES SEPTEMBER 11TH, 2002.

Notes: [1]Mel Allen (broadcaster), Edward Barrow (general manager), Yogi Berra, Bill Dickey, Whitey Ford, Lefty Gomez, Ron Guidry, Elston Howard, Reggie Jackson, Joe McCarthy, Roger Maris, Don Mattingly, Billy Martin, Thurman Munson, Allie Reynolds, Phil Rizzuto, Red Ruffing, Jacob Ruppert (owner), Bob Sheppard (PA announcer), Casey Stengel, visit of Pope Paul VI in 1965, visit of Pope John Paul II in 1979; [2]Billy Martin (1), Babe Ruth (3), Lou Gehrig (4) Joe DiMaggio (5), Mickey Mantle (7), Yogi Berra (8), Bill Dickey (8), Roger Maris (9), Phil Rizzuto (10), Thurman Munson (15), Whitey Ford (16), Don Mattingly (23), Elston Howard (32), Casey Stengel (37), Reggie Jackson (44), Ron Guidry (49).

A B C D E F G H I J K L M N O P Q R S T U V W X Y Z

Year Of The Lord

Byron Nelson's Winning Streak

In 1945, PGA great Byron Nelson won 11 golf tournaments in a row, earning $30,250 in the process. Lord Byron actually won his next tournament as well, but it is not counted in his streak because the purse was below the PGA minimum. (He tied for fourth in Memphis a week after that.) Here are the victories:

1. Miami Four Ball with Jug McSpaden, Miami Springs Course
2. Charlotte Open, Myers Park Golf Course
3. Greensboro Open, Starmount Country Club
4. Durham Open, Hope Valley Country Club
5. Atlanta Open, Capital City Course
6. Montreal Open, Islemere Golf & Country Club
7. Philadelphia Inquirer Invitational, Llanerch Country Club
8. Chicago Victory National Open, Calumet Country Club
9. PGA Championship, Moraine Country Club, Dayton, Ohio
10. Tam O'Shanter Open, Tam O'Shanter Country Club, Chicago
11. Canadian Open, Thornhill Country Club, Toronto

Yore Names Here

Origins Of Nicknames For Major Sports Teams

MLB

Los Angeles Angels: After Los Angeles ("the angels" in Spanish).

Oakland Athletics: After athletic club workers in Philadelphia (where the team began) who formed city's first pro baseball team.

Houston Astros: After Houston's space program industry.

Toronto Blue Jays: For a bird found throughout Canada.

Atlanta Braves: Named for the Braves, an obsolete political group, by James Gaffney, who bought team in 1912.

Milwaukee Brewers: After Milwaukee's beer industry.

St. Louis Cardinals: For the color of early red uniforms.

Chicago Cubs: Reference to numerous young players in club's early days. (The team adopted newspapers' nickname for them.)

Tampa Bay Devil Rays: For a fish found in Tampa Bay.

Arizona Diamondbacks: For a rattlesnake found in Arizona desert.

Los Angeles Dodgers: A reference to pedestrians who dodged trolleys in the team's native Brooklyn.

San Francisco Giants: Early manager, Jim Mutrie, referred to players as "My big fellows! My giants!"

Cleveland Indians: Reference to Louis Frances Sockalexis, first Native American major leaguer, who played

for Cleveland Spiders in late 1800s.

Seattle Mariners: For local maritime industry.

New York Mets: Reference to New York metropolitan area.

Washington Nationals: Because Washington D.C. is the national capital; also a reference to prior local team.

Baltimore Orioles: For the state bird of Maryland.

San Diego Padres: The Spanish word for priests, who were instrumental in founding San Diego.

Philadelphia Phillies: Obsolete term for inhabitants of Philadelphia.

Pittsburgh Pirates: Reference to an early owner's pirating of rival players.

Texas Rangers: After the elite Texas lawmen.

Boston Red Sox: Reference to the uniform leggings.

Cincinnati Reds: From Red Stockings, see above. Term coined by the press.

Colorado Rockies: A reference to the Rocky Mountains.

Kansas City Royals: After Kansas City's American Royal livestock show and parades.

Detroit Tigers: Because the team's original black and brown striped socks looked like the markings of a tiger.

Florida Marlins: After fish found off the coast of Florida.

Minnesota Twins: Because Minneapolis is one of the Twin Cities.

Chicago White Sox: Originally White Stockings, reference to the team's leggings.

New York Yankees: Bestowed by a sportswriter for unknown reasons.

NBA

Charlotte Bobcats: For a fierce animal with 10-foot leap native to the Carolinas.

Milwaukee Bucks: Because male deer are "spirited, good jumpers, fast and agile."

Chicago Bulls: Reference to Chicago's livestock and meatpacking industry.

Cleveland Cavaliers: Because "cavaliers represent a group of daring, fearless

········➤

A
B
C
D
E
F
G
H
I
J
K
L
M
N
O
P
Q
R
S
T
U
V
W
X
Y
Z

Yore Names Here, continued from page 243

men, whose life's pact was to never surrender, no matter what the odds."

Boston Celtics: For the Irish heritage of Boston.

Los Angeles Clippers: For San Diego's history as a harbor for clipper ships, after the franchise relocated to that city from Buffalo (and before it moved to Los Angeles).

Memphis Grizzlies: For grizzly bears native to British Columbia, where team started.

Atlanta Hawks: Originally the Tri-Cities Blackhawks were located along Iowa-Illinois border, near where Black Hawk, a Sauk Indian chief, fought for his settlement in 1831.

Miami Heat: Ever been to Miami?

New Orleans Hornets: After a British general's remark during the Revolutionary War about resistance in the Carolinas (where the team started): "There's a rebel behind every bush, it's a veritable nest of hornets!"

Utah Jazz: After the music history of New Orleans, where the team began.

Sacramento Kings: Name changed from Royals to Kings to avoid confusion with Kansas City Royals and Omaha Royals, the team's prior incarnations.

New York Knicks: After knickerbockers worn by 17th-century Dutch settlers in New York.

Los Angeles Lakers: After state motto of Minnesota ("Land of 10,000 Lakes") where the team started.

Orlando Magic: Inspired by owner's daughter's visit to Disney's Magic Kingdom.

Dallas Mavericks: After the legend of Samuel Maverick, a Texan who refused to brand his cattle.

New Jersey Nets: For the basketball net and because it rhymes with other local pro teams.

Denver Nuggets: A tribute to 19th century mining boom in Colorado.

Indiana Pacers: For the Indianapolis 500 pace car and the state history of producing harness racing pacer horses.

Detroit Pistons: After first owner Fred Zollner's piston-making plant.

Toronto Raptors: Inspired by the popularity of *Jurassic Park* and dinosaurs among kids.

Houston Rockets: After Atlas Rockets made in San Diego, where the team started.

Philadelphia 76ers: For 1776, when the Declaration of Independence was signed in Philadelphia.

San Antonio Spurs: Reference to Texas cowboys.

Phoenix Suns: Reference to Phoenix area known as Valley of the Sun.

Seattle SuperSonics: Reference to a local aircraft maker's proposed work on supersonic jets.

Minnesota Timberwolves: For an animal native to Minnesota.

Portland Trail Blazers: A tribute to those famous travelers of Oregon Trail, Lewis and Clark, and the ruggedness of Pacific Northwest.

Golden State Warriors: Carryover of a BAA team in Philadelphia, where the team started.

Washington Wizards: Because wizards are magical.

NFL

Chicago Bears: Reference to the Chicago Cubs and that football players are bigger than baseball players.

Cincinnati Bengals: After a previous pro team in Cincinnati.

Buffalo Bills: After Buffalo Bill Cody.

Denver Broncos: After a defunct local pro baseball team.

Cleveland Browns: After team's first coach and GM, Paul Brown.

Tampa Bay Buccaneers: Because buccaneers take no prisoners.

Arizona Cardinals: Reference to the original uniform colors.

San Diego Chargers: Reference to fans yelling "Charge!"

Kansas City Chiefs: Because original Kansas City Mayor H. Roe Bartle was known as The Chief.

Indianapolis Colts: Reference to history of horse breeding and racing in Baltimore region, where the team started.

Dallas Cowboys: Name was chosen to distinguish team from Dallas Rangers, its original name and also the name of the local baseball team.

Miami Dolphins: Because a dolphin is one of the fastest and smartest sea creatures.

Philadelphia Eagles: A Depression-era tribute to National Recovery Administration, which had an eagle as its symbol.

Atlanta Falcons: Because a falcon is proud and courageous.

San Francisco 49ers: After the 1849 California gold rush.

New York Giants: After New York's baseball team of the same name.

Jacksonville Jaguars: Because jaguars are ferocious.

New York Jets: Reference to planes that flew in and out of airports near Shea Stadium, the team's first home.

Detroit Lions: Because the lion is a monarch of the jungle.

Carolina Panthers: Because panthers are ferocious.

Green Bay Packers. After original team sponsor, the Indian Packing Company.

New England Patriots: A reflection of local heritage during American Revolution.

Oakland Raiders: Chosen by an early owner for an unknown reason.

St. Louis Rams: After Fordham Rams, loved by team's first general manager.

Baltimore Ravens: After Edgar Allan Poe's "The Raven," written in Baltimore.

Washington Redskins: Derived from the first team name, Braves, which itself was tribute to local baseball team.

New Orleans Saints: Because the franchise was awarded on All Saints' Day and New Orleans is known for its jazz, as in the song "When the Saints Go Marching In."

Seattle Seahawks: For the fierce osprey, nicknamed the seahawk.

Pittsburgh Steelers: Reference to the local steel industry.

Houston Texans: Ever notice where they play?

Tennessee Titans: Because owner Bud Adams wanted a name that reflected "strength, leadership and other heroic qualities."

Minnesota Vikings: Because so many Minnesotans trace their heritage to Scandinavia.

........➤

Yore Names Here, continued from page 245

NHL

Colorado Avalanche: For avalanches that occur in local mountains.

Chicago Blackhawks: For the Army Regiment—Black Hawk Battalion—of an early owner.

Columbus Blue Jackets: For the color of Union Army jackets, in tribute to Ohio citizens who fought in Civil War.

St. Louis Blues: For the town's music heritage, from famous song by W.C. Handy.

Boston Bruins: Because early owner Charles Adams wanted a name synonymous with "size, strength, agility, ferocity, and cunning."

Montreal Canadiens: For the team's location and nationality of the original team members.

Vancouver Canucks: For Canadian folk hero Johnny Canuck.

Washington Capitals: Because Washington D.C. is the U.S. capital.

Phoenix Coyotes: For an animal that roams the Southwestern desert.

New Jersey Devils: After the Jersey Devil, part-man, part-beast said to haunt the state of New Jersey.

Anaheim Ducks: Named after *The Mighty Ducks* movie produced by original team owner Disney.

Calgary Flames: For the Civil War burning of Atlanta, where the team started.

Philadelphia Flyers: Chosen by the owner because the name conveys fast motion.

Carolina Hurricanes: For hurricanes that often hit the Carolinas.

New York Islanders: For the team's location on Long Island.

Los Angeles Kings: Chosen by owner Jack Cooke in 1967 to signify royalty.

Tampa Bay Lightning: For frequent lightning storms in Tampa.

Toronto Maple Leafs: For Canada's Maple Leaf Regiment of World War I.

Edmonton Oilers: After the oil industry in the region.

Florida Panthers: For an endangered wildcat native to Florida.

Pittsburgh Penguins: Because the home arena is nicknamed The Igloo for its shape.

Nashville Predators: A reference to the fangs and bones of a saber-tooth tiger found on the site of arena.

New York Rangers: After first owner, Tex Rickard; sportswriters referred to the team as Tex's Rangers.

Detroit Red Wings: Named by the owner in honor of team he played for in Montreal, the Winged Wheelers.

Buffalo Sabres: Because the owners wanted a name not currently being used in the pros that wasn't Buffaloes or Bisons.

Ottawa Senators: After the Canadian Senate, located in Ottawa.

San Jose Sharks: After the shark population of the Bay Area.

Dallas Stars: After a motto ("Star of the North") of Minnesota, where the team started.

Atlanta Thrashers: For the state bird of Georgia, the Brown Thrasher.

Minnesota Wild: Reference to the vast Minnesota wilderness.

Youthful Ideas

Satchel Paige's Six Tips For Staying Young

If anyone knew anything about staying young, it was Negro Leagues legend Satchel Paige (1906?-82), who played competitive baseball until age 59. Here are his six prescriptions for eternal youth, as they appeared in his autobiography, Maybe I'll Pitch Forever: A Great Baseball Player Tells the Hilarious Story Behind the Legend.

1. Avoid fried meats, which angry up the blood.
2. If your stomach disputes you, lie down and pacify it with cool thoughts.
3. Keep the juices flowing by jangling around gently as you move.
4. Go very light on the vices, such as carrying on in society. The social ramble ain't restful.
5. Avoid running at all times.
6. Don't look back. Something might be gaining on you.

Z-Boys

Z-Boys

The Original Members Of The Zephyr Skateboarding Team

In 1972, Jeff Ho, Skip Engblom, and Craig Stecyk III opened Jeff Ho Surfboards and Zephyr Productions in the Dogtown section of Venice, California. A Zephyr surfing team soon followed, with members competing in local contests and exhibitions. And then, magic: After the invention of urethane wheels launched a resurgence in skateboarding, the Z-Boys took to skating as a post-surfing distraction. What started as a hobby soon revolutionized the sport. The aggressive riding style of the Z-Boys (whose ranks included one girl) elevated skateboarding to unprecedented heights. They skated streets, schoolyards, and empty pools, and appeared on magazine covers. Eventually, the stress of fame and money broke up the team, but not before the Z-Boys had become legends. They are:

- Jay Adams
- Tony Alva
- Bob Biniak
- Paul Constantineau
- Shogo Kubo
- Jim Muir
- Peggy Oki
- Stacy Peralta
- Nathan Pratt
- Wentzle Ruml IV
- Allen Sarlo
- Chris Cahill

Zealous Collectors

Highest-priced Sports Memorablia Items

When it comes to sports collectibles, there's stuff blessed by the Babe and then there's everything else. Here, according to sports memorabilia auction house SCP Auctions, are the highest prices paid for various pieces at public auction:

Trading Card: 1909-11 Honus Wagner T206 PSA near mint/mint (sold for $2.35 million; 2007)

Game-Used Ball: 1998 Mark McGwire Home Run No. 70 ($3,005,000; 1999)

Game-Used Bat: 1923 Babe Ruth; hit first HR in Yankee Stadium ($1,265,000; 2004)

Game-Used Jersey: 1932 Babe Ruth; the "Called Shot" jersey ($940,000; 2005)

Signed Ball: Babe Ruth PSA mint-plus 9.5 ($150,000; 2005)

Signed Bat: 1920 Babe Ruth game-used bat ($216,000; 2004)

Signed Photograph: 1920 oversized Babe Ruth ($149,500; 2004)

Document: 1920 Babe Ruth Sale Agreement ($996,000; 2005)

Zee End

PLAYERS LISTED LAST ALPHABETICALLY IN VARIOUS SPORTS LEAGUES

LPGA
Veronica Zorzi (2006-present)

MLB
Dutch Zwilling (OF; Chicago White Sox, Chicago Chi-Feds/Whales, Chicago Cubs; 1910, 1914-16)

MLS
Martin Zuniga (goalkeeper; Chivas USA; 2005-present)

NASCAR
Ralph Zrimsek (1949)

NBA
Matt Zunic (forward; Washington Capitols; 1948-49)

NFL
Jim Zyntell (guard; New York Giants, Philadelphia Eagles; 1933-35)

NHL
Andrei Zyuzin (D; San Jose Sharks, Tampa Bay Lightning, New Jersey Devils, Minnesota Wild, Calgary Flames; 1997-present)

PGA
Tate Zyroll (2003)

PBA
Sam Zurich (1980-87)

TENNIS
John Zwieg (ATP, 1970)
Joanna Zyndzo (WTA, 2000-01)

Zero Better

ALL-TIME RECORD HOLDERS IN SEVEN SPORTS

PGA

Jack Nicklaus (66 records)

Career: 18 Major championships, 4 U.S. Open wins, 6 Masters wins, 5 PGA Championships, Major championships amateur and professional (20), second-place finishes in Majors (19), top-3 finishes in Majors (48), top-5 finishes in Majors (56), top-10 finishes (73), career grand slams (2), consecutive years finishing in top-10 on money list (17), years finishing in top 10 on money list (18), years leading money list (8)

Masters: wire-to-wire wins (1), youngest second-time winner (25 years, 2 months, 21 days), youngest third-time winner (26 years, 2 months, 20 days), youngest fourth-time winner (32 years, 2 months, 19 days), oldest winner (46 years, 2 months, 23 days), under par for first nine (12), successive wins (2), runner-up finishes (4), largest lead at 36 holes (5), eagles (24), birdies (502), top-5 finishes (15), top-10 finishes (22), top-25 finishes (29), cuts made (37), low first-round as senior, 50 and over (67), low fourth-round as senior (68), low middle 36 holes as senior (139), low final 36 holes as senior (138), low first 54 holes as senior (211), low 72 holes as senior (283)

········➤

A B C D E F G H I J K L M N O P Q R S T U V W X Y Z

Zero Better, continued from page 251

U.S. Open: lowest 72-hole score by amateur (282), runner-up finishes (4), top-5 finishes (11), top-10 finishes (18), top-25 finishes (22), winner of U.S. Open and U.S. Amateur (1), lowest 72-hole score (272), lowest 18-hole score (63), lowest first-round score by winner (-7), lowest score to lead field after 18 holes (-7), consecutive starts (44), finished starts (35), longest span from first to last win (18 years), sub-par rounds in career (37), rounds in the 60s (29), sub-par 72-hole totals (7)

PGA Championship: runner-up finishes (4), largest margin of victory (7), sub-par rounds (52), rounds in the 60s (41), lowest career scoring average (71.33), appearances (37), rounds played (126), top-3 finishes (12), top-5 finishes (14), top-10 finishes (15), top-25 finishes (23), cuts made (27), wire-to-wire winner (1)

British Open: second-place finishes (7), career rounds in the 60s (33), top-5 finishes (16)

Note: Stats through 2006 PGA Tour.

NHL

Wayne Gretzky (60 records)

Career: goals (894), goals by center (894), goals including playoffs (1,016), playoff goals (122), playoff assists (260), 40-goal seasons (12), consecutive 40-goal seasons (12), 50-goal seasons (9), 60-goal seasons (5), consecutive 60-goal seasons (4), 100-point seasons (15), consecutive 100-point seasons (13), 3-or-more-goal games (50), assists (1,963), assists by center (1,963), assists including playoffs (2,223), consecutive games with assist (23), points (2,857), points by center (2,856), points including playoffs (3,239), point-scoring streak (51), point-scoring streak from start of season (51), assists per game (1.320), overtime assists in career (15), playoff points (382), playoff game-winning goals (24), 3-or-more goal games in playoffs (10), All-Star game goals (13), All-Star game points (25)

Season: goals (92), goals by center (92), goals including playoffs (100), goals in 50 games from start of season (61), goals in one period (4), 3-or-more-goal games (10), assists (163), assists by center (163), assists in one playoff year (31), assists in one playoff series other than Finals (14), assists in Finals series (10), assists in one playoff game (6), assists in one playoff period (3), assists including playoffs (174), regular season points (215), regular season points by center (215), points including playoffs (255), goals-per-game average (1.18), assists per game (2.04), points-per-game (2.77), playoff points in one year (47), points in Finals series (13), shorthanded goals in one playoff year (3)

Game: assists (7), assists in road game (7), assists by player in first NHL season (7), points in one playoff period (4), shorthanded goals in one playoff game (2), All-Star game goals (4), All-Star Game goals one period (4), All-Star Game points one period (4).

Note: Stats through 2005-06 NHL season.

NBA

Wilt Chamberlain (50 records)

Career: rebounds per game (22.9), total rebounds (23,924), seasons leading in rebounding (11), 50-point games (118), 40-point games (271), 1,000-rebound seasons (13), consecutive 50-point games (7), consecutive 40-point games (14), consecutive games 30-plus points (65), consecutive games 20-plus points (126), seasons leading league in minutes (8), consecutive seasons leading league in minutes (5), minutes per game (45.8), consecutive seasons leading league in scoring (7), seasons leading field goal percentage (9), consecutive seasons leading league in field goal percentage (5), consecutive seasons leading league in field goals (7), consecutive seasons leading league in field goal attempts (7), seasons leading league in free throw attempts (9), consecutive seasons leading league in free throw attempts (6)

Season: scoring average (50.4), points (4,029), minutes (3,882), minutes per game (48.5), field goal percentage (.727), field goals (1,597), field goal attempts (3,159), free throw attempts (1,363), rebounds (2,149), rebounds per game (27.2), rookie scoring average (37.6), points by rookie (2,707), rebounds by rookie (1,941), complete games (79), 50-point games (45), 40-point games (63), most consecutive field goals no misses (35)

Game: points (100), most points in a half (59), rebounds (55), field goals (36), field goal attempts (63), field goal attempts in a half (37), field goal attempts in a quarter (21), free throw attempts (34), free throws (28), points by rookie (58), field goal percentage (1.000), most field goals no misses (18), field goals in a half (22)

Note: Stats through 2005-06 NBA season.

MLB

Babe Ruth (36 records)

Career: seasons leading majors in slugging percentage (12), consecutive seasons leading majors in slugging percentage (6), most seasons leading league in slugging percentage (13), consecutive seasons leading league in slugging percentage (7), slugging percentage, majors (.690), highest slugging percentage, league (.692), seasons with slugging percentage .700 or higher (9), seasons with slugging percentage .600 or higher (13), consecutive seasons .600 or higher slugging percentage (7), seasons leading majors in runs (8), consecutive seasons leading majors in runs (3), seasons leading league in runs (8), consecutive seasons leading league in runs (3), consecutive seasons leading majors in extra-base hits (4), consecutive seasons leading league in extra-base hits (4), seasons leading majors in total bases (6), consecutive seasons leading majors in total bases (2) , seasons leading majors in home runs (11), seasons leading league in home runs (12), seasons with 50 or more home runs (4), seasons with 40 or more home runs (11), consecutive seasons with 40 or more home runs (7), games with two or more home runs (72), games with two or more home runs, league (71), consecutive games with grand slam (2), seasons leading majors in runs batted

········➤

A B C D E F G H I J K L M N O P Q R S T U V W X Y Z

Zero Better, continued from page 253

in (5), seasons leading league in runs batted in (5), consecutive seasons with 150 or more runs batted in (3), seasons leading majors in walks (11), consecutive seasons leading majors in walks (4), seasons leading league in walks (11), seasons with 100 or more walks (13), seasons leading majors in strikeouts (4)

Season: times reaching base safely (379), extra-base hits (119), total bases (457)

Note: Stats through 2006 MLB season.

LPGA

Annika Sorenstam (28 records)

Career: lowest score for 72 holes (-27), lowest score for 54 holes (-24), lowest score for 36 holes relation to par (-20), 36 holes raw score (124), lowest score for 18 holes relation to par (-13), 18 holes raw score (59), 54-hole winning score (-24, 192), consecutive wins at same tournament (Mizuno Classic; 4), largest come-from-behind win (10 strokes), lowest second round (59, -13), lowest first round by winner (62, -10), consecutive rounds in 60s (14), birdies in one round (13), most sub-par holes in one event (29), most Rolex Player of the Year Awards (7)

Season: lowest scoring average (68.70), official earnings ($2,863,904), first to reach $2 million, fastest to $200,000 (2 events), fastest to $300,000 (3 events), fastest to $400,000 (3 events), fastest to $500,000 (4 events), fastest to $600,000 (5 events), fastest to $700,000 (6 events), fastest to $800,0000 (7 events), fastest to $900,000, fastest to $1 million (8 events), fastest to $2 million (15 events).

Note: Stats through 2006 LPGA season.

NASCAR

Richard Petty (15 records)

Career: wins (200), super speedway wins (55), short track wins (139), pole wins (126), short track pole wins (97), races won from pole (61)

Season: wins (27), consecutive wins (10), wins from pole (15), consecutive wins at one track (Martinsville; 7), wins at one track (Martinsville, North Wilkesboro; 15), consecutive wins from pole (4), years with a win from pole (16), races in career (1,177), years leading circuit in wins (7)

Note: Stats through 2006 NASCAR season.

NFL

Jerry Rice (14 records)

Career: TDs (208), TD receptions (197), total yards from scrimmage (23,540), receiving yards (22,895), receptions (1,549), receiving TDs (197), 1,000-yard receiving seasons (14), 100-yard receiving games (76), 50-reception seasons (17), consecutive games with reception (274), most consecutive games with a receiving TD (13)

Season: receiving TDs (22), receiving yards (1,848)

Game: receiving TDs (5)

Note: Stats through 2005-06 NFL season.

Zzzzzzzz ...

ESPN's First 24 Hours Of Programming

September 7–8, 1979, All Times ET

7 pm: SportsCenter
7:30 pm: NCAA preview
8 pm: Slo-Pitch World Series
11 pm: FILA wrestling
11:30 pm: SportsCenter
Midnight: NCAA soccer: UCLA vs. Saint Louis University
2 am: SportsCenter (replay)
2:30 am: NCAA preview (replay)
3 am: Monte Carlo tennis
7 am: Munster hurling
8 am: FILA wrestling (replay)
8:30 am: Irish cycling
9 am: SportsCenter
9:30 am: Slo-Pitch World Series (replay)
12:30 pm: Men's volleyball: Korea vs. Japan
3 pm: Marathon: A Personal Test
3:30 pm: NCAA soccer: UCLA vs. University of Connecticut
5:30 pm: FILA wrestling
6 pm: SportsCenter
6:30 pm: Women's volleyball: USA vs. USSR

A B C D E F G H I J K L M N O P Q R S T U V W X Y Z

ACKNOWLEDGMENTS

We're just going to come right out and say it: A book like this wouldn't happen if it wasn't for all the people who made it happen. More specifically, this collection of disparate and often unwieldy material would not have come together were it not for the idea generation, creativity, and thoroughness of our primary collaborators: Lane Strauss, Andy Kamenetzky, Brian Kamenetzky, Morty Ain, Eddie Matz, and Ari Yolkut. As always, we're amazed at their professionalism and consistent willingness to go far beyond our expectations.

We'd also like to thank our crack research team, led by the incomparable Craig Winston and his colleague Roger Jackson: Matt Beardmore, Dale Brauner, Jordan Brenner, Anna Katherine Clemmons, Matthew Cole, Charles Curtis, Shauna DeGeorge, Zach Ewing, Mary Fenton, John Hassan, Adesina Koiki, Mike Lynch, Gueorgui Milkov, Doug Mittler, Bartley Morrisroe, Tim Sultan, Daniel Sweren-Becker, Darrell Trimble, Michael Woods and Noor Zaidi. Copy editor Beth Adelman had the good misfortune to take on this project and her high standards produced more saves than Patrick Roy on his best night. And an extra special thanks to Simon Brennan, who treated this manuscript as if it were his name on the cover rather than ours. We can't think of a higher compliment—or a better backstop.

We shouldn't—and won't—forget the good folks at ESPN Books, including Gary Hoenig, Michael Solomon, Jessica Welke, Chris Raymond, Glen Waggoner, John Glenn, Andrew Chaikivsky, Bill Vourvoulias, and Sandy DeShong. They supported this book throughout and did their damnedest to make sure we didn't look like fools in the finished project. Michael, in particular, lent a helpful and much-needed critical eye to our collection of sports triviata.

Sam Eckersley at Rogers Eckersley Design did a stellar job with what can only be described as a complex manuscript and collection of information. We're proud to have been a conduit for his creativity, and grateful he never thought to throw us under a bus. Or at least never actually threw us. A tip of the cap as well to Stuart Rogers, Jose Antonio Contreras, and Jane Huschka.

Nicole Salzano's insights into the organization of this book were invaluable. Better still, she was a great sport to work with. As usual. And Russell Roberts lent his keen insight and puckish sensibility in critiquing the manuscript and offering helpful suggestions for additional entries.

Perry van der Meer and his operations/copy crew at *ESPN The Magazine* ensured that everything that could be done to make this book as accurate and readable as possible was, in fact, done. We're very grateful. Any errors of commission or omission in the book are entirely ours, to the extent that we can be blamed for any one thing, given our numerous failings. We promise to try harder next time.

REFERENCES

Page 3, American Pine Language: United States Bowling Congress

Page 16, Banner Carriers: Pete Fournier, author of *The Handbook of Mascots and Nicknames*, 2nd edition

Page 17, Baseball Originals: *The Elias Book of Baseball Records*; MLB

Pages 18–19, Belt Bucklers: WWE

Pages 26–27, Canton Classics: Pro Football Hall of Fame

Pages 31–34, Cereal Stars: General Mills

Page 35, Cooperstown Pioneers: Baseball Hall of Fame

Pages 44–45, Dubious Distinction: Professional Football Researchers Association

Page 49, Engraved Errors: Hockey Hall of Fame; NHL.com

Pages 50–51, Entry Points: MLB

Pages 54–55, Extinct Teams: *Total Football II*

Page 59, Felt Tips: www.hickoksports.com; www.bca-pool.com

Pages 60–61, First On Ice: *NHL Official Guide and Record Book*

Page 63, Football Originals: *Total Football II*

Page 65, Fore Thoughts: British Golf Museum

Pages 70–71, Global Game: NBA

Page 74, Greek Goners: Olympics.org; *The Complete Book of the Summer Olympics*

Page 75, Green Bay Watch: VinceLombardi.com

Pages 80–81, Hardwood Regulations: Naismith Memorial Basketball Hall of Fame; NCAA.org

Page 82, Hit Parade: www.enlexica.com ("The Language of Baseball")

Page 85, Hoop Hellraisers: NBA.com

Page 86, Hoops Originals: NBA.com; *The Official NBA Encyclopedia*; RememberTheABA.com

Page 89, Huddle Parties: Pro Football Hall of Fame

Page 89, Huge Affronts: International Federation of Bodybuilding and Fitness

Page 92, Ice Guys: Hockey Hall of Fame

Pages 100–101, Jinx Alerts: All text except Auto Racing reprinted with permission of Information Please Database, © 2006 Pearson Education, Inc. All Rights reserved.

Page 103, Jump Master: American Motorcyclist Association; ESPN.com

Page 104, Jumping The Line: MLB.com

Page 105, Jumps For Joy: United States Parachute Association

Page 110, Kennel Club Champs: westminsterkennelclub.org

Pages 118–119, League Of Nations: Tod Maher, Associate Editor, *ESPN Pro Football Encyclopedia*

Pages 122–123, Lure Language: Reprinted with permission of Gibbs Smith, publisher, 2005

Pages 126–127, Mailed-In Monuments: The United States Postal Service

Page 129, Monday Best: ESPN/ABC Sports

Page 138, Net Gains: NHL

Page 148, Obsessed Aquatics: Channel Swimming Association, Dover (England) Museum websites

Pages 150–151, Oval Office Politics: *Baseball's Greatest Quotations* by Paul Dickson; *Baseball: The Presidents Game* by William B. Mead and Paul Dickson

Page 165, Pounds For Pounding: *The Boxing Register*

Page 169, Questionable Math: *NFL Record & Fact Book*

Pages 170–171, Quotable Yankee: Yogi Berra Museum & Learning Center

Page 174, Rapier Bits: Craig Harkins, founder Fencing.net

Page 177, Rink Requirements: Earl Zukerman, McGill University Department of Athletics

Page 178, Round-Trippers: Excerpted from *The New Dickson Baseball Dictionary* © 1999 by Paul Dickson. Reprinted with permission of Harcourt, Inc.

Page 180, Run Factories: The Elias Sports Bureau

Page 185, Screen Gems: boxofficemojo.com

Page 191, Springfield Walk-Ons: TheSimpsons.com; imdb.com

Page 199, Tournament Topplers: *NCAA Official Men's Final Four Records Book*

Pages 200–201, Traveling Batsmen: Pete Palmer, co-editor, *The ESPN Baseball Encyclopedia*

Page 203, Two Timers, Part One: Little League

Page 207, United Skates: Hockey Hall of Fame; NHL

Page 210, Unparalleled Leadership: *The Sporting News*; ESPN Classic

Page 215, Vanished Bowls: *NCAA Football Records Book*

Page 216, Visionary Moments: Museum of Broadcast Communications

Page 220, Voracious Appetites: Major League Eating

Page 224, Waist Materials: American Tae Kwon Do Association; American Shotokan Karate Alliance; American Jujitsu Association

Page 230, Winter War: Justin Anderson, World PowerSports Association

Page 242, Year Of The Lord: Masters.org

Gary Belsky is an executive editor at *ESPN The Magazine* and an adjunct professor of journalism at New York University. He is the author of several books, including *On Second Thought: 365 of the Worst Promises, Predictions, And Pronouncements Ever Made.* He lives in New York City.

Neil Fine is also an executive editor at *ESPN The Magazine.* Along with Gary Belsky, he is one of the co-authors of *Answer Guy: Extinguishing the Burning Questions of Sports With the Water Bucket of Truth,* but he is not as much of a know-it-all.